INSIDERS' GUIDE®

OFF THE BEATEN PATH® SERIES

W9-BNU-153

Off the Beaten Path®

EIGHTH EDITION

new york

A GUIDE TO UNIQUE PLACES

WILLIAM G.

AND

KAY SCHELLER

INSIDERS' GUIDE®

GUILFORD, CONNECTICUT
AN IMPRINT OF THE GLOBE PEQUOT PRESS

The prices, rates, and hours listed in this guidebook were confirmed at press time. We recommend, however, that you call establishments to obtain current information before traveling.

To buy books in quantity for corporate use or incentives, call **(800) 962–0973, ext. 4551,** or e-mail **premiums@GlobePequot.com.**

INSIDERS' GUIDE®

Copyright © 1994, 1997, 1999, 2001, 2003, 2005 by William G. Scheller

Text design by Linda Loiewski
Maps created by Equator Graphics © The Globe Pequot Press
Illustrations by Carole Drong
Spot photography throughout © Mike Dobel/Masterfile

ISSN 1540-9201
ISBN 0-7627-3533-3

Manufactured in the United States of America
Eighth Edition/First Printing

To Sally—always there for us,
always ready to go.

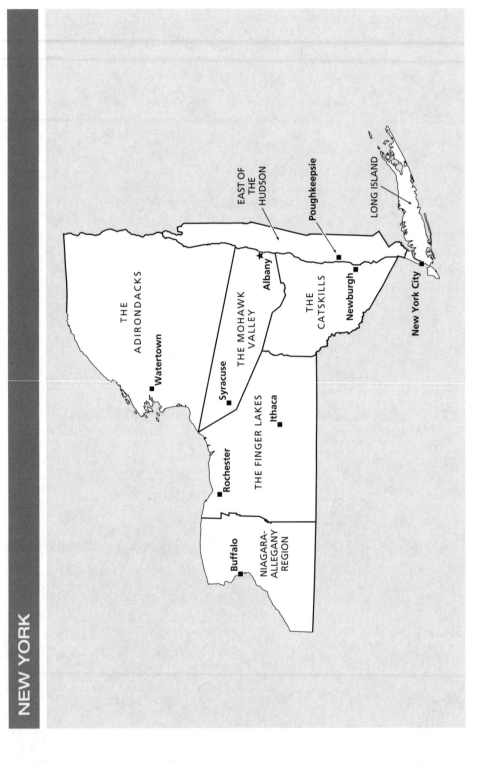

THE
ADIRONDACKS

Watertown

THE MOHAWK
VALLEY

Syracuse

Albany

EAST OF
THE
HUDSON

Poughkeepsie

THE FINGER LAKES

Ithaca

Rochester

THE
CATSKILLS

Newburgh

LONG ISLAND

New York City

NIAGARA-
ALLEGANY
REGION

Buffalo

Contents

Introduction vii

East of the Hudson 1

The Adirondacks 35

The Mohawk Valley 71

The Finger Lakes 99

The Niagara-Allegany Region 135

The Catskills 161

New York City and Long Island 189

Indexes

    General 241

    Museums 250

    Parks and Nature Preserves 253

About the Authors 254

Introduction

Back in 1986, when we researched the first edition of *New York Off the Beaten Path,* the challenge seemed to be to find enough places that would meet the title's criterion. After all, the paths that run between Montauk and Niagara, between Binghamton and Massena, are among the most heavily beaten in the United States. Could there be any stones left unturned in such a place?

Of course there were. And over the course of seventeen years and seven revisions, we've been able to find pathways ever more untrammeled and obscure. After nearly two decades of combing the backstreets and two-lane blacktops of the Empire State, we've seen this book evolve in ways that have allowed us to delete many better-known attractions and replace them with the kind of places you aren't likely to find in any other guide. Here are bald eagles and buffalo, guideboats and glassblowers, places famous for making kazoos and carousels, and a kaleidoscope as big as a silo (actually, it is a silo). Along the way we've turned up the kind of restaurants and overnight accommodations favored by aficionados of the less-traveled roads. There are more eateries and lodging places than ever in these pages, and not one of them serves portion-controlled meals or offers a room identical to one you've stayed in on an interstate in Nebraska.

New York occupies a unique position in American history, a position between that of the small, densely settled New England states and the western expanses left untamed well into the nineteenth century. With the exception of the Dutch settlements at New Amsterdam and along the Hudson Valley, New York remained a virtual frontier until the late 1700s. When it was settled, the newcomers were not colonists from abroad but in many cases migrating New Englanders, men and women setting the pattern for the next hundred years of

Vital Stats

New York State encompasses 49,476 square miles.

The state has four mountain ranges: Adirondack, Catskill, Shawangunk, and Taconic.

Mount Marcy in the Adirondacks, at 5,344 feet above sea level, is the highest point in the state.

The state has 70,000 miles of rivers and streams, 127 miles of Atlantic Ocean coastline, and, including lake, bay, and oceanfront, 9,767 miles of shoreline.

The Making of an Empire

While touring New York in 1784, George Washington referred to it as the "Seat of the Empire." Hence the nickname—The Empire State.

westward expansion. New York thus became a transitional place between old, coastal America and the horizons of the West.

More than that, the future "Empire State" became a staging area for the people, ideas, and physical changes that would transform the United States in the nineteenth century. Its position between the harbors of the Atlantic coast and the Great Lakes ensured early prominence in the development of canals and, later, railroads. New York's vast resources made it an industrial power, while its size and fertility guaranteed its importance as a farm state. It began its growth early enough to create an infrastructure of small towns connected by back roads, rivers, and canals and remained vigorous in a modern era conducive to the rise of great cities along busy trunkline railroads. All the while, the state's geographical diversity allowed its different regions to assume varied and distinct personalities.

The spiritual and intellectual atmosphere in New York was no less responsive to change. This is where the quietist Shakers played out much of their experiment in plain living, where Washington Irving proclaimed a native American literature, where the artists of the Hudson River School painted American nature as it had never been painted before, and where Elbert Hubbard helped introduce the Arts and Crafts movement to the United States.

This book is about the rich legacy of tangible associations that all of this activity has left behind. New York is crammed as are few other states with the homes, libraries, and workshops of famous individuals, with battlefields and

It's Official

The rose—wild and cultivated—was declared New York's state flower in 1955.

The native brook trout, also known as brookies or speckles, is New York's official state fish.

A popular winter visitor, the red-breasted bluebird, is the official state bird.

The apple muffin is the official state muffin.

the remnants of historic canals, with museums chronicling pursuits as divergent as horse racing, gunsmithing, and wine making. In a place where people have done just about everything, here are reminders of just about everything they've ever done—and since this isn't merely a history book, it will introduce you to plenty of New Yorkers who are still hard at work building their state and filling it with interesting things.

Within each of the regional chapters of this book, the order of individual listings has been determined geographically, as explained in the chapter introductions. Few readers will be proceeding dutifully from site to site, so no attempt has been made to provide detailed linking directions. Still, it's nice to know what's near what if a slightly longer drive would make visits to several destinations possible.

Seventeen years, eight editions. By way of reminding ourselves how much time has gone by since *New York Off the Beaten Path* first appeared, we recall that in 1986, while we were getting the first edition ready for publication the following spring, we had to take a few days off when our son Dave was born . . . and Dave is off to college this fall. Fortunately, the route from our house in Vermont to his school, the University of Toronto, passes through New York State. That will give all of us a chance to scout out a few new places for the ninth edition.

East of the Hudson

The first of our seven New York State regions begins in the crowded bedroom communities of Westchester County and extends northward into the western foothills of the Berkshires and the Green Mountains. Hilly itself throughout, it encompasses the eastern slopes of one of the most beautiful river valleys in the world. Anyone in need of convincing should drive north along the length of the Taconic State Parkway, which runs through the high country midway between the Hudson and the Connecticut and Massachusetts borders. Along with the more easterly and meandering State Route 22, the Taconic makes for a nice backdoor entry into New England and an even more scenic trip than the more heavily traveled New York State Thruway on the other side of the river. Many of the attractions described in this chapter, however, are clustered along the river itself and are mainly accessible via U.S. Route 9, once the carriage road that connected the feudal estates of Old Dutch New York. Franklin D. Roosevelt's Hyde Park and the sumptuous Vanderbilt estate are two of the valley's best-known latter-day country seats; in this chapter, though, we'll concentrate on less publicized homesteads and other points of interest. The orientation is from south to north.

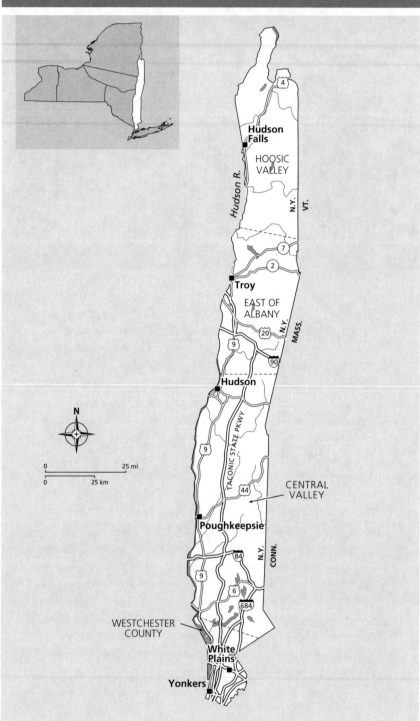

Westchester County

Just beyond the New York City limits, in Yonkers, the *Hudson River Museum* occupies the magnificent 1876 Glenview Mansion. As the preeminent cultural institution of Westchester County and the lower Hudson Valley, the museum's resources reflect the natural, social, and artistic history of the area.

A visit to the Hudson River Museum includes a walk through the four meticulously restored rooms on the first floor of the mansion itself. You'll hardly find a better introduction to the short-lived but influential phase of Victorian taste known as the Eastlake style, marked by precise geometric carving and ornamentation—the traceries in the Persian carpets almost seem to be echoed in the furniture and ceiling details.

Aside from the furnishings and personal objects that relate to the period when the Trevor family lived in the mansion, the museum's collections have grown to include impressive holdings of Hudson River landscape paintings, including works by Jasper Cropsey and Albert Bierstadt.

In contrast to the period settings and historical emphases of the older parts of the museum, the state-of-the-art Andrus Planetarium features the Zeiss M1015 star projector, the only one of its kind in the Northeast. A contemporary orientation is also furthered by as many as thirty special art, science, and history exhibitions each year, centered on the work of American artists of the nineteenth and twentieth centuries. There are concerts in summer and a Victorian Holiday celebration each December.

The Hudson River Museum, 511 Warburton Avenue, *Yonkers,* (914) 963–4550, is open October through April, Wednesday through Sunday noon to 5:00 P.M.; and May through September, Wednesday through Sunday noon to 5:00 P.M., Friday until 9:00 P.M. Admission to the museum galleries is $4.00 for

AUTHORS' FAVORITES EAST OF THE HUDSON

American Museum of Firefighting	Old Drovers Inn
Chuang Yen Monastery	Old Rhinebeck Aerodrome
Donald M. Kendall Sculpture Gardens	Rodgers Book Barn
Harralds	Sunnyside
Locust Grove	Wing's Castle
Olana	

The Real "FDR Drive"

The Taconic Parkway offers motorists the most scenic of several routes along the east side of the Hudson River. Begun in 1927, the road was planned as an offshoot of the Bronx Parkway, but a major extension was under consideration even before ground was broken. In 1924 the Taconic State Park Commission was formed, and its commissioner, Franklin D. Roosevelt, was eager to push the parkway north as far as Albany. It didn't get quite that far—in 1963 the Taconic eventually reached its northernmost point at the intersection with Interstate 90 in Chatham. It was FDR, however, who insisted on the road's scenic path through some of the most majestic portions of his beloved Hudson Valley. He even prescribed the rustic, thickly mortared stone bridges that help make the Taconic such a handsome rural thoroughfare.

adults, $3.00 for senior citizens and children under 12. Admission to the planetarium is $4.00 for adults, $1.50 for senior citizens and children under 12. There is a free planetarium star show Friday at 7:00 P.M. Other planetarium shows are held Saturday and Sunday at 1:30, 2:30, and 3:30 P.M. Admission for both museum and star show is $7.00 for adults and $3.00 for seniors and children under 12.

Hundreds of years before Glenview Mansion was built, the Philipse family assembled a Westchester estate that makes Glenview's twenty-seven acres seem puny by comparison. Frederick Philipse I came to what was then New Amsterdam in the 1650s and began using his sharp trader's instincts. By the 1690s his lands had grown into a huge estate, including a 52,500-acre tract that encompassed one-third of what is now Westchester County.

In 1716 Philipse's grandson Frederick Philipse II assumed the title of Lord of the Manor of Philipsborough, greatly enlarged the cottage built by his grandfather, and used ***Philipse Manor Hall*** as a summer residence. Col. Frederick Philipse (III) rebuilt and further enlarged the Georgian manor house, planted elaborate gardens, and imported the finest furnishings for the hall. His tenure as Lord of the Manor ended when he decided to side with the Tory cause at the beginning of the American Revolution.

Confiscated along with the rest of its owner's properties after the war, Philipse Manor Hall was auctioned by the State of New York and passed through the hands of a succession of owners until 1908 when the state bought the property back. The state has since maintained the mansion as a museum of history, art, and architecture. Home to the finest papier-mâché rococo ceiling in the United States, inside and out it remains one of the most perfectly preserved examples of Georgian style in the Northeast.

Philipse Manor Hall State Historic Site, 29 Warburton Avenue, P.O. Box 496, Yonkers 10701, (914) 965–4027, is open April through October, Wednesday through Saturday noon to 5:00 P.M. and Sunday 1:00 to 4:00 P.M. Admission is free. Group tours are available by appointment.

Fans of the nineteenth-century, New York–born Hudson River School painter and architect *Jasper F. Cropsey* will want to make appointments to visit Ever Rest, his Gothic *home and studio,* and the *Newington Cropsey Foundation Gallery of Art.* Ever Rest is preserved as it appeared when the artist lived here and exhibits his paintings, watercolors, and sketches. The handsome Gallery of Art, with its octagonal gallery built to resemble "Aladdin," Cropsey's studio in Hastings-on-Hudson, New York, houses the world's largest collection of the artist's works.

They're both in *Hastings-on-Hudson:* His home and studio, 49 Washington Avenue, (914) 478–1372, is open by appointment only from February through July and September through November weekdays 10:00 A.M. to 1:00 P.M. The gallery, 25 Cropsey Lane, (914) 478–7990, offers forty-five-minute tours by appointment only (at least a week in advance) from February through July and September through December weekdays from 1:00 to 5:00 P.M. Visitors are welcome to tour the grounds weekdays from 1:00 to 5:00 P.M. without an appointment.

Donald M. Kendall, former chairman of the board and chief executive officer of PepsiCo, Inc., had a dream that extended far beyond soft drinks. He wanted to create a garden whose atmosphere of stability, creativity, and experimentation would reflect his vision of the company. In 1965 he began collecting sculptures; today more than forty works by major twentieth-century artists are displayed on 168 acres of magnificent gardens—many created by internationally renowned designers Russell Page and François Goffinet, who picked up where Mr. Page left off.

Alexander Calder, Jean Dubuffet, Marino Marini, Alberto Giacometti, Auguste Rodin, Henry Moore, and Louise Nevelson are just a few of the artists

Imagine Big Letters on a Hillside Spelling "Mamaroneck"

Back in the early days of the movies, D.W. Griffith set up a movie studio complex on Orienta Point in Mamaroneck. Lillian and Dorothy Gish, Mary Pickford, and many other stars of the silent screen made films here, and on location around Westchester County.

ANNUAL EVENTS EAST OF THE HUDSON

MAY

Rhinebeck Antiques Fair,
Dutchess County Fairgrounds,
Rhinebeck,
(845) 876–4001

JUNE

Clearwater Festival,
Poughkeepsie,
(800) 677–5667

Crafts at Rhinebeck,
Dutchess County Fairgrounds,
Rhinebeck,
(845) 876–4001

Riverfront Arts Festival,
Troy,
(518) 273–0552

JULY

Falcon Ridge Folk Festival,
Hillsdale,
(860) 364–0366;
www.falconridgefolk.com

AUGUST

Bard Music Festival,
Annandale-on-Hudson,
(800) 445–3131;
www.dutchesstourism.com

SEPTEMBER

Battle of Saratoga Anniversary Encampment,
Stillwater,
(518) 664–9821, ext. 224

whose works are displayed in the ***Donald M. Kendall Sculpture Gardens.*** Mr. Kendall's artistic vision has truly been realized.

The Donald M. Kendall Sculpture Gardens, PepsiCo World Headquarters, 700 Anderson Hill Road, ***Purchase*** (914) 253–2000, is open daily year-round from 9:00 A.M. to dusk. There is no admission fee.

In 1838 the great Gothic Revival architect ***Alexander Jackson Davis*** designed ***Lyndhurst.*** Overlooking the broad expanse of the Tappan Zee from the east, this beautiful stone mansion and its landscaped grounds, built for former New York City mayor William Paulding, represented the full American flowering of the neo-Gothic aesthetic that had been sweeping England since the closing years of the eighteenth century.

Lyndhurst is unusual among American properties of its size and grandeur in having remained under private ownership for nearly a century and a quarter. Paulding and his son owned the estate until 1864, when it was purchased by a wealthy New York merchant named George Merritt. Merritt employed Davis to enlarge the house and to add its landmark tower; he also constructed a large greenhouse and several outbuildings. The greatest legacy of his stewardship, however, was the commencement of an ambitious program to develop an English-inspired romantic landscape to complement the Gothic architecture of the main house.

One of the most notorious of America's railroad robber barons, ***Jay Gould,*** acquired Lyndhurst in 1880 and maintained it as a country estate. Upon his death in 1892, Lyndhurst became the property of his oldest daughter, Helen, who left it in turn to her younger sister Anna, duchess of Talleyrand-Perigord, in 1938. The duchess died in 1961, with instructions that the estate become the property of the National Trust for Historic Preservation.

Lyndhurst, 635 South Broadway (Route 9 just south of the Tappan Zee Bridge), Tarrytown, (914) 631–4481, is open mid-April through October, Tuesday through Sunday 10:00 A.M. to 5:00 P.M., and November through mid-April, Saturday and Sunday 10:00 A.M. to 4:00 P.M. Open on Monday holidays. Closed Thanksgiving, Christmas, and New Year's. Guided tours and self-guided audio tours are available. Lunch is served in the historic Carriage House from April through October. Admission is $10.00 for adults, $9.00 for senior citizens, and $4.00 for children 12 to 17, under 12 free with paying adult.

Far less imposing than Lyndhurst but a good deal homier, ***Sunnyside*** stands just to the north in ***Tarrytown*** and offers a fascinating glimpse of the last twenty-three years in the life of its owner, ***Washington Irving.*** Irving described his country retreat as "a little old-fashioned stone mansion, all made up of gable ends, and as full of angles and corners as an old cocked hat." Not surprising for the man who wrote *The Legend of Sleepy Hollow, Rip Van Winkle,* and *Diedrich Knickerbocker's History of New York,* Sunnyside is a step-gabled Dutch Colonial affair, ivied with time and possessed of more than a little whimsy.

Washington Irving spent two periods of retirement at Sunnyside: the years 1836–42 and the last thirteen years of his life, 1846–59. It was here that he wrote *Astoria,* his account of the Pacific Northwest, as well as *The Crayon Miscellany, Wolfert's Roost,* and *The Life of George Washington.* Here, too, the author entertained such visitors as Oliver Wendell Holmes, William Makepeace Thackeray, and Louis Napoleon III. In the time not taken up with work and hospitality, he planned his

Lyndhurst

own orchards, flower gardens, and arborways. These survive to this day, as do favorite Irving possessions such as the writing desk and piano on view in the house.

Sunnyside, West Sunnyside Lane (1 mile south of the Tappan Zee Bridge on Route 9), Tarrytown, (914) 591–8763 is open daily 10:00 A.M. to 5:00 P.M. from April through October except Tuesday and major holidays. In March it is open weekends from 10:00 A.M. to 4:00 P.M. and in November and December, daily except Tuesday from 10:00 A.M. to 4:00 P.M. The last tour of the day leaves at one hour before closing. Admission is $9.00 for adults, $8.00 for seniors, and $5.00 for children ages 5 to 17. A grounds pass is available for $4.00. Boat trips to Sunnyside via New York Waterway leave from Manhattan and New Jersey spring, summer, and fall. An overnight tour with an inn stay is also offered. For information call (800) 53–FERRY.

One of the area's most luxurious lodgings is the **Castle at Tarrytown,** a Norman-style mansion built between 1900 and 1910 on ten acres of land overlooking the Hudson River. Surrounded by a stone wall and a magnificent arboretum, the castle features a 40-foot Grand Room with a vaulted ceiling, stained-glass windows, and a musicians' balcony. One of the dining rooms has paneling taken from a house outside Paris that was given by France's Louis XIV to James II of England after the latter's removal from the throne in 1688. Breakfast, lunch, dinner, and Sunday brunch are served in the elegant Equus Restaurant. High tea is served Wednesday from 2:30 to 5:00 P.M. The castle is at 400 Benedict Avenue in Tarrytown, (914) 631–1980; www.castleonthehudson.com. Call for rates.

There are two wonderful old churches in Sleepy Hollow, which prior to a recent name change was known as **North Tarrytown.** The **Old Dutch Church of Sleepy Hollow** on Route 9 (845–631–1123), built in 1685, is still heated by a woodstove. Washington Irving's *The Legend of Sleepy Hollow* is read in the church during Halloween season. A service is held Sunday at 10:15 A.M. the third week of June through the first week of September. Tours are given Saturday and

They Trod Shod

In the summer of 1938, to celebrate the 250th anniversary of the settling of New Rochelle, a group of children made a pilgrimage to New York City. They were commemorating the long trek the region's first settlers, the Huguenots, had to make to attend church. According to tradition, these early churchgoers made the trek barefooted. But the children put on their shoes after the first block.

Sunday from Memorial Day through October from 2:00 to 4:00 P.M.; and Memorial Day until Labor Day, Monday, Wednesday, and Thursday from 1:00 to 4:00 P.M. or by appointment. Call for holiday schedule. Donations are accepted.

The **Burying Ground,** adjacent to the Old Dutch Church is the final resting place of Washington Irving and other luminaries, including William Rockefeller and Andrew Carnegie.

The tiny **Union Church of Pocantico Hills** on Route 448 (914–631–8200) has a magnificent collection of stained-glass windows by Henri Matisse and Marc Chagall, which were commissioned by the Rockefeller family. It's open daily except Tuesday from April through December, weekdays 11:00 A.M. to 5:00 P.M., Saturday 10:00 A.M. to 5:00 P.M., and Sunday 2:00 to 5:00 P.M. Admission is $4.00. Church activities may preempt visiting hours.

The menu at the lovely **Crabtree's Kittle House Restaurant and Country Inn** changes daily, but the food, ambience, and service remain consistently superb. Guests can choose a cold salad or hot appetizer, with offerings such as butternut squash ravioli or grilled West Coast oysters. Entrees might include braised lamb shank; a portobello mushroom, spinach, and red pepper gâteau; or filet mignon. For many, dessert is the high point of a meal in this 1790 mansion, with fanciful confections such as a poached pear under spun sugar or a delicious warm pecan pie. *Wine Spectator* magazine awarded the restaurant its "Grand Award of Excellence" several times for having one of the most outstanding restaurant wine lists in the world—more than 30,000 bottles and 1,300 selections.

Crabtree's Kittle House Restaurant and Country Inn, 11 Kittle Road, Route 117, **Chappaqua,** (914) 666–8044, has twelve guest rooms with private bath that rent for $147 per night. Lunch is served weekdays, dinner nightly, and brunch on Sunday from noon to 2:30 P.M. Reservations are highly recommended, especially on weekends. There's live jazz in the Tap Room Friday and Saturday evenings.

In 1826 the State of New York built **Sing Sing Prison,** in **Ossining,** using convict labor. The prison became famous when "Father" Pat O'Brien walked "gangster" Jimmy Cagney "the last mile" to its electric chair in the movie *Angels with Dirty Faces*. Today a replica of the chair is part of a fascinating exhibition at **Ossining Heritage Area Park Visitors Center.** Divided into two themes, "Down the River: The Old Croton Aqueduct" and "Up the River: Sing Sing Prison," the first part focuses on the construction of the city's aqueduct, historic downtown buildings, and the prison. The second part includes weapons made by prisoners and replicas of an 1825 and a present-day cell.

The Ossining Heritage Area Park Visitors Center, 95 Broadway, Ossining, (914) 941–3189, is open daily except Sunday from 10:00 A.M. to 4:00 P.M. Admission is free.

While it's off the beaten path, the Croton Dam is not easily overlooked—it's the second-largest hand-hewn structure in the world. The 297-foot-high, 2,168-foot-long dam was built in 1892 just outside Ossining, and it's estimated that it has as much stone in it as Egypt's Great Pyramid. The reservoir behind the dam supplies about 400 million gallons of water to New York City each day. The dam is part of **Croton Point Park** and the trailhead for the 26-mile-long Old Croton Aqueduct Trail, which ends at 173rd Street in Manhattan.

Croton Point Park, Route 129, Croton, (914) 862–5290, is open dawn to dusk. There is an $8.00 fee per car from Memorial Day to Labor Day.

Peekskill is home to more than seventy artists who work in a variety of media. Many of them host **Open Artist Studio Tours** the third Saturday of each month, and there's a two-hour guided art tour, which leaves from the Paramount Theater at 10:45 A.M. ($10.00; seniors $8.50) from May through October. If you're visiting between mid-June and October, stop at the **Peekskill Farmer's Market** on Bank Street. For information contact The Peekskill Business Improvement District at (914) 737–2780.

Another important figure of the early Republic, political rather than literary, made his country home to the northeast at **Katonah.** This was **John Jay,** whom George Washington appointed to be the first chief justice of the United States and who, with Alexander Hamilton and James Madison, was an author of the *Federalist Papers.* Jay retired to the farmhouse now known as the **John Jay Homestead** in 1801, after nearly three decades of public service, and lived here until his death in 1829.

His son William and his grandson John Jay II lived at the old family homestead, as did John II's son Col. William Jay II, a Civil War officer of the Union Army. The last Jay to live at the Katonah estate was Eleanor Jay Iselin, the colonel's daughter. After her death in 1953, the property was purchased by Westchester County and turned over to the State of New York as a state historic site.

Having survived so long in the Jay family, the John Jay Homestead is still well stocked with furnishings and associated items that date back to the days when the great patriot lived here. Sixty acres of John Jay's original 900-acre farm are part of the state historic site.

The John Jay Homestead State Historic Site, 400 Route 22, Katonah, (914) 232–5651, is open April through October, with tours Wednesday through Sunday 10:00 A.M. to 4:00 P.M. Call for off-season hours. Tours are given every hour on the hour. Group tours are by advance reservation. There is a fee of $3.00 for adults, $2.00 for seniors, and $1.00 for children. The grounds are open from dawn to dusk year-round.

Almost Better Than His Pulitzer

When people talk about the romance of the rails, they seldom have commuter trains in mind. But New York's Metro-North, which hauls thousands of suburbanites in and out of Grand Central Station each day, has taken on a bit more panache ever since it began naming individual cars after prominent people associated with its territory along the Hudson Valley.

None of these cars is more freighted with poignant associations for Westchester commuters than the John Cheever. Cheever, a longtime resident of Ossining, was the great chronicler of postwar suburban life. His heroes and heroines poured into Grand Central from places like Shady Hill and Bullet Park, imaginary in name only, and rode back each night to seek love and redemption among their rhododendrons.

If you're walking along the Hudson at twilight and see the *John Cheever* roll by, raise a phantom glass (very dry, with an olive) to those phantom commuters and to the man who made their longings universal.

In 1907 financier J.P. Morgan built a stone-and-brick Tudor mansion on a hillside overlooking the Hudson River Valley for his friend and minister, William S. Rainsford. The mansion was privately owned until 1973, when it was restored and reborn as a French restaurant called *Le Chateau.* Today, with its dogwood-lined approach, patio and gardens, richly paneled rooms, and elegantly set tables, the restaurant affords patrons the opportunity to enjoy a rapidly diminishing phenomenon—a true dining experience. At Le Chateau, classic French food is prepared and presented in a grand style that matches the atmosphere in which it is served.

Among the house specialties at Le Chateau are lobster bisque; snails with garlic butter; roasted sea scallops; and Chateaubriand for two. Elegant desserts include a chocolate and Grand Marnier soufflé and crème brûlée (caramelized custard). A three-course a la carte dinner averages $47. Sunday brunch ($34) includes a dessert buffet.

Le Chateau, Route 35 at the junction of Route 123, *South Salem,* (914) 533–6631, serves dinner nightly except Monday and a seasonal Sunday brunch. Reservations are a must, and jackets are required.

Muscoot Farms is an agricultural holdout in the rapidly suburbanizing Westchester landscape. Dating to the early 1900s, the 777-acre working farm has a twenty-three-room main house, barns and outbuildings, antique equipment, a large demonstration vegetable garden, and lots of animals. Weekends are a busy time; in addition to hayrides, agricultural programs cover topics such as sheepshearing and harvesting. There's also a full roster of seasonal festivals. The farm, on Route 100 in Katonah, (914) 232–7118, is open daily Memorial Day through Labor Day 10:00 A.M. to 6:00 P.M. Donations are welcome. Groups must preregister.

The largest Buddha statue in the Western hemisphere is 37 feet high and is surrounded by 10,000 small statues of the Buddha on a lotus terrace. Surrounding the pedestal of the Great Buddha are twelve bas-reliefs of Bodhisattvas. It is only fitting that such a statue be housed in a building of great stature, and the Hall of Ten Thousand Buddhas Encircling Buddha Vairocana (also known as "the Great Buddha Hall") fits the bill. Done in the style of architecture of the Tang Dynasty (A.D. 618–A.D. 907), it is 84 feet tall, contains 24,000 square feet of space, and can fit 2,000 people in the main hall. Murals by Professor C. G. Chen, including one 8 feet high and 104 feet long depicting scenes from the "Pure Land," or Amitabha Buddha, cover the walls. Professor Chen also designed and created the Great Buddha and the little Buddhas.

All this and more are at the Buddhist Association of the United States' *Chuang Yen Monastery.* Another building, Kuan-Yin Hall, also in the style of the Tang Dynasty, houses a number of rare pieces of art, including a statue dating from the Tang Dynasty itself and a colored porcelain statue dating from the Ming Dynasty.

The Chuang Yen Monastery, Route 301, *Carmel,* (845) 225–1819, welcomes visitors who wish to tour the buildings and grounds and/or to stay, study, and meditate.

Central Valley

It takes an interesting region to supply the wherewithal for an interesting regional museum, and Brewster in southern Putnam County has done a good job of filling the bill for the *Southeast Museum.* The town has been the center of a diverse number of enterprises, including mining, railroading, circuses, and even the manufacture of condensed milk. Reminders of these phases of local history are on exhibit at the museum, which is housed in the 1896 Old Town Hall of Southeast, although the area is commonly referred to as *Brewster,* for the family that rose to prominence in the 1840s and 1850s.

The first settlers came about 1725. For more than one hundred years, their main pursuits were agriculture and modest cottage industries. In the mid-nineteenth century, Brewster's economic horizons expanded through the arrival of the Harlem Railroad, which became part of Commodore Vanderbilt's vast New York Central system, and the Putnam Line Railroad, a division of the New York and New Haven Line. Railroad days in Brewster are represented at the museum by the artifacts in the David McLane collection.

Brewster was also winter quarters for a number of circuses in the past century. Many of these small local enterprises were later consolidated by **P.T. Barnum,** who hailed from Bridgeport, just across the state line in Connecticut. This most colorful aspect of Brewster's past is recalled in the museum's collection of early American circus memorabilia.

The Southeast Museum is at 67 Main Street, Brewster, (845) 279–7500 and is open April through December. Call for hours and information on special events. Suggested donation is $2.00. Village walking tours are available.

Your six-course meal at **Harralds,** in **Stormville,** includes a choice of eight delicious appetizers, a hot or chilled soup, a selection from fifteen main courses, and a variety of cheeses, elegant desserts (including an excellent cheesecake), fresh fruits, port wine, and fresh ground coffee. The menu changes daily and each night is wheeled to your table on a blackboard. As you would expect of a restaurant that has consistently earned high accolades since it opened in 1968, everything is deliciously prepared, artfully presented, and graciously served. A three-course menu is also available.

Harralds is housed in a large, timbered, 200-year-old cottage with a big stone hearth, brass chandeliers, and a candlelit patio. The custom-built wine house across the way stores more than 250 different wines, most under $30. Harrald Boerger is general manager of the restaurant; his wife, Eva Durrschmidt Boerger, is presiding chef. They work together to ensure diners a splendid gastronomic experience.

Harralds, Route 25, Stormville, (845) 878–6595, serves dinner Wednesday through Saturday from 6:00 to 9:00 P.M. Reservations are a must, jackets are required, and credit cards are not accepted. The six-course fixed-price meal is $65 per person, not including wine. The three-course dinner is $40 per person.

Not all of the Hudson Valley landowners were well-to-do. Most were burghers of a far more modest stamp. The legacy of the life led by one such family is preserved in the **Van Wyck Homestead Museum,** a National Historic Site, east of the river in **Fishkill.** The house was begun in 1732 by Cornelius Van Wyck, who had purchased his nearly 1,000 acres of land from an earlier 85,000-acre Dutchess County estate, and was completed in the 1750s with the construction of the West Wing. For all the land its owners possessed, the homestead is nevertheless a modest affair, a typical Dutch country farmhouse.

Like so many other farmhouses, the Van Wyck Homestead might have been forgotten by history had it not played a part in the American Revolution. Located as it was along the strategic route between New York City and the

Champlain Valley, the house was requisitioned by the Continental Army to serve as headquarters for General Israel Putnam. Fishkill served as an important supply depot for General Washington's northern forces from 1776 to 1783. Military trials were held at the house; one such event was reputedly the source used by *James Fenimore Cooper* for an incident in his novel *The Spy.*

Another factor leading to the homestead's preservation was its having reverted to the Van Wyck family after the revolution ended. Descendants of its builder lived here for more than 150 years. Today it is operated by the Fishkill Historical Society as a museum of colonial life in the Hudson Valley. The house features a working colonial kitchen fireplace with a beehive oven, which is used during special events. An interesting sidelight is the exhibit of Revolutionary War artifacts unearthed in the vicinity during archaeological digs sponsored by the society.

The Van Wyck Homestead Museum, 504 Route 9, (near the intersection of Routes 9 and 84), Fishkill, (845) 896–9560, is open Memorial Day through October on Saturday and Sunday from 1:00 to 4:00 P.M. and by appointment. There is an admission charge of $2.00. Special events include September and holiday craft fairs, a June midsummer festival, and a St. Nicholas Day holiday tour.

Lewis Country Farms, a sixteen-acre farm with restored 1861 barns (complete with silo, original post-and-beam ceiling supports, and fieldstone walls), is an all-season kids' stop and shopping mecca.

There are live farm animals for petting, a gift and flower shop, a deli, a greenhouse and garden center, and when you get hungry, the folks at Lewis Country Farms will serve up homemade soups and chili and sandwiches.

Lewis Country Farms, Overlook and DeGarmo Roads, *Poughkeepsie,* (845) 452–7650, is open daily 9:00 A.M. to 5:00 P.M.

In 1847 *Samuel F. B. Morse,* inventor of the telegraph and Morse code, purchased one hundred acres of land and a seventeen-year-old Georgian house. With the help of his friend, architect Alexander Jackson Davis, he transformed the original structure into a Tuscan-style villa. Today, **Locust Grove, Samuel Morse Historic Site,** a unique combination of 150 acres of nature preserve, historic gardens, landscaped lawns, vistas, and architecture, is one of the most handsome of the Hudson River estates. In 1963 it became the first in the valley to be designated a National Historic Landmark.

Thirty years after Morse's death, his family sold the property to the Young family, who preserved it essentially as it had been in Morse's time, until 1975, when the estate was bequeathed to a trust "for the enjoyment, visitation, and enlightenment of the public."

Original family furnishings of the Youngs and the Morses are exhibited in period room settings and include rare Duncan Phyfe and Chippendale pieces.

Paintings include works by Mr. Morse—a fine painter in his own right—as well as by artists such as George Inness. There's also a rare bound collection of *Birds of America* by J.J. Audubon. A replica of "the invention of the century" is on exhibit in the Morse Room.

Locust Grove, Samuel Morse Historic Site, 2683 South Road (Route 9), Poughkeepsie, (845) 454–4500, is open daily May through Thanksgiving, from 10:00 A.M. to 3:00 P.M. Admission is $7.00 for adults, $6.00 for seniors, and $3.00 for those between the ages of 3 and 18. There is no fee to walk the grounds, which are open from 8:00 A.M. to dusk.

You're now in *The Culinary Institute of America* country. Founded in 1946, it's the oldest culinary college in the United States and the only residential college in the world devoted entirely to culinary education. The public is invited to sample the fare from any or all of its four student-staffed restaurants and its cafe on the 150-acre Hyde Park campus, which serve lunch from 11:30 A.M. to 1:00 P.M. and dinner from 6:30 to 8:30 P.M.

St. Andrew's Cafe features a simple and elegant selection of dishes, emphasizing fresh seasonal ingredients with a touch of Asian inspiration. The restaurant is open Monday through Friday for lunch and dinner. Reservations are recommended.

The *Ristorante Caterina de' Medici* spotlights seasonal ingredients and indigenous flavor combinations of the various regions of Italy. The restaurant is open Monday through Friday for lunch and dinner. It is in the new Colavita Center for Italian Food and Wine. Reservations are required.

The casual *Al Forno Room* serves pizza, salad, and antipasti. (Reservations are not required for Al Forno.)

The *Escoffier Restaurant,* open Tuesday through Saturday, highlights classic French cuisine prepared according to the principles of legendary chef Auguste Escoffier, but with a lighter contemporary touch. Lunch and dinner are served. Reservations are required.

The *American Bounty Restaurant* serves a variety of regional American dishes as well as a daily special from the Julia Child Rotisserie kitchen.

You Never Know Where You'll End Up

Pierre Teilhard de Chardin, the great Jesuit theologian and philosopher who wrote *The Future of Man*, was buried beneath a simple marker in the graveyard of the Jesuit seminary at St. Andrews-on-Hudson. But it isn't a seminary any longer—the complex was sold by the order some years ago, and now Teilhard rests alongside the Culinary Institute of America.

The restaurant serves lunch and dinner Tuesday through Saturday. Reservations are required,

The **Apple Pie Bakery Cafe** features daily fresh-baked breads, cakes, cookies, and pies; lunch items such as soups, sandwiches, and salads; and confections. Specialty beverages include coffees, teas, local cider, wine, beer, and soft drinks. Hours are Monday through Friday 8:00 A.M. to 6:30 P.M. No reservations taken.

The Culinary Institute of America is on Route 9 in Hyde Park, (845) 452–9600. Reservations are recommended at all of the restaurants and can be made by calling (845) 471–6608 Monday through Friday 8:30 A.M. to 5:00 P.M. Enter through the main gate and follow signs for the restaurants.

Those who love cooking—or eating—will enjoy poking through the Culinary Institute of America's **Conrad N. Hilton Library.** The $7.5 million, 45,000-square-foot facility houses one of the largest collections of culinary works in the country. In addition to more than 68,000 volumes, the library has a video viewing center and a video theater.

The Conrad N. Hilton Library is open Monday through Thursday 8:00 A.M. to 11:00 P.M., Friday 8:00 A.M. to 5:00 P.M., Saturday 9:00 A.M. to 5:00 P.M., and Sunday noon to 8:00 P.M. The research staff is available Monday through Friday from 8:30 A.M. to 5:00 P.M. The library is immediately on your left after you pass through the main gate.

Whenever Eleanor Roosevelt took time out from the many causes she championed before, during, and after her husband's presidency, she retreated to Val-Kill, a small, fieldstone cottage that F.D.R. had built for her in 1925 by a stream on the grounds of the Roosevelt family estate. The cottage became the permanent home for two dear friends, New York Democratic Committee co-workers Nancy Cook and Marion Dickerman, and whenever Eleanor returned home, she would opt to stay here rather than in the nearby family mansion presided over by Franklin's autocratic mother, Sara Delano Roosevelt.

In 1926 the women, along with Caroline O'Day, built a second, larger building to house Val-Kill Industries, intended to teach farm workers how to manufacture goods, thus keeping them from migrating to large cities in search of work. Until the business closed in 1936—a victim of the Great Depression—the workers manufactured replicas of Early American furniture, weavings, and pewter pieces. At this point, Mrs. Roosevelt converted the building into apartments for herself and her secretary Malvina "Tommy" Thompson, and added several guest rooms. She renamed the building Val-Kill Cottage and wrote to her daughter: "My house seems nicer than ever and I could be happy in it alone! That's the last test of one's surroundings." Among the visitors to Val-Kill were John F. Kennedy, Adlai Stevenson, Nikita Khrushchev, and Jawaharlal Nehru.

After Mrs. Roosevelt died in 1962 several developers tried to take over her home, but they were thwarted when a group of concerned citizens organized to preserve the site. In 1977 President Jimmy Carter signed a bill creating the ***Eleanor Roosevelt National Historic Site.*** Today visitors can tour the cottages and grounds.

Eleanor Roosevelt National Historic Site, Route 9G, 519 Albany Post Road, Hyde Park, (845) 229-9115 or (800) 967–2283 (reservations only), is open May through October, daily 9:00 A.M. to 5:00 P.M.; and from November through April, Saturday and Sunday 9:00 A.M. to 5:00 P.M. Admission is $8.00 adults, children under 17, free.

Heading north past ***Hyde Park,*** we're back in mansion territory, but with a difference. Homes such as Philipse Manor Hall were built by men whose fortunes were founded in vast landholdings, but palaces such as the ***Mills Mansion State Historic Site*** in Staatsburg represent the glory days of industrial and financial captains—the so-called Gilded Age of the late nineteenth century. The idea behind this sort of house building was to live not like a country squire but like a Renaissance doge.

Ogden Mills's neoclassical mansion was finished in 1896, but its story begins more than a hundred years earlier. In 1792 the property on which it stands was purchased by Morgan Lewis, great-grandfather of Mills's wife, Ruth Livingston Mills. Lewis, an officer in the revolution and the third postindependence governor of New York State, built two houses here. The first burned in 1832, at which time it was replaced by an up-to-date Greek Revival structure.

Mills Mansion State Historic Site

This was the home that stood on the property when it was inherited by Ruth Livingston Mills in 1890.

But Ogden Mills had something far grander in mind for his wife's legacy. He hired a firm with a solid reputation in mansion building to enlarge the home and embellish its interiors—a popular firm among wealthy clients, one that went by the name of **McKim, Mead, and White.**

The architects added two spacious wings and decked out both the new and the old portions of the exterior with balustrades and pilasters more reminiscent of Blenheim Palace than anything previously seen in the Hudson Valley. The interior was (and is) French, in Louis XV and XVI period styles—lots of carving and gilding on furniture and wall and ceiling surfaces, along with oak paneling and monumental tapestries.

The last of the clan to live here was Ogden L. Mills, at one time U.S. secretary of the treasury, who died in 1937. One of his surviving sisters donated the home to the State of New York, which opened it to the public as a state historic site.

The Mills Mansion State Historic Site, off Route 9, Staatsburg, (845) 889–8851, is open from mid-April through Labor Day, Wednesday through Saturday 10:00 A.M. to 5:00 P.M. and Sunday noon to 5:00 P.M. From Labor Day through the last Sunday in October, the mansion is open Wednesday through Sunday noon to 5:00 P.M. It is also open in December, Wednesday through Sunday noon to 5:00 P.M. Admission is $5.00 for adults, $4.00 for seniors and students; $1.00 for children ages 5 to 12; 4 and under free.

If touring the area's numerous mansions has left you with "mansion envy," reserve a room at **Belvedere Mansion,** a grand Greek Revival hilltop estate overlooking the Hudson River. Guests can choose one of the beautifully appointed "cottage" rooms—each with its own entrance and private bath—in a separate building facing the mansion, or one of the smaller "cozies." A full country breakfast is served fireside in the winter and, in warmer months, alfresco in a pavilion gazebo overlooking a fountain and pond. A candlelit dinner in the elegant restaurant might include delicacies such as an appetizer of gâteau of wild mushrooms and chèvre with a truffle vinaigrette and entrees such as braised lamb shank with saffron risotto, artichokes, and mint.

Belvedere Mansion in **Staatsburg** (mailing address: P.O. Box 785, Rhinebeck 12572), (845) 889–8000; www.belvederemansion.com, is open year-round. Rates range from $75 to $95 for the "cozies" to $275 in the mansion. Rooms in the Carriage House range from $150 to $195; in the Hunting Lodge, there are four suites, including one with a fireplace, for $250 to $450; there is a two-night minimum stay on weekends and a three-night minimum on holiday weekends. Guests have use of the tennis court and outdoor pool.

Troutbeck, on the banks of the trout-filled Webatuck River in Amenia, is an English-style country estate that functions as a corporate conference center during the week and as a country inn on weekends. The 422-acre retreat, with its slate-roofed mansion with leaded windows, is a perfect place for a romantic weekend. There are nine fireplaced bedrooms, many rooms with canopy beds, an oak-paneled library, gardens—even a pool and tennis courts. And, of course, gourmet dining.

The former home of poet-naturalist Myron B. Benton, Troutbeck was a gathering place for celebrities during the early decades of the twentieth century. Ernest Hemingway, Sinclair Lewis, and Teddy Roosevelt are said to have been houseguests of the Springarn family, who owned the house from 1902 to 1978.

The restaurant, open to the public for lunch and dinner Wednesday through Saturday and Sunday brunch, has an excellent kitchen and features dinner entrees such as smoked Maine lobster and oven-braised Black Angus veal shanks. The dessert menu, with "everything that you always wanted to try," includes goodies such as Georgia peach and ginger-cream strudel.

Troutbeck, Leedsville Road, *Amenia,* (845) 373–9681 or (800) 978–7688; www.troutbeck.com, is open year-round. Weekend rates include two nights' lodging and meals, and range from $650 to $1,050 a couple.

The Wetmore family, who own **Cascade Mountain Winery and Restaurant,** say of their product, "Regional wine is a way of tasting our seasons past. Last summer's sunshine, the snows of winter, rain, and frost; it's all there in a glass." You can sample Hudson Valley's seasons past at the vineyard, which offers tours and tastings daily year-round from 10:00 A.M. to 5:00 P.M. They also serve lunch Thursday through Sunday noon to 3:00 P.M. and dinner Saturday from 6:00 to 8:30 P.M.

Don't look for hamburgers on the menu; the kitchen takes pride in serving gourmet meals with a regional touch. Menu samplings might include chilled smoked sturgeon with red rice salad, fresh asparagus, and horseradish cream; house smoked baby back ribs with Dijon potato salad; and grilled spice-rubbed porterhouse steak with demi-glaze, cilantro red rice, and vegetables. Happy

Basso Profundo

The year 2003 saw a new New York State record for striped bass caught in freshwater, when a 55-pounder was taken on the Hudson River. The record saltwater striper, taken off Montauk Point on Long Island, tipped the scales at 76 pounds.

Dropping in on Ms. Day

Three college friends and I were driving along the Hudson's eastern shore, one day in the spring of 1970, when one of our group remarked that we weren't far from the old mansion where Dorothy Day, the journalist and social reformer who was the guiding spirit behind the radical newspaper called the *Catholic Worker,* ran a summer settlement house for troubled urban youth. He had worked with Ms. Day in New York City and suggested we stop in and meet her. She greeted us at the door, made tea, and served cake she had made that morning. At 73, Dorothy Day came across less as a legend of the American Progressive movement, which she was, than as a gracious hostess, more than happy to chat with unexpected guests.

—Bill Scheller

hour features music, hot and cold hors d'oeuvres, tours and tastings, and, of course, wine.

Cascade Mountain Winery and Restaurant is on Cascade Mountain Road in Amenia, (845) 373–9021.

Although its location is off the beaten path, the **Old Drovers Inn** is very much on the main track for those who love gourmet dining and superb accommodations. Winner of some of the industry's most prestigious awards, including AAA's Four Diamond Award and an award of excellence for its wine list and cellar from *Wine Spectator,* the inn, a Relais and Chateau property, was also named one of the five Gourmet Retreats of the Year in Andrew Harper's *Hideaway Report.*

The beautifully restored colonial inn, in continuous use since it was built in 1750, was originally a stop for cattle drovers, who purchased cattle and swine from New England farmers and drove the animals down the post roads to markets in New York City.

The inn's signature dishes, cheddar cheese soup and browned turkey hash, reflect its colonial heritage. Dinner entrees such as grilled magret of duck reflect the kitchen's blending of American and European styles. A tavern menu is also available at lunch and dinner.

Like the food, the four guest suites are elegant. Prices range from $150 midweek for the intimate, antique-filled Rose Room to $475 on weekends and holidays for the Meeting Room, with a unique barrel-shaped ceiling and fireplace. American breakfast and full dinner are included on weekends. Pets are permitted for a fee of $25 per day with advance approval.

Old Drovers Inn, Old Route 22, **Dover Plains,** (845) 832–9311; www.old droversinn.com serves lunch Friday, Saturday, and Sunday, and dinner nightly except Tuesday and Wednesday.

When Peter Wing returned from fighting in Vietnam, he was twenty-one years old and wanted to build a place where he could retreat from the world. He and his wife, Toni, worked for the next twenty-five years to create **Wing's Castle,** a fabulously eccentric stone castle overlooking the Hudson Valley. Eighty percent of the structure is made of salvaged materials from antique buildings.

Peter wasn't successful in retreating, however. Visitors from around the world stop in for tours and are surprised to learn that the castle is also the Wings' home. It's furnished with Victorian pieces, more than 2,000 antiques, and mannequins dressed in period clothing. A 7-foot-deep moat that runs under the castle serves as a swimming pool, and 12- and 13-foot hand-hewn rocks that Peter removed from an old building are arranged in a circle to create Stonehenge East.

Wing's Castle, 717 Bangall Road, **Millbrook,** (845) 677–9085, is open Wednesday through Sunday June 1 through September 1, noon to 5:00 P.M.; September through December 20, weekends only, noon to 4:30 P.M. Tours are given on the half hour. Admission is $7.00 for adults and $5.00 for children ages 4 to 11.

At **Innisfree Garden,** Eastern design concepts combine with American techniques to create a "cup garden," which has origins in Chinese paintings dating back a thousand years.

The cup garden draws attention to something rare or beautiful, segregating it so that it can be enjoyed without distraction. It can be anything—from a single rock covered with lichens and sedums to a meadow. Each forms a three-dimensional picture. Innisfree Garden is a series of cup gardens—streams, waterfalls, plants—each its own picture and each a visual treat.

Innisfree Garden, Tyrrel Road, Millbrook, (845) 677–8000, is open early May to October 20, Wednesday through Friday 10:00 A.M. to 4:00 P.M. and weekends and legal holidays 11:00 A.M. to 5:00 P.M. It is closed Monday and Tuesday except legal holidays. Admission is $3.00 for those 6 years and older on weekdays and $4.00 on weekends and holidays. A picnic area is open to visitors.

"There I was, minding my own business. I was standing by the side of the road, investigating a potential dinner, when some lunatic in a rusty Plymouth knocked me 10 feet into the air."

Thus begins a column by Elizabeth T. Vulture in the *Raptor Report,* news bulletin of the **Hudson Valley Raptor Center.** Luckily for Elizabeth—whose vision was never quite the same—she was rescued and given a home at the center. In addition to caring for injured raptors and returning as many as possible to the wild, the center offers the public a chance to meet and learn about all birds of prey, including bald eagles, red-tailed hawks, peregrine falcons, and great horned owls. It houses more than one hundred raptors of twenty species, many of which are threatened or endangered.

The Hudson Valley Raptor Center, 148 South Road, Route 53 (R.R. 1, Box 437B), Lafayetteville, (845) 758–6957, is open April through October on Saturday and Sunday from 1:00 to 4:00 P.M., and in July and August, Wednesday through Friday 1:00 P.M. to 4:00 P.M. There is a raptor demonstration at 2:00 P.M. Admission is $7.00 for adults, $5.00 for seniors and students, and $2.50 for children ages 12 and under. Off-season hours by appointment.

The *Old Rhinebeck Aerodrome,* 3 miles upriver from the town of *Rhinebeck,* is more than just a museum—many of the pre-1930s planes exhibited here actually take to the air each weekend.

The three main buildings at the aerodrome house a collection of aircraft, automobiles, and other vehicles from the period 1900–37 and are open throughout the week. On Saturday and Sunday, though, you can combine a tour of the exhibits on the ground with attendance at an air show featuring both original aircraft and accurate reproductions. Saturdays are reserved for flights of planes from the Pioneer (pre–World War I) and Lindbergh eras. On Sundays the show is a period-piece melodrama in which intrepid Allied fliers do battle with the "Black Baron." Where else can you watch a live dogfight?

All that's left at this point is to go up there yourself, and you can do just that. The aerodrome has on hand a 1929 New Standard D-25—which carries four passengers wearing helmets and goggles—for open-cockpit flights of fifteen minutes' duration. The cost is $40 per person, and rides are available on weekends, before and after the show.

Old Rhinebeck Aerodrome, 44 Stone Church Road, Rhinebeck, (845) 758–8610, is open daily May 15 through the end of October from 10:00 A.M. to 5:00 P.M. On Saturday and Sunday from mid-June through mid-October, the air show begins at 2:00 P.M. and includes a fashion show, in which ladies from the audience dress up in vintage clothing. Weekday admission is $6.00 for adults, $5.00 for seniors, $2.00 for children ages 6 to 10, and free for children under 6. Admission for weekend air shows is $15.00 for adults, $10.00 for seniors, and $5.00 for children ages 6 to 10. The plane rides cost extra, as mentioned above.

America's oldest continuously operated hotel, the *Beekman Arms,* opened for business as the Traphagen Inn in 1766. A meeting place for American Revolutionary War generals, the Beekman was also the site of Franklin Delano Roosevelt's election eve rallies from the beginning of his career right through his presidency. Visitors can choose from one of fourteen rooms in the inn, the motel, or in the fourty-four room *Delamater Inn* (845–786–7080), a block away, built in 1844 and one of the few early examples of American Gothic residences still in existence. The inn's accomodatiaons include seven guest houses, serveral with fireplaces, clustered around a courtyard.

The Beekman Arms and Delamater Inn, Route 9, Rhinebeck, (845) 876–7077; www.beekmandelamaterinn.com is open year-round. Rates range from $120 to $170 in the Arms, $100 to $125 in the contemporary motel, and $95 to $180 in the Delamater House. All rooms have private bath, TV, phone, and a complimentary decanter of sherry. A two-night minimum stay is required weekends from May through October and holiday weekends. Lunch, dinner, and Sunday brunch are served in the restaurant, and there is a cozy tap room.

China Rose, which bills itself as "a Chinese Bistro," serves delicious classic dishes from regions throughout China. Among the standouts are Hunan pork dumplings with hot sauce and Peking-style duck. For the kids there's lo mein; for those who like it hot, pork in tiger sauce and hot and sour soup. The restaurant, at 1 Schatzel Avenue, Rhinecliff, (845) 876–7442, opens for dinner nightly at 5:00 P.M. except Tuesday. Reservations aren't accepted, so go early. A second location, at 608 Ulster Avenue in Kingston (845) 338–7443, serves lunch and dinner. Hours are Monday through Friday 11:30 A.M. to 10:00 P.M.; Saturday 3:00 to 10:00 P.M.; closed Sunday.

John and Jan Gilmor create a variety of mouth-blown and hand-pressed stemware, tableware, decorative vessels, and ornaments from glass that John formulates from scratch, working with his wife to develop unique colors and finishes. Their pieces are featured in international and presidential collections. At **Gilmor Glassworks,** at the corner of Routes 22 and 44 in **Millerton,** (518) 789–6700, visitors are invited to watch the artists while they work at the glass furnaces but are urged to call ahead to find out when the "hot process" can be observed. First-quality and irregular pieces are on sale. Shop hours are Monday through Saturday 10:00 A.M. to 5:00 P.M. and Sunday 11:00 A.M. to 5:00 P.M.

Kaatsbaan is "dedicated to the growth, advancement, and preservation of professional dance." Facilities at the 153-acre site overlooking the Hudson River include a 160-seat performance theater and three dance studios.

Write to Kaatsbaan International Dance Center at P.O. Box 482, Tivoli 12583. A list of events is posted on their Web site; www.Kaatsbaan.org; or call (845) 757–5106.

There was a time when every schoolchild worthy of a gold star on his or her reports knew the name *Clermont*. Of course, it was the first successful steamboat, built by **Robert Fulton** and tested on the Hudson River. Less commonly known, however, is that the boat formally registered by its owners as *The North River Steamboat of Clermont* took its name from the estate of **Robert R. Livingston,** chancellor of New York and a backer of Fulton's experiments. **Clermont,** one of the great family seats of the valley, overlooks the Hudson River near Germantown.

The story of Clermont begins with the royal charter granted to Robert Livingston in 1686, which made the Scottish-born trader Lord of the Manor of Livingston, a 162,000-acre tract that would evolve into the entire southern third of modern-day Columbia County. When Livingston died in 1728, he broke with the English custom of strict adherence to primogeniture by giving 13,000 acres of his land to his third son. This was Clermont, the Lower Manor, on which Robert of Clermont, as he was known, established his home in 1728.

Two more Robert Livingstons figure in the tale after this point: Robert of Clermont's son, a New York judge, and *his* son, a member of the Second Continental Congress who filled the now-obsolete office of state chancellor. It was the chancellor's mother, Margaret Beekman Livingston, who rebuilt the house after it was burned in 1777 by the British (parts of the original walls are incorporated into the present structure).

The Livingston family lived at Clermont until 1962, making various enlargements and modifications to their home over time. In that year the house, its furnishings, and the 500 remaining acres of the Clermont estate became the property of the State of New York.

The mansion at Clermont State Historic Site (also a National Historic Landmark) has been restored to its circa 1930 appearance; however, the collections are primarily half eighteenth- and half nineteenth-century French and early American. Tours of Clermont include the first and second floors. An orientation exhibit and a short film are given at the visitor center. There are formal gardens, woodsy hiking trails, and spacious landscapes (perfect for picnics) on bluffs overlooking the Hudson.

Clermont, 1 Clermont Avenue, off Route 9G, *Germantown,* (518) 537–4240, is open Tuesday through Sunday and on Monday holidays from 11:00 A.M. to 5:00 P.M. (last tour at 4:30). From November through March, hours are 11:00 A.M. to 4:00 P.M. (last tour at 3:30), weekends only. The grounds are open and free daily year-round from 8:30 A.M. to sunset. The Visitor Center is open from April through October, Tuesday through Sunday and Monday holidays 10:30 A.M. to 5:00 P.M. and November through March, weekends 11:00 A.M. to 4:00 P.M. The Heritage Music Festival is held in mid-July. Admission to the mansion is $5.00 for adults, $4.00 for seniors, and $1.00 for children ages 5 to 12.

Want to paddle a sea kayak around the Statue of Liberty? How about past Sing Sing Prison or up through the northern Hudson Highlands past Bannerman's Castle on Pollepel Island? *Atlantic Kayak Tours,* the largest sea kayaking business in the tri-state area, offers these tours and many more throughout the waters of Connecticut, New Jersey, and the Empire State, and you don't need any experience to join up. They're at 320 West Saugerties Road in Saugerties, (845) 246–2187. The company also offers kayak tours and lessons on the

Lower Hudson River at Annsville Creek Paddlesport Center on the grounds of Hudson Highlands State Park. That facility is open weekends in April; daily from May through August; Saturday, Sunday, and Wednesday through Friday in September and October; and Saturday, Sunday, Thursday, and Friday from October 12 through the end of October. Check out their Web site: www .AtlanticKayakTours.com.

History generally conditions us to expect the great houses of the world to belong to industrialists and landholders, while artists—so the cliché has it—starve in garrets. One artist who built many fanciful garrets and starved in none of them was the Hudson River School master ***Frederic Edwin Church,*** whose Persian Gothic castle, ***Olana,*** commands a magnificent view of the river south of the town of Hudson. What the popular landscape painter did here was nothing less than sculpt the perfect embodiment of his tastes and then go on to live in it for the rest of his life.

Olana draws heavily upon Islamic and Byzantine motifs. Persian arches abound, as do Oriental carpets, brasswork, and inlaid furniture. The overall setting is typically Victorian, with no space left empty that could possibly be filled with things. What makes Olana atypical, of course, is the quality of the things.

Although Church employed as a consultant ***Calvert Vaux,*** who had collaborated with ***Frederick Law Olmsted*** on the design of New York's Central Park, the artist was the architect of his own house. When scholars describe Olana as a major work of art by Church, they are not speaking figuratively; the paints for the interior were mixed on his own palette.

Olana

Olana State Historic Site, Route 9G, Hudson, (518) 828–0135, is open *by guided tour only* from April through October, Tuesday through Sunday 10:00 A.M. to 5:00 P.M. Tours are limited to twelve people, so reservations are advised. An admission fee of $7.00 for adults, $5.00 for seniors, and $2.00 for children ages 5 to 12 is charged. The grounds are open year-round from 8:00 A.M. until sunset.

More than seventy antiques shops fill five historic walking blocks on Warren Street in **Hudson.** Furniture, clocks, porcelains, rugs, ephemera . . . the antiques district is a collector's dream. Most shops are open Thursday through Tuesday. For information call the **Hudson Antique Dealers Association** at (518) 822–9397 or check their Web site: www.hudsonantiques.net. For a complete list of shops, contact Columbia County Tourism Department at (800) 724–1846.

On July 13, 1865, Barnum's American Museum, located at the corner of Ann Street and Broadway in Manhattan and filled with the "wonders of the world," caught fire. Volunteer fire companies, some in newly introduced steam engines, rushed to the rescue and managed to save, among other things, "Old Glory," the flag that was flying from a mast on the roof.

Today Old Glory is one of just 2,500 fire-related articles on display at the **American Museum of Firefighting,** which documents nearly 300 years of firefighting history and houses one of the country's largest collections of firefighting apparatuses and memorabilia. Of the sixty-eight firefighting engines on display, the majority are nineteenth-century hand pumpers, ladder trucks, and hose carts, including a 1725 Newsham, the first successful working engine used in New York.

The museum is next door to the Volunteer Firemen's Home, a health care facility for volunteer firefighters who continue to volunteer, this time as museum guides.

The American Museum of Firefighting, 125 Harry Howard Avenue, Hudson, (518) 828–7695 or (800) 479–7695, is open 9:00 A.M. to 4:30 P.M. daily except major holidays. Admission is free.

The road less traveled can sometimes lead us to the nicest places. Route 23 out of **Hillsdale** to Craryville is such a road. It goes—via a right turn off Route 23 onto Craryville Road, and then a left onto West End Road and then right onto Rodman Road (or just follow the signs)—to **Rodgers Book Barn,** a secondhand shop considered by many bibliophiles to be one of the best in the country. The barn—a two-story affair—is packed from floor to ceiling with some 50,000 books. The collection is wonderfully eclectic: There are inexpensive '50s potboilers, tomes on European and American history, gardening books, and rare out-of-print editions in dozens of categories. The shop's owner, Maureen Rodgers, encourages browsing to the point of inviting patrons to bring along a lunch to enjoy in the grape arbor next to the herb garden.

Rodgers Book Barn, Rodgers Road, Hillsdale, (518) 325–3610, is open November through March, Friday noon to 5:00 P.M. and Saturday and Sunday 10:00 A.M. to 5:00 P.M.; April through October, Monday, Thursday, and Friday noon to 6:00 P.M.; Saturday 10:00 A.M. to 6:00 P.M.; and Sunday 11:00 A.M. to 6:00 P.M.

The *Crandall Theater* first opened its doors on Christmas Day 1926. Today, Columbia County's oldest and largest movie theater, a Spanish-style building of brick and stucco, remains proudly independent in a world of chain-owned, cookie-cutter megaplexes. Get there early, grab a bag of freshly popped popcorn and head for the balcony. You'll get a true blast from the past along with a first-run movie for only $3.50 a ticket ($2.50 for kids under 12). The theater is on Main Street in Chatham; (518) 392–3331.

Donald W. Fisher, Ph.D., knows his rocks and fossils: He's New York's State Paleontologist Emeritus. He's stocked *Fisher's O.K. Rock Shop* (O.K. stands for *Old Kinderhook*) with a wide variety of rock specimens, as well as minerals from around the world (but principally from New York, New England, Ontario, and Quebec) and fossils. Dr. Fisher also sells school kits, mineral and fossil jewelry (including Herkimer "diamonds"), geologic time charts and posters, rockhounding supplies, and a wide variety of related specialty items. And visitors to Fisher's shop can mine him for information on the best mineral and fossil sites in the state.

Fisher's O.K. Rock Shop, 2 Chatham Street (Route 9), Old Kinderhook, (518) 758–7657 (residence, 518–758–9044), is open Sunday, Monday, and Tuesday by appointment only; Wednesday through Friday noon to 5:30 P.M.; and Saturday 10:00 A.M. to 5:30 P.M. Between Thanksgiving and Christmas the shop is open Monday through Saturday 10:00 A.M. to 5:30 P.M., Friday until 8:00 P.M., and Sunday from 12:30 to 4:00 P.M.

East of Albany

The *Shaker Museum and Library* in *Old Chatham* is housed in a collection of buildings located just 12 miles from *Mt. Lebanon,* New York, where the Shakers established one of their first U.S. communities.

The Shakers, formally known as the United Society of Believers in Christ's Second Appearing, were a sect founded in Britain and transplanted to America just prior to the revolution. A quietist, monastic order dedicated to equality between the sexes, sharing of community property, temperance in its broad sense, and the practice of celibacy, the sect peaked in the middle nineteenth century with about 6,000 members. Today there are fewer than a dozen Shakers living in a community at Sabbathday Lake, Maine.

Ironically, it is the secular aspects of Shaker life that are most often recalled today. The members of the communities were almost obsessive regarding simplicity and purity of form in the articles they designed and crafted for daily life; "Shaker furniture" has become a generic term for the elegantly uncluttered designs they employed. In their pursuit of the perfect form dictated by function, they even invented now ubiquitous objects such as the flat broom.

The Shaker Museum has amassed a collection of more than 18,000 objects, half of which are on display. The main building contains an orientation gallery that surveys Shaker history and provides highlights of the rest of the collection. The museum's library contains one of the two most extensive collections of Shaker material in the world. The cafe serves snacks and beverages.

The Shaker Museum and Library, 88 Shaker Museum Road (off County Route 13), Old Chatham, (518) 794–9100, is open daily except Tuesday late May to late October, from 10:00 A.M. to 5:00 P.M. Admission is $8.00 for adults, $6.00 for senior citizens, $4.00 for children ages 8 to 17, and free for children under 8. Family admission (two adults and two children) is $18.00.

In 1624 Dutchmen sailed up the Hudson River and established a fur-trading station called Fort Orange at present-day Albany. Within twenty-five years it was a thriving community. Across the river is the town of **Rensselaer,** named for the family who held the "patroonship," or feudal proprietorship, of the vast area on the east bank. **Crailo,** built in the early eighteenth century by the first Patroon's grandson, recalls a time when the Dutch were still the predominant cultural presence in the area.

Crailo changed with time and tastes. A Georgian-style east wing added, in 1762, reflected the increasing influence of the English in the area; Federal touches were added later in the century. Since 1933 the house has served as a museum of the Dutch in the upper Hudson Valley. Exhibits include seventeenth- and eighteenth-century prints and archaeological artifacts, many from the Fort Orange excavation of 1970–71.

Crailo State Historic Site, 9½ Riverside Avenue, Rensselaer, (518) 463–8738, is open mid-April through late October, Wednesday through Saturday from 10:00 A.M. to 5:00 P.M. Crailo is also open on Tuesday in July and August. From

Ring around the Collar

According to local lore Mrs. Hannah Lord Montague of Troy spawned a new industry when, in 1825, she cut the soiled collars off her husband's otherwise clean shirts so she would only have to wash the dirty parts.

Born in the USA

During the War of 1812, Troy brickmaker Samuel Wilson opened a slaughterhouse and sold meat to a government contractor named Elbert Anderson. All of his beef and pork were stamped us-ea, and soldiers made up a story that the us, which stood for United States, actually stood for "Uncle Sam" Wilson, and thus was Uncle Sam born. A monument to his memory stands at the head of 101st Street in Troy.

November through March, visits are by appointment Tuesday through Friday 10:00 A.M. to 4:00 P.M. Tours are given on the hour and half-hour; the last tour is at 4:00 P.M. It is also open Memorial Day, Independence Day, and Labor Day. Admission is $3.00 for adults, $1.00 for children ages 5 to 12, and $2.00 per person for tour buses and New York State seniors.

Natural and social history are the focus of a **_Troy_** institution geared specifically to young people. This is **_The Junior Museum,_** a hands-on learning center that has everything from a reproduction of a circa 1850 log cabin to constellation shows in the planetarium.

The main gallery of the museum features annually changing art, history, and science exhibits. Topics range from space exploration to Hudson Valley habitat restoration; the GE Animal Nursery features a live animal collection. Exhibits on Mohican life are centered around a 12-foot bark wigwam replica, where story-telling and Indian craft activities are focused. For information on special exhibits, visit the museum's Web site at www.juniormuseum.org.

The Junior Museum, 105 Eighth Street, Troy, (518) 235–2120, is open from July 1 through Labor Day Monday through Saturday, 10:00 A.M. to 5:00 P.M.; the rest of the year Thursday 10:00 A.M. to 2:00 P.M. and Friday through Sunday 10:00 A.M. to 5:00 P.M. Admission is $6.00. Children under 3 are admitted free. Admission includes shows in the planetarium and shows with live animals.

Hoosic Valley

Most of us know that the Battle of Bunker Hill was not actually fought on Bunker Hill (it took place on Breed's Hill, also in Charlestown, Massachusetts), but how many can identify another military misnomer of the revolution?

We're talking about the 1777 Battle of Bennington, an American victory that laid the groundwork for the defeat and surrender of General Burgoyne at Saratoga that October. The battle, in which American militiamen defended their ammunition and supplies from an attacking party made up of British troops,

Tory sympathizers, mercenaries, and Indians, took place not in Bennington, Vermont, but in Walloomsac, New York. True, the stores that the British were after were stashed in the Vermont town, but the actual fighting took place on New York soil.

The State of New York today maintains the site of the battle as an official state historic site. It's on a lovely hilltop in eastern Rensselaer County's Grafton State Park, and is studded with bronze and granite markers that explain the movements of the troops on the American militia's triumphal day. The spot is located on the north side of Route 67 and is open May 1 through Labor Day, daily 10:00 A.M. to 7:00 P.M.; Labor Day to Veterans Day, weekends only 10:00 A.M. to 7:00 P.M. Visitors can check road conditions by calling **Bennington Battlefield State Historic Site** at (518) 279–1155 or get general information at (518) 686–7109. On a clear day you can enjoy fine views of the Green Mountain foothills, prominent among which is Bennington's obelisk monument. Drive over to visit the monument and give the Vermonters their due—but really, doesn't "Battle of Walloomsac" have a nice ring to it?

Will Moses, a great-grandson of the renowned primitive painter Grandma Moses, is a folk artist whose minutely detailed paintings reflect the charm and beauty of the tiny rural community where he lives. Lithographs, printed by master lithographers from original oil paintings done by Will, are exhibited and sold, along with offset prints, at **Mt. Nebo Gallery,** 60 Grandma Moses Road, **Eagle Bridge,** (518) 686–4334 or (800) 328–6326. The gallery is open Monday through Friday 9:00 A.M. to 4:00 P.M., Saturday 10:00 A.M. to 5:00 P.M., and Sunday noon to 5:00 P.M.

Our next stop on this ramble up the east shore of the Hudson offers proof that in this part of the world the monastic spirit did not pass into history with the Shakers. **Cambridge** is the home of the **New Skete Communities,** a group of monks, nuns, and laypeople organized around a life of prayer, contemplation, and physical work. Founded in 1966 within the Byzantine Rite of the Roman Catholic Church, the New Skete Communities have been a part of the Orthodox Church in America since 1979.

Visitors to New Skete are welcome at the community's two houses of worship. The small Temple of the Transfiguration of Christ, open at all times, contains a number of icons painted by the monks and nuns, while the larger Church of Christ the Wisdom of God—open to visitors only during services—has, imbedded in its marble floor, original pieces of mosaic that were brought from the A.D. 576 Church of Saint Sophia (Holy Wisdom) in Constantinople. Worship services are usually twice daily.

As in many monastic communities, the monks and the nuns of New Skete help support themselves through a wide variety of pursuits. An important part of their life is the breeding of German shepherds and the boarding and training of all breeds of dogs. The monks have even written two successful books, *How to Be Your Dog's Best Friend* and *The Art of Raising a Puppy*. At their gift shop they sell their own cheeses, smoked meats, fruitcakes, the famous New Skete cheesecakes, dogbeds, and religious cards made by the nuns, and original painted icons.

The New Skete Communities are in Cambridge. The convent is accessible from the village of Cambridge via East Main Street on Ash Grove Road, and the monastery is farther out of town on New Skete Lane. For information call the monks at (518) 677–3928 or the nuns at (518) 677–3810. The nuns' bakery is open Tuesday through Friday 9:00 A.M. to 4:00 P.M., and Saturday 10:00 A.M. to 4:00 P.M. Their Web site is www.newskete.com.

At the **Log Village Grist Mill,** built in 1810 by Hezekiah Mann, a 17-foot wooden waterwheel still provides power to three millstones that grind cornmeal, wheat flour, and buckwheat. A museum in the mill barn houses an exhibit of old farm machinery and household items, and the cider mill, built in 1894, still has the original cider press, powered by a seven-horsepower single-cylinder gas engine. Have a picnic, take a tour, and watch as several "obsolete" machines crank and grind their way through the twenty-first century.

The Log Village Grist Mill, County Route 30, **East Hartford,** (518) 632–5237, is open Saturday and some holidays from 10:00 A.M. to 6:00 P.M. and Sunday noon to 6:00 P.M. Memorial Day weekend through mid-October, and by appointment. Allow several hours to visit the mill. Adult admission is $2.50, children, 50 cents.

Places to Stay East of the Hudson

AVERILL PARK

Gregory House
Route 43
(518) 674–3774

Hillsdale Aubergine
Route 22 and 23
(518) 325–3412

HOPEWELL JUNCTION

Le Chambord
2075 Route 523
(845) 221–1941

HUDSON

Hudson House Inn
2 Main Street
(845) 265–9355

Inn at Blue Stores
2323 Route 9
(518) 537–4277

MILLERTON

Simmons' Way Village
Inn & Restaurant
33 Main Street
(518) 789–6235

POUGHKEEPSIE

Inn at the Falls
50 Red Oaks Mill Road
(800) 344–1466

Sheraton Hotel
40 Civic Center Plaza
(845) 485–5300

RHINEBECK

Gables at Rhinebeck
6358 Mill Street
(845) 876–7577

Rhinebeck Motel
117 Route 9
(845) 876–5900

Whistle Wood Farm
11 Pells Road
(845) 876–6838

TROY

Olde Judge Mansion
3300 6th Avenue
(518) 274–5698

Places to Eat East of the Hudson

AMENIA

Xe Sogni
Route 44
(845) 373–7755

BREWSTER

Red Rooster Diner
Route 22
(845) 279–8046

GARRISON

Bird & Bottle Inn
Old Albany Post Road
(845) 424–3000

KATONAH

Blue Dolphin Diner
175 Katonah Avenue
(914) 232–4791

MILBROOK

Slammin' Salmon Gourmet to Go
Franklin Avenue
(845) 677–5400

OSSINING

Brasserie Swiss
118 Croton Avenue
(914) 941–0319

PAWLING

The Corner Bakery
10 Charles Colman Boulevard
(845) 855–3707

McKinney & Doyle Fine Foods Cafe
10 Charles Colman Boulevard
(845) 855–3875

POUGHKEEPSIE

Le Pavillon
230 Salt Point Turnpike
(845) 473–2525

RED HOOK

The Village Diner
39 North Broadway
(845) 758–6232

RHINEBECK

Le Petit Bistro
8 East Market Street
(845) 876–7400

TIVOLI

Santa Fe
52 Broadway
(845) 757–4100

WHITE PLAINS

Sam's of Gedney Way
52 Gedney Way
(914) 686–2277

REGIONAL TOURIST INFORMATION— EAST OF THE HUDSON

Dutchess County Tourism,
3 Neptune Road,
Poughkeepsie,
(800) 445–3131
www.dutchesstourism.com

Poughkeepsie Area Chamber of Commerce,
110 Main Street,
Poughkeepsie,
(845) 454–1700
www.pokchamb.org

Rensselaer County Tourism,
1600 Seventh Avenue,
Troy,
(518) 270–2959
www.hightechonthehudson.com

Bardavon 1869 Opera House,
35 Market Street,
Poughkeepsie,
(845) 473–5288

Boscobel,
1601 Route 9D, Garrison,
(845) 265–3638

**FDR's Home and Library
(Springwood),**
4097 Albany-Post Road (Route 9),
Hyde Park,
(845) 229–8114 or (800) 337–8474

**Frances Lehman Loeb Art Center,
Vassar College,**
124 Raymond Avenue,
Poughkeepsie,
(845) 437–5632

Lebanon Valley Dragway,
1746 Route 20,
West Lebanon,
(518) 794–7130

Madame Brett Homestead,
50 Van Nydeck Avenue,
Beacon,
(845) 831–6533

Mary Flagler Cary Arboretum,
Route 44A,
Millbrook,
(845) 677–5359

Montgomery Place,
River Road,
Annandale-on-Hudson,
(845) 758–5461

Taconic State Park,
Route 344 off Route 22
near Copake Falls,
(518) 329–3993

**Vanderbilt Mansion National
Historic Site,**
Route 9,
Hyde Park,
(845) 229–9115 or (800) 967–2283

Wilderstein,
64 Morton Road,
Rhinebeck,
(845) 876–4818

The Adirondacks

North of the Mohawk Valley, spread between Lake Champlain and the St. Lawrence River, New York's Adirondack Mountains make up one of the nation's great expanses of near-wilderness and surely the largest slice of backcountry in the northeastern states. The state-protected **Adirondack Forest Preserve** alone accounts for more than two million acres of mountains, woodlands, and lakes, and this is only part of the six-million-acre Adirondack State Park. For sheer vastness and emptiness, the Adirondack region is rivaled in this part of the country only by the northern interior of Maine; but while inland Maine—except for Mt. Katahdin—is generally flat or gently rolling, the northern counties of New York contain forty-two peaks more than 4,000 feet in height. (The highest is **Mt. Marcy,** near Lake Placid, at 5,344 feet.) As in northern Maine, parts of the Adirondacks are still logged, although many areas have returned to a near approximation of what they looked like when white men first saw them.

Ironically, the Adirondacks have benefited from being left on the sidelines during the "discovery" of nearby Vermont and New Hampshire in the years following World War II. The two New England states have acquired a certain cachet, and they have been more heavily developed and populated as a result.

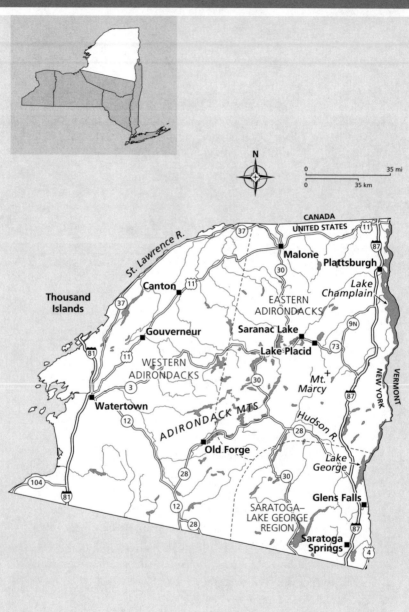

N

0   35 mi
0   35 km

CANADA
UNITED STATES

St. Lawrence R.

37

Malone

Plattsburgh

11

87

30

Canton

11

Lake
Champlain

Thousand
Islands

37

EASTERN
ADIRONDACKS

Gouverneur

Saranac Lake

9N

81

11

Lake Placid

73

WESTERN
ADIRONDACKS

Mt.
Marcy

NEW YORK

3

30

VERMONT

Watertown

12

87

ADIRONDACK MTS.

Hudson R.

28

Old Forge

Lake
George

28

30

104

Glens Falls

81

12

SARATOGA–
LAKE GEORGE
REGION

87

28

Saratoga
Springs

4

The equally beautiful Adirondacks, meanwhile, have drifted along in the public consciousness largely as the place where the famous summer chairs come from (it seems they really did originate here) and as the locale for Gilded Age "camps" on estates running into the tens of thousands of acres. Throw in the Thousand Islands, Saranac Lake, and Lakes Placid and George, and the perception is complete.

But there's so much more. In addition to being a "hidden" wilderness recreation land of such vast proportions, the Adirondacks played their part in history as well, from the French and Indian Wars through the American Revolution and the War of 1812. Once a point of friction between British Canada and the United States, today's border is marked by the engineering marvel of the St. Lawrence Seaway and by the binational resort area that has sprung up around the Thousand Islands. The southeastern gateway to the Adirondacks, Saratoga, is one of the horse-racing capitals of America. Farther north are museums that chronicle the life of the Iroquois, the art of Frederic Remington, and Adirondacks craftsmanship, boatbuilding, and pioneer life.

Head north beyond Saratoga, then, for the real "upstate" New York, a domain that rivals the expansiveness of the West yet is rooted in the traditions of the East.

(*Note:* The overall place-to-place direction followed in this chapter is counterclockwise—south to north to west.)

Saratoga–Lake George Region

North of the confluence of the Mohawk and Hudson Rivers, near the present-day towns of Mechanicville and **Stillwater,** one of the most decisive battles of world history was fought in the early days of October 1777. **The Battle of**

AUTHORS' FAVORITES—ADIRONDACKS

Adirondack Museum	National Museum of Racing and Thoroughbred Hall of Fame
Fort Ticonderoga	
Frederic Remington Art Museum	Sagamore
Hattie's	Stillwater Reservoir
Moose River Recreation Area	Thousand Islands Inn
	Whetstone Gulf State Park

Saratoga holds its place in history as a watershed, a turning point in the prolonged and peripatetic series of military campaigns that made up the American Revolution. The battle, the sites of which are commemorated in *Saratoga National Historical Park*, offered the first conclusive proof that American forces could triumph over the British in a major engagement and led to the French entering the war on behalf of the United States.

A 10-mile tour road in the 3,200-acre Saratoga National Historical Park encompasses the sites that were crucial during the Battle of Saratoga. The 1777 Philip Schuyler House can be toured Saturday and Sunday in summer months.

Saratoga National Historical Park Visitor Center, 648 Route 32, Stillwater, (518) 664–9821, is open daily except Thanksgiving, Christmas, and New Year's Day from 9:00 A.M. to 5:00 P.M. The tour road is open from early April through mid-November, dawn to dusk, weather permitting. Between May 1 and October 31, admission is $5.00 per car; $3.00 per person on foot or bicycle for the tour road; $10.00 annual pass. Children 16 and under are admitted free. There is no charge to visit the Schuyler House.

Tradition says the Indians of the Saratoga region visited High Rock Spring as early as 1300 to gain strength from the "Medicine Spring of the Great Spirit." Four hundred seventy years later, in 1771, Sir William Johnson, suffering from a wound received in the Battle of Lake George, was carried on a litter by Mohawk Indians from Johnstown to High Rock Spring. After a short stay his health improved noticeably, and the reputation of the spring quickly grew.

The first person to recognize the commercial value of the mineral waters at Saratoga Springs may well have been *John Arnold,* who in 1774 purchased a crude log cabin built on a bluff overlooking High Rock Spring, improved it, and opened an inn. Thirteen years later, Revolutionary War hero Alexander Bryan purchased the inn. He is generally recognized as the first permanent white resident of Saratoga Springs, and his inn was the only Saratoga hotel until 1801, when Gideon Putnam built the Grand Union Hotel. Throughout the years the inn has operated sporadically as a lodge, tavern, restaurant, and private dwelling. Today you can enjoy prime rib, Gorgonzola New York sirloin, home-style turkey dinner, or a host of other delicious dishes at *The Olde Bryan Inn.*

The Olde Bryan Inn, 123 Maple Avenue, Saratoga Springs, (518) 587–2990, is open Sunday through Thursday 11:00 A.M. until 10:00 P.M., and Friday and Saturday 11:00 A.M. to 11:00 P.M. The tavern is open daily until midnight.

Between 1823 and 1889 mineral waters from approximately thirty springs in Saratoga County were bottled and distributed around the world, and an industry was born. The *National Bottle Museum,* housed in a 1901 former hardware store in *Ballston Spa's* historic district, documents the rise and decline of that industry. Through exhibits of antique bottles and glassmaking

The Olde Bryan Inn

tools, videos, and artifacts, it tells the story of a time past, when young men were indentured to the owners of glass factories and apprenticed for fifteen years in order to become glassblowers in the glasshouses that made bottles and jars by hand. It re-creates an industry and a way of life that have vanished from the American scene.

The National Bottle Museum, 76 Milton Avenue, Ballston Spa, (518) 885–7589, is open daily from June 1 to September 30, 10:00 A.M. to 4:00 P.M.; October 1 to May 31, open Monday through Friday 10:00 A.M. to 4:00 P.M. and closed weekends. Recommended donation is $2.00 for adults and $1.00 for children ages 6 to 12. No donation for children under 6. If you're really intrigued by the glassmaking process, sign up for one of the four-hour, weekend or evening glass-blowing courses given by guest artisans in the museum's flameworking shops. Call the above nunber to reserve a spot; students must pay in advance.

If you think the grand era of Saratoga spas is long past, you haven't been to *The Crystal Spa,* the resort town's newest privately owned mineral bath-house. Opened in 1988 to take advantage of the Rosemary Spring, discovered in 1964, the spa offers eighteen different treatments, including private thirty-minute mineral baths, aromatherapy saunas, full-body massages, European facials, moor mud or seaweed body wraps, honey almond and pumpkin apri-cot scrubs, and stress reduction scalp treatments. Treatments can be combined as packages, and you can also take the oldest and most direct mineral water treatment of all, drinking from the Rosemary Spring fountain housed beneath a restored Victorian gazebo.

The Crystal Spa, 120 South Broadway (next to the Grand Union Motel), Saratoga Springs; (518) 584–2556 is open daily September to June except

A Gas Explosion

The discovery of a process to extract carbonic gas from Saratoga Springs's waters in 1890 was almost the resort's death knell. Over the next few decades, many of its wells were being pumped dry. In 1910, to protect its natural resources, the state purchased 163 springs and 1,000 acres of land surrounding them, and constructed baths, a research institute, a Hall of Springs, and the Gideon Putnam hotel.

Wednesday and Thursday from 8:30 A.M. to 4:30 P.M. (to 3:30 P.M. on Sunday); in July, daily except Wednesday 8:30 A.M. to 4:30 P.M.; and daily in August, 8:30 A.M. to 5:30 P.M. Reservations are strongly recommended, and may be made up to two months in advance. Call for prices of individual treatments and packages.

After a nice mineral bath and massage, you'll be all set for a night at the track. Horse racing is Saratoga's other raison d'être, and the history and traditions of the sport are thoroughly chronicled at the *National Museum of Racing and Thoroughbred Hall of Fame*, directly across from the Saratoga Race Course. Patrons enter the museum through an actual starting gate, complete with life-size representations of a horse, jockey, and starter. Some of the highlights: paintings of outstanding horses, the saddle and boots used by jockey Johnny Loftus on Man o' War, a Hall of Fame, and the actual skeleton of a thoroughbred. *Race America,* filmed at racetracks and stud farms across the country, is shown in the theater. Video booths lining the walls provide films of some of racing's greats.

The National Museum of Racing and Thoroughbred Hall of Fame, 191 Union Avenue, Saratoga Springs, (518) 584–0400, is open year-round. From January 1 through the end of July, hours are Monday through Saturday 10:00 A.M. to 4:00 P.M. and Sunday noon to 4:30 P.M.; during racing season, daily 9:00 A.M. to 5:00 P.M.; and September 1 through December 31, Monday through Saturday 10:00 A.M. to 4:00 P.M. and Sunday noon to 4:00 P.M. Admission is $7.00 for adults and $5.00 for senior citizens, students, and children 6 to 18.

Folks in Saratoga Springs have been flocking to *Hattie's* for Southern fried chicken and biscuits since 1938, and we're assured by the present owner, Jasper Alexander, that Hattie's New Orleans recipes haven't changed. "We've kept her most popular dishes, like fried chicken and pan-fried pork chops, and added some Creole specialties," explains Jasper. And indeed they're all here, a combination of Southern and New Orleans favorites—slow-cooked barbecued spare ribs, Hoppin' John (black-eyed peas with chopped onion, salt and pepper, butter, and pork), blackened catfish, Creole jambalaya, gumbo—all authentically prepared and moderately priced.

Hattie's, 45 Phila Street, Saratoga Springs, (518) 584–4790, is open during the summer months daily from 8:00 A.M. to 1:00 P.M. and 5:00 to 10:00 P.M.; after Labor Day weekend through mid-June, Wednesday through Sunday from 5:00 to 10:00 P.M.

The *Petrified Sea Gardens* consists of the exposed remains of a sea reef that thrived here beneath the Cambrian Sea 500 million years ago, give or take a year or two. Known since 1825 and properly identified in 1883, the "gardens" are the fossilized remains of cabbagelike plants related to modern algae. The reef they formed when alive teemed with trilobites, brachiopods, and rudimentary snails, the fossils of some of which are visible among the plant fossils at this site. When the primordial seas receded, the vegetation was exposed, fossilized beneath layers of sediment, and eventually exposed again by the shearing action of the glaciers.

ANNUAL EVENTS IN THE ADIRONDACKS

LATE APRIL

St. Clement's Saratoga Horse Show,
Saratoga Springs,
(518) 587–2623

MAY

The Adirondack Paddle Fest,
Inlet,
(315) 357–6672

Maple Festival,
Croghan,
(315) 346–6060

JUNE

Americade Motorcycle Rally,
Lake George,
(518) 798–7888
(www.tourexpo.com)

LARAC Arts Festival,
Glens Falls,
(518) 798–1141

Lake Placid Film Festival,
various lodfations around Lake Placid,
(518) 523–3456

JULY

Willard Hammes Guide Boat and Canoe Race,
Saranac Lake,
(518) 891–1990

AUGUST

Adirondack Art & Craft Festival,
Saratoga Springs,
(802) 425–3399;
www.craftproducers.com

Lake Placid Art and Craft Frestival,
Lake Placid,
(802) 425–3399;
www.craftproducers.com

SEPTEMBER

Adirondack Canoe Classic,
Old Forge,
(518) 891–1990

OCTOBER

World's Largest Garage Sale,
Warrensburg,
(518) 623–2161

A Chip by Any Other Name . . .

One day "Aunt Kate" Weeks, a cook at a hotel on Saratoga Lake, tried to make perfectly crisp French fried potatoes. Instead she created "Saratoga Chips," now known as potato chips.

At the Petrified Sea Gardens, visitors can walk among these ancient plants, which can easily be distinguished by the untrained eye. Just look for gray, layered nodules that look as if they might be broken, protruding sections of petrified cabbage. Among the vegetation is the "Iroquois Pine," one of the largest in the Adirondacks and estimated to be 300 years old. There are hands-on activities for children in the nature center.

Petrified Sea Gardens, 42 Petrified Sea Gardens Road (off Route 29), Saratoga Springs, (518) 584–7102, is open May (starting Mother's Day weekend) Saturday, Sunday, and Memorial Day 11:00 A.M. to 5:00 P.M.; June, Thursday through Monday 11:00 A.M. to 5:00 P.M.; July and August, daily 11:00 A.M. to 5:00 P.M.; September to mid-October, Thursday through Monday 4:00 A.M. to 5:00 P.M.; and late October to early November, weekends 11:00 A.M. to 5:00 P.M. Admission is $3.50 for adults, $2.50 for senior citizens and college students with I.D., and $1.75 for children 6 to 16. Call for group rates.

In June 1885, suffering from throat cancer and longing for fresh air and a healthier climate, President *Ulysses S. Grant* left his home in New York City for Saratoga County. He and his family moved into a summer cottage on top of Mt. McGregor, 8 miles from Saratoga Springs. At the cottage he continued work on his memoirs and, two weeks after completing them, died on July 23, 1885.

The house at **Grant Cottage State Historic Site** is preserved as Grant left it, from the bed where he died to the floral pieces sent from around the country. It is operated by the Friends of the Ulysses S. Grant Cottage, in cooperation with the New York State Office of Parks, Recreation, and Historic Preservation.

Grant Cottage State Historic Site, Mt. McGregor Road, **Wilton** (mailing address: P.O. Box 990, Saratoga Springs 12866), (518) 587–8277, is open Memorial Day through Labor Day, Wednesday through Sunday 10:00 A.M. to 4:00 P.M.; through Columbus Day weekend, from 10:00 A.M. to 4:00 P.M. Groups, by advance reservation, are accepted spring and fall only. Admission is $2.50 for adults, $2.00 for senior citizens, and $1.00 for children over 5.

Just north of Saratoga, where so much turn-of-the-century money was spent on the sporting life, is the town of **Glens Falls,** where a small fortune was instead disbursed on a remarkable collection of art. Glens Falls was the home of Charlotte Pruyn, heiress to a local paper fortune, who married Louis Fiske

Hyde of Boston in 1901. In 1907 the Hydes returned to Glens Falls, and in 1912 they began building the Florentine villa that today houses the **Hyde Collection.** Influenced by the home-as-museum philosophy of the Boston tastemaker Isabella Stewart Gardner, and with the help of connoisseurs such as Bernard Berenson, the Hydes filled their home with an eclectic and assiduously acquired collection of American and European art spanning five centuries.

The Hydes bought art with experts' eyes, concentrating not so much upon any individual period or school but upon the most expressive work of whichever painter or sculptor caught their attention. The end result was a collection that appears to have been amassed not by members of the upstate gentry but by a prince with a state treasury at his disposal.

The Hyde Collection opened its doors to the public after Mrs. Hyde's death, at the age of ninety-six, in 1963, and underwent extensive restoration and renovations in 2004. And so it is that in Glens Falls you can enjoy works by such artists as Rubens, Botticelli, Rembrandt, Seurat, Degas, Homer, Whistler, Picasso, Cézanne, and Matisse.

The Hyde Collection, 161 Warren Street, Glens Falls, (518) 792–1761, is open year-round 10:00 A.M. to 5:00 P.M., and Sunday noon to 5:00 P.M.; closed Monday and national holidays. Admission is free.

To really get an off-the-beaten-path view of the Adirondacks, get a horse. **Bennett's Riding Stable** conducts guided trail rides—everything from a one-hour ride for $25, to a 2½-hour ride up Beech Mountain for $50, to a half-day ride for $70 or a full day for $125. The 3½-hour sunset ride for $70 includes a steak barbecue. Reservations are advised for longer rides, and families are welcome (helmets are available). The stable is on Route 9N in **Lake Luzerne,** (518) 696–4444. The stable is open daily in summer; call for times the rest of the year.

At the age of nineteen, Marcella (Kochanska) Sembrich made her operatic debut in Athens, Greece, singing in a number of the great opera houses in Europe before joining New York's Metropolitan Opera Company for its first season in 1883. She returned to Europe until 1898 and then rejoined the Metropolitan Opera until 1909, when her farewell was the occasion for the most sumptuous gala in the Met's history. She was founder of the vocal departments of the Juilliard School in New York and the Curtis Institute in Philadelphia and was a preeminent teacher of singing for twenty-five years. She often brought students to a studio near her summer home in **Bolton Landing** on Lake George. The **Marcella Sembrich Opera Museum,** in Mme. Sembrich's converted studio, displays operatic memorabilia she collected from her debut to her death in 1935.

Summer events include studio talks, a lakeside lecture series, a master class in voice, and occasional recitals or chamber concerts.

The Marcella Sembrich Opera Museum, 4800 Lake Shore Drive, Route 9N, Bolton Landing, (518) 644–9839 (office: P.O. Box 417, Bolton Landing 12814, 518–644–2492), is open daily June 15 through September 15, 10:00 A.M. to 12:30 P.M. and 2:00 to 5:30 P.M. Suggested donation is $2.00 for adults 16 and over.

Eastern Adirondacks

Fort Ticonderoga, which stands on a promontory jutting into the southern end of Lake Champlain, was built by the French in 1755 when the colonial administration in Quebec needed a southern defense in its struggle against Great Britain for control of Canada. Called Fort Carillon, it was built of earth and timbers in the classic French fortress design, and later upgraded to stone, with four pointed bastions presenting an interlocking field of fire against attackers.

In 1758 the Marquis de Montcalm repelled a massive attack by the British, but a year later Lord Jeffrey Amherst captured the fort and renamed it "Ticonderoga." Seventeen years later—three weeks after the Battles of Lexington and Concord—Ethan Allen and Benedict Arnold captured "Fort Ti" from the British "in the name of the Great Jehovah and the Continental Congress," giving the Americans their first victory of the revolution.

Last garrisoned in 1777, Fort Ti might be little more than a roadside marker had it not been for the efforts of the Pell family to protect the site since 1820 and the commitment of Stephen and Sarah Pell to restore it beginning in 1908. At today's handsome reconstruction, guides in eighteenth-century clothing and a host of events, such as live artillery demonstrations and fife and drum musters, help bring the fort to life.

Visitors can stride along the ramparts, view the earthworks built during both the French and Indian Wars and the American Revolution, examine the barracks, and visit the museum, which houses North America's largest collection of eighteenth-century artillery as well as paintings, furniture, and military memorabilia. Just outside the fort is the battlefield where, in 1758, Montcalm devastated the 42nd Highland ("Black Watch") Regiment.

Tours of the 600-acre garrison grounds, offered daily, include the "King's Garden," a 1920s-era formal flower garden, and demonstration vegetable gardens including a Native American garden, children's garden, and garrison garden. Throughout the season there are numerous special events, including a Grand Encampment of the French and Indian War in late June, a Memorial Military Tattoo the weekend following the Fourth of July, and a Revolutionary War Encampment in September. Call for information.

Fort Ticonderoga, Route 74, Ticonderoga, (518) 585–2821, is open from early May through late October, daily 9:00 A.M. to 5:00 P.M. Admission is $12.00

And He Probably Thought They Killed Cats in the Catskills

Back in the early 1970s, I was in graduate school at the University of Vermont with a fellow from Philadelphia who is now a well-known Hollywood screenwriter. We used to enjoy the view across Lake Champlain from the university's hilltop campus in Burlington; on a clear day, nearly all the high peaks of the Adirondacks were visible.

"So those are the Adirondacks," he said to me early in our first semester. "You know, before I got here I thought people were referring to the *Outer Ondacks,* and that there were *Inner Ondacks* somewhere."

So far, he hasn't set any scripts in the Ondacks, Inner or Outer.

—Bill Scheller

for adults, $10.80 for seniors, $6.00 for children ages 7 to 12, and free for children under 7. The Log House is open for breakfast, lunch, and snacks.

As a sidelight to a Fort Ticonderoga visit, drive to the summit of nearby *Mt. Defiance* for a panoramic view of the Champlain Valley. Hop aboard the M/V *Carillon* to visit *Mt. Independence,* site of a Revolutionary War fort, across Lake Champlain in Vermont.

Located west of *Ticonderoga,* deeper in the Adirondacks, *Garnet Hill Lodge,* a remote resort on 600 acres of land, was built by members of the Barton family in 1933 when they came to the area to mine garnet. The architecture of the main lodge is rustic Adirondack-style, but some of the rooms, complete with whirlpool baths and hot tubs, are anything but rustic. The resort offers a host of activities, including tubing, mountain biking, and a special course on fly-fishing. The lodge, at 13th Lake Road in North River, (800) 497–4207, is open year-round. MAP (Modified American Plan, i.e., breakfast and dinner are included in the rate) rates range from $110 to $200.

Visitors can tour the *Barton Mines* and look for gemstones in the open pits at Garnet Mine Tours on Barton Mines Road. The mines are open daily from late June through Labor Day, 9:30 A.M. to 5:00 P.M. Monday through Saturday; 11:00 A.M. to 5:00 P.M. Sunday; and on weekends through Columbus Day. A fee is charged for a lecture. Visitors must be escorted in the mines. Call (518) 251–2706 for information.

At *Jasco Minerals* Jim and Judy Shaw sell minerals and fossils from around the world, and Judy, a gemologist, handcrafts jewelry. The shop, on Route 28 in *North River,* (518) 251–3196, is open year-round, weather permitting: July and August from 9:00 A.M. to 7:00 P.M. and the rest of the year from 9:00 A.M. to 5:00 P.M. If the shop isn't open, knock on the door or yell.

Brandied French toast with sautéed apples is the breakfast specialty at **Goose Pond Inn,** a charming, antiques-filled, turn-of-the-century bed-and-breakfast just a mile from Gore Mountain Ski Center. The inn, open year-round, is on Main Street in **North Creek,** (518) 251–3434. Rates range from $85 to $95 for a mid-week double to $95 to $140 on weekends; holidays to $150.

In North Creek, hop aboard the **Upper Hudson River Railroad** for a two hour, 17-mile round-trip scenic ride along the Hudson River to Riverside and back (the ride will be expanded during the 2005–2006 season). The train leaves from the restored historic **North Creek Railroad Station,** where Vice President Theodore Roosevelt began his journey back to Washington, D.C., after President McKinley was shot. The "stick style" station, built in 1874, was the northernmost terminus of the Adirondack Branch of the D&H Railroad. It now houses a local history and train museum. Trains run May through October. Call (518) 251–5334 for the schedule; check the Web site at www.uhrr.com for details.

Superb food, an award-winning wine list, and elegant accommodations are hallmarks of **Chestertown's Friends Lake Inn,** built in the 1860s as a board-inghouse to accommodate the tanners who worked in the city's major industry.

The inn has seventeen guest rooms with turn-of-the-century furnishings, private baths, and queen-size four-poster beds. Many rooms have panoramic views of the lake.

The dining room serves a New American cuisine featuring homemade pâtés, breads, and international desserts and has the largest wine cellar in northern New York. A full country breakfast, with treats like locally smoked bacon and mango crepes with raspberry *coulis*, is included in the rate.

The inn has a private beach for summer fun, a sauna, and outdoor pool, and in winter its Nordic Ski Center grooms 32 kilometers of cross-country ski trails.

The Friends Lake Inn is on Friends Lake Road, Chestertown, (518) 494–4751; www.friendslake.com. Rates range from $295 to $425 per couple per night MAP; B&B rates are available, as are ski packages.

For some distance north of Ticonderoga, Lake Champlain remains narrow enough for a single military installation to have commanded both shores and governed the passage of ship traffic in the eighteenth century. This was the purpose of the fortifications that now lie in ruins at **Crown Point State Historic Site.**

In the late 1600s the staging area for French raids on English settlements in New England and the Hudson Valley, Crown Point became the location of the French Fort St. Frederic, begun in 1734 and finished in 1737. The fort was designed as a stone citadel within outer walls, defended by fifty cannons and swivel-mounted guns and a garrison of 80 to 120 soldiers.

In 1759 General *Jeffrey Amherst* seized the fort for the British, after it was abandoned by the French, and ordered it enlarged. In 1775 American militiamen captured the fort from the British and used it as headquarters for the navy under Benedict Arnold until 1776.

The survival of the walls, foundations, and partial structures that we see at **Crown Point** today is due to the 1910 conveyance of the property to the state by private owners who wished to see the ruins preserved. In 1975 the area officially became a state historic site. The following year the new visitor center and museum were opened. Highlights of the museum exhibits include artifacts uncovered at the site during extensive archaeological digs.

The visitors' center at Crown Point State Historic Site, at the Lake Champlain Bridge, 4 miles east of Routes 9N and 22, Crown Point, (518) 597–3666, is open May through October, Wednesday through Saturday 10:00 A.M. to 5:00 P.M., Sunday 1:00 to 5:00 P.M. Also open Memorial Day, Independence Day, and Labor Day. Open during the rest of the year by appointment only. Grounds are open all year from 9:00 A.M. to dusk. There is a $4.00 admission fee for each car on weekends and holidays; an admission fee is charged for the museum at all times. Group visits by advance reservation.

Tiny *Essex,* in the foothills of the Adirondacks on the shore of Lake Champlain, is one of the state's loveliest villages. Founded in the eighteenth century and one of the earliest European settlements on the lake, it is listed on the National Register of Historic Places and offers visitors a fascinating architectural overview: The streets are lined with homes and public buildings in a multitude of styles including Federal, Greek Revival, Italianate, and French Second Empire. One of the homes, an 1853 Greek Revival twenty-room mansion with 18-inch-thick cut stone walls called *Greystone* (Elm Street, 518–963–8058 or 963–4650), took four years to complete and is being restored by its present owners, who have opened it for tours by appointment.

There are several lodging options in town, including the *Essex Inn* (Box 234, Essex 12936, 518–963–8821), which has been operating almost continuously since it was built in 1810, making it one of the longest lived structures in town. Extensively renovated in 1986, the inn has nine guest rooms (seven with private bath) and rates, ranging from $85 to $135, include a full breakfast. There are several restaurants in town, including one at the inn, which serves meals alfresco when the weather permits.

If you want to take a short boat ride, the *Essex-Charlotte Ferry* (802–864–9804) in town crosses the lake in just twenty minutes to Charlotte, Vermont.

If you're on foot, there's not much to see on the other side, but you can hop off and catch a return ferry in a half hour. The ferry does not operate when there is ice on the lake.

For general information contact the Lake Placid/Essex County Convention and Visitors Bureau, Lake Placid, Olympic Center, Main Street, Lake Placid, (518) 523–2999 or (800) 447–5224.

Most museums seek to interpret a particular era, if history is their subject, or the artifacts surrounding a particular event or series of events. Not so the **Adirondack Museum** at **Blue Mountain Lake** in the heart of the mountain region. This institution's ambition, at which it has succeeded admirably, is the chronicling of the entire Adirondack experience throughout the years in which the area has been known to humanity. Located on a ridge overlooking Blue Mountain Lake, the museum rambles through twenty-two separate exhibit buildings on a thirty-acre compound and has been called the finest regional museum in the United States.

The museum takes as its focus the ways in which people have related to this incomparable setting and made their lives here over the past two centuries. As befits an institution that began in an old hotel, the museum tells the story of how the Adirondacks were discovered by vacationists in the nineteenth century, especially after the 1892 completion of the railroad to nearby Raquette Lake.

Examples of nineteenth-century hotel and cabin rooms are shown, and a restored turn-of-the-century cottage houses a large collection of rustic "Adirondack furniture," currently enjoying a revival among interior designers. Financier August Belmont's private railroad car *Oriental*—a reminder of the days when grand conveyances brought the very wealthy to even grander Adirondack mansions and clubs—is also on exhibit.

The workaday world of the Adirondacks is recalled in mining, logging, and boatbuilding exhibits. The museum possesses an excellent collection of handmade canoes and guideboats, including some of the lightweight masterpieces of nineteenth-century canoe-builder J. H. Rushton. The lovely sloop *Water Witch* hangs in the renovated gatehouse.

Special attention is given to what has been written and painted using Adirondack subjects. The museum's picture galleries display the work of artists from the Hudson River School and later periods.

The Adirondack Museum, Route 28N/30, Blue Mountain Lake, (518) 352–7311, is open daily from Memorial Day weekend through Columbus Day, 10:00 A.M. to 5:30 P.M. Admission is $14 for adults; $13 age 62 and over; $7 ages 7 to 17, students and military personnel; under 7 free. Allow three to five hours for your visit.

Of the roughly thirty-five Gilded Age Adirondack "Great Camps" that survive, one of the most spectacular—and least known—is *Camp Santanoni,* which stands within a 12,900-acre estate that is now part of the Adirondack Forest Preserve. The property, located in Newcomb, was developed as an estate by Robert and Anna Pruyn of Albany. The Pruyns commissioned architect Robert H. Robertson to design their camp, a partly Japanese-inspired, six-building log complex on the shores of Newcomb Lake. The main lodge buildings, completed in 1893, required 1500 spruce trees for their construction. The buildings' common roof, covering 16,000 square feet and composed of fifty-eight distinct planes, was conceived to resemble a bird in flight.

Saved from demolition and placed on the National Register of Historic Places following their 1972 acquisition by the state, the more than forty-five buildings standing on the estate are under the care of an organization called Adirondack Architectural Heritage, which has undertaken a massive program of stabilization and restoration.

Santinoni is unusual even among remote Great Camps in that its main buildings are inaccessible except by nonmotorized travel. From the rambling gate lodge—itself a mammoth six-bedroom structure incorporating a stone gateway arch—visitors must continue for nearly 5 miles to reach the lake and main lodge. This means hiking, mountain biking, or cross-country skiing to traverse the generally flat terrain. In summer you can rest for the night before beginning the trip back, or go on to Moose Pond, which is even deeper within the preserve. There are eight designated primitive campsites around Newcomb Lake.

Interns posted at the gate lodge and main lodge during the summer months can provide interpretive information on the property, and a program of three guided tours is offered. For tour schedules and general information on Santanoni, contact Adirondack Architectural Heritage, 1790 Main Street, Keeseville 12944; (518) 834–9328.

Studying a subject in a museum is a great way to learn about it. But experience is often the best teacher—even the best museum in the world can't convey how it *feels* to walk among mountains that are almost one million years old. *Siamese Ponds Wilderness Region* in western Warren County is a wilderness area in the true sense of the word: There are hundreds of miles of state-maintained trails and tote roads winding over hills and mountains, past streams, ponds, and lakes. Rockhounds will love exploring the passageways and valleys through a wide variety of rock formations. They were carved by glaciers of the Ice Age and by erosion caused by aeons of tumbling rocks carried along mountain streams, and hikers have found numerous exposed veins of minerals and semiprecious stones.

Siamese Ponds Wilderness Region has entrance points from Stony Creek, Thurman, Wevertown, Johnsburg, North Creek, and North River. Information is available in the *Guide to Adirondack Trails: Central Region*, published by the Adirondack Mountain Club, RD 3, Box 3055, Luzerne Road, Lake George 12845, (518) 668–4447.

Much of the 98-mile-long shoreline of **Raquette Lake** is inaccessible by road. But everyone knows the U.S. mail always gets through—this time with the help of the Bird family, who has been providing mail service since 1942. The original delivery boat was a Gar Wood speedboat. Today Bird family members deliver the mail Monday through Saturday and also offer tours of the lake by appointment. The fare is $12.00 for adults and $6.00 for children under 12. The livery also rents canoes, pontoons, motor and pedal boats, and sells bait. **Bird's Boat Livery** is on Route 28, Raquette Lake, (315) 354–4441.

Great Camp Sagamore, on Raquette Lake, is a prototypical Adirondack Great Camp. The National Historic Site with twenty-seven buildings was built in 1897 by William West Durant, who sold it in 1901 to Alfred Vanderbilt as a wilderness retreat. After Vanderbilt died on the *Lusitania* in 1915, his widow continued to entertain family and friends as "the hostess of the gaming crowd" for the next thirty-nine years.

Visitors to Sagamore can take a two-hour guided tour and, with reservations, stay overnight in one of the double-occupancy rooms (twin beds, bathroom down the hall). Buffet meals are served in the dining hall overlooking the lake. There are 20 miles of hiking trails, canoeing, and a semi-outdoor bowling alley! Request a program catalog to learn about special events.

Sagamore, Sagamore Road, P.O. Box 40, Raquette Lake 13436, (315) 354–5311, has guided tours at 10:00 A.M. and 1:30 P.M. daily from late June to Labor Day and weekends from Labor Day to Columbus Day. Admission is $12.00 for adults, $6.00 for children 12 and under. Should you wish to stay overnight, the proprietors remind you that "Sagamore is not a hotel, motel, or resort. It is, instead, a complete experience in living a 'bit of history' in an incomparable setting." For further information on acccomodations, check the Web site; www.sagamore.org.

More than 435 species of plants and trees, 18 varieties of orchids, and 28 varieties of ferns thrive in the Adirondacks' largest block of remote public land—the 50,000-acre **Moose River Recreation Area,** which is also home to several rare butterfly species, including the Arctic Skipper and the carnivorous Harvester. There are more than 40 miles of roads and 27 miles of trails to explore, and camping is provided at 140 primitive sites.

Nearby, just off Uncas Road in Inlet, is ***Ferd's Bog,*** where a newly built 500-foot boardwalk permits visitors to traverse a rare open bog mat. Among the numerous unusual plants growing here are several species of rare orchids, including the white-fringed, rose Patagonia, and grass pink. Also watch for bug-eating pitcher plants.

Both of these areas are administered by New York State's Department of Environmental Conservation. For information call (315) 354–4611.

The Artworks, an artists' cooperative on Main Street in downtown Old Forge, features art and craftwork by Adirondack artists. Media include pottery, stained glass, jewelry, fine arts, basketry, folk art, fabric art, and photography. The shop is open year-round. For hours call (315) 369–2007.

"A Living Museum of Functional and Aesthetic Necessities: Everything from Abacuses to Zoom Binoculars" is how ***Old Forge Hardware*** describes itself. "The Adirondacks' Most General Store," serving the area since 1900, is fun to poke through anytime, but it's a haven on a rainy day. Old Forge Hardware, Main Street, Old Forge, (315) 369–6100, is open daily year-round except Easter, Thanksgiving, Christmas, and New Year's. Hours vary with the season, so call ahead.

Stillwater Reservoir, which abuts Pigeon Lake Wilderness, Five Ponds Wilderness, Pepperbox Wilderness, and Independence River Wild Forest, more than qualifies as an off-the-beaten-path destination. Both routes to the reservoir, from either Lowville or the Old Forge–Eagle Bay area, include 10-mile drives along narrow dirt roads through the wilderness. But we certainly can't say it's undiscovered. The site's very remoteness has contributed to its increasing popularity over the years, and the New York Department of Environmental Conservation, which oversees the area, recently restricted camping along the shoreline to designated sites, or to at least 150 feet inland from the reservoir's high-water mark.

Camping beyond this perimeter, however, remains relatively unrestricted and affords some of the region's best opportunities for wilderness tenting, as well as fine flat-water canoeing, motorboating (proceed with caution; there are numerous navigational hazards), fishing (splake, bass, perch, and bullheads), snowmobiling, and cross-country skiing.

Campsites at the 6,700-acre reservoir are free of charge and available on a first-come, first-served basis. Permits, however, are required, and can be obtained, along with specific driving instructions, at the Stillwater Forest Ranger Headquarters; call (315) 376–8030.

Explore one of the world's largest ice arena complexes at the ***Olympic Center Sports Complex*** in downtown ***Lake Placid.*** The site of the 1932 and 1980 Winter Olympic Games has four indoor rinks, a museum, cafeteria, and gift shop and is open for public skating from late June through early September on weekdays for just $5.00 (skate rental is $3.00). There are ice shows here most Saturday nights throughout the summer months.

If you're looking for a bit more stimulation, how about rocketing down the only dedicated bobsled run in America on a wheeled sled at a speed of more than 45 mph? The sleds at *Verizon Sports Complex* are piloted by professional drivers and brakemen and operate from late June through mid-October, Wednesday through Sunday from 10:00 A.M. to 12:30 P.M. and 1:30 to 4:00 P.M. The rate is $30 per person and the ride is subject to weather and bobsled run conditions. Call (518) 523–4436 for information.

Other activities at the complex include biathlon target shooting (late June through Labor Day), Wednesday through Sunday 10:00 A.M. to 4:00 P.M. with a charge of $5.00 for five rounds; and mountain biking on Mt. Van Hoevenberg (rentals available). From early July through late August, freestyle aerial skiing demonstrations (the skiers end up in the pool) are held on Wednesday at the MacKenzie-Intervale Ski Jumping complex, and, on Saturday, Nordic ski jumping is held at the 90-meter jump.

Visitors can defray costs for all of the above activities as well as take a ride up the chairlift at Whiteface Mountain, visit the Skydeck observation area at the Olympic Jumping Complex, and ride up Whiteface Mt. Veteran's Memorial Highway by purchasing a Kodak Summer Passport for just $19 a person.

For information on all of these activities as well as special events, call the Olympic Center Main Office, Lake Placid, at (518) 523–1655 or (800) 462–6236.

In an age of superstores and megamalls, it's always a treat to find a small, independent shop that specializes in some of the things we love best. At *With Pipe and Book,* on Lake Placid's Main Street, the aromas of fine pipe tobacco and old books and manuscripts blend together in a heady and inviting combination well known to devotees of true relaxation. In addition to custom-blended tobacco, imported cigars, and old and rare books, the shop carries the area's largest selection of Adirondack prints and maps.

With Pipe and Book, 91 Main Street, Lake Placid, (518) 523–9096, is open Saturday and Sunday throughout the year from 9:30 A.M. to 5:30 P.M.; call for extended seasonal hours.

It is surprising to drive north and find a spot near Lake Placid and *Saranac Lake* whose principal connections are with events that occurred hundreds of miles from the Adirondacks. Here are the homestead and grave of the militant abolitionist *John Brown,* who was executed for his part in the 1859 raid on the U.S. arsenal at Harpers Ferry, Virginia. The homestead and grave are maintained today as the *John Brown Farm State Historic Site.*

Brown and several of his sons had organized their followers to stage the raid in the hope that the captured arms might be used to launch a war of liberation on behalf of black slaves in the South. But his involvement in the abolitionist cause began years before the failed Harpers Ferry attack. His sons had homesteaded in Kansas during the period in the 1850s when the territory earned the name "Bloody Kansas" because of the struggle to decide whether it would be admitted to the Union as a slave or a free state; Brown went to fight on the abolitionist side and took part in the desperate struggle at Osawatomie. But Brown wasn't a Kansan himself. Inasmuch as he had a permanent home during that turbulent period, it was his farm at **North Elba,** near Lake Placid. He had moved here in 1849 to participate in a plan to settle free blacks in an agricultural community called Timbucto. The benevolent scheme hadn't worked, but Brown still considered North Elba home and had requested that he be buried there. Two of his sons, killed at Harpers Ferry, are also interred at the farm, as are several of his followers, whose remains were moved here in 1899.

The farmhouse at the John Brown Farm State Historic Site, 2 John Brown Road, Lake Placid, (518) 523–3900, is open from May 1 to October 31, daily (except Tuesday) 10:00 A.M. to 5:00 P.M. The grounds are open all year during daylight hours. Admission for house tours is $2.00 for adults, $1.00 for children and seniors.

At the **Adirondack Guideboats Woodward Boat Shop,** Chris Woodward builds Adirondack guide boats using the same techniques that Willard Hanmer, one of the boat's original builders, used back in the 1930s. And he's making them in the same building. The boats—the style is indigenous to the region between Saranac Lake and Old Forge—are used for hunting and guiding. Chris also makes and sells paddles, seats, and oars and sells boat accessories. The shop, at 9 Algonquin Avenue (Route 3), Saranac Lake, (518) 891–3961, is open weekdays 9:00 A.M. to 5:00 P.M. or by appointment. Call ahead to make sure he'll be there.

Sure Beats the Classroom

At Paul Smith's College, a small, private institution located near Saranac Lake, students can major in recreation, adventure travel, and ecotourism. A typical project might be a canoe trip down the Hudson from the Adirondacks to the Statue of Liberty, or along the Erie Canal from Buffalo to Troy.

In 1887 Robert Louis Stevenson set sail from Bournemouth, England, for a small farmhouse in Saranac Lake, the village he dubbed "the Little Switzerland in the Adirondacks." He lived here with his family, writing *The Master of Ballantrae* and *The Wrong Box,* skating at nearby Moody Pond, and enjoying life in the mountains. He wrote to a friend of his life here: "We are high up in the Adirondack Mountains living in a guide's cottage in the most primitive fashion. The maid does the cooking (we have little beyond venison and bread to cook) and the boy comes every morning to carry water from a distant spring for drinking purposes. It is already very cold but we have calked the doors and windows as one calks a boat, and have laid in a store of extraordinary garments made by the Canadian Indians."

Today the cottage, preserved in its original state, holds the country's largest collection of Stevenson's personal mementos, including his Scottish smoking jacket, with a sprig of heather in the breast pocket, original letters, and his yachting cap. There's a plaque here by sculptor Gutzon Borglum, donated by the artist who regarded the writer as "the great sculptor of words."

The **Robert Louis Stevenson Memorial Cottage,** Stevenson Lane, Saranac Lake, (518) 891–1462 or (800) 347–1992, is open July through Columbus Day, Tuesday to Sunday 9:30 A.M. to noon and 1:00 to 4:30 P.M. The rest of the year it is opened by appointment. Admission is $5.00 for adults; children under 12, free. Group rates are available.

It's difficult to suggest that a forest preserve encompassing almost six million acres—roughly the size of the state of New Hampshire—is off the beaten

Robert Louis Stevenson Memorial Cottage

path. But **Adirondack State Park** includes some of the state's finest out-of-the-way attractions and offers some of its best opportunities to leave civilization behind. The park is a unique mixture of public and private lands. Approximately 130,000 year-round residents live in 105 towns and villages, but 43 percent of the total acreage is state owned, constitutionally protected "forever wild" land.

howit'sdone

Park administrators from throughout the world have come to New York State to study the management of Adirondack State Park.

To best get a sense of the park, stop at one of the two **Visitor Interpretive Centers:** Paul Smiths VIC, Route 30, **Paul Smiths,** (518) 327–3000; or Newcomb VIC, Route 28N, **Newcomb,** (518) 582–2000. Both are open daily year-round from 9:00 A.M. to 5:00 P.M. except Thanksgiving and Christmas. Admission is free. If you're interested in camping at one of the 500 campsites spread over forty-eight islands on three of the Adirondack's most scenic lakes, request the brochure "Camping in the New York State Forest Preserve."

The Adirondacks and, in fact, much of New York State were once the territory of the **Iroquois Confederacy.** Perhaps the most politically sophisticated of all the tribal groupings of North American Indians, the Iroquois actually comprised five distinct tribes—the Mohawks, Senecas, Onondagas, Oneidas, and Cayugas—who were later joined by the Tuscaroras to form the "six nations" of the confederation. The history and contemporary circumstances of the Iroquois are documented in the **Six Nations Indian Museum,** a "living museum" that presents its material from a Native American point of view.

The museum, opened in 1954, was built by the Faddens, members of the Mohawk Nation, and is still operated and staffed by members of that family. The museum's design reflects the architecture of the traditional Haudenosaunee (Six Iroquois National Confederacy) bark house. The longhouse is a metaphor for the Confederacy, symbolically stretching from east to west across ancestral territory.

A visit to the museum—jam-packed with artifacts—is a reminder that for centuries before Europeans arrived, the Iroquois were building a society. Throughout the season Native Americans visit to talk about their histories, cultures, and their people's contributions to contemporary society.

The Six Nations Indian Museum, Roakdale Road (County Route 30), **Onchiota,** (518) 891–2299, is open daily except Monday from July 1 through Labor Day, 10:00 A.M. to 5:00 P.M. and by appointment in June and September. Admission is $2.00 for adults and $1.00 for children.

Once a part of the corridor used by trading and war parties in the days of the French and Indian Wars, the area around **Plattsburgh,** on Lake Champlain, had settled into a peaceful mercantile existence by the end of the eighteenth century. It was in Plattsburgh that the **Kent-Delord House** was built in 1797 by William Bailey. Following several changes of ownership, the house was purchased in 1810 by Henry Delord, a refugee from the French Revolution who had prospered as a merchant and served as a justice of the peace in Peru, New York, before moving to Plattsburgh. Delord remodeled the house in the fashionable Federal style of the era and in 1811 moved in, thus beginning more than a century of his family's residence here.

Just three years after the Delords moved into their new home, the War of 1812 came to Plattsburgh in the form of a southward thrust by British forces along Lake Champlain. But the enemy was repelled later that month by the Delords' friend Commodore Thomas Macdonough in the Battle of Plattsburgh.

Aside from the wartime seizure of the house, the story of the Kent-Delord House might be that of any home of a provincial bourgeois family during the nineteenth century. The difference, of course, is that this house has survived remarkably intact. It offers a fine opportunity to see how an upper-middle-class family lived from the days just after the revolution through the Victorian age and, not incidentally, houses a distinguished collection of American portrait art, including the work of John Singleton Copley, George Freeman, and Henry Inman.

The Kent-Delord House Museum, 17 Cumberland Avenue, Plattsburgh, (518) 561–1035, is open March until December, Tuesday through Saturday from noon to 4:00 P.M.; the last tour begins at 3:15 P.M. Admission is $5.00 for adults, $3.00 for students, and $2.00 for children under 12. The museum is closed during January and February.

Downtown Plattsburgh was never known as a must-stop specialty food destination—never, that is, until Zaidee and Trevor Laughlin opened **The**

But What about Bridesmaids?

In earlier times, the mothers of Iroquois maidens arranged the marriages of their daughters. A girl would acknowledge her mother's choice by putting a basket of bread at the door of the prospective bridegroom's door. If he and his mother accepted, they would send a basket of food back to the girl and her family. If the offer was turned down, the girl's offering would remain untouched.

Grand Onion a few years ago. The little shop, tucked onto a side street and jammed to the rafters with gourmet comestibles, is now known to just about every educated palate in the North Country, leaving us to wonder whether the gentrification of the lakeshore city gave us the Grand Onion, or the other way around. Don't plan a picnic without stopping here first: You'll find fresh artisan breads, imported and domestic deli meats, including pungent Italian salamis, cheeses from around the world (and around the Lake Champlain region), and homemade salads. If you're lucky, the Laughlins might have a couple of white chocolate macadamia nut cookies to end your picnic on a sweet note. Or, if lunch is long past and it's time for a carryout dinner, head straight to the back of the store, where Trevor serves up his entree of the week: There may be smoked salmon cakes, chicken piccata, or duck confit with leeks.

The Grand Onion however, isn't just a picnic provisioner. There are plenty of goodies here to bring home too, ranging from walnut oil to tamarind paste, Venezuelan chocolate to Derbyshire biscuits, and loose British teas to Austrian elderflower syrup. And, if your timing is good, you'll be popping in on one of those occasional Saturdays when the Laughlins slice open an aged wheel of English cheddar or Parmigiano Reggiano for all to try.

The Grand Onion, 21 Bridge Street, Plattsburgh, (518) 56–ONION, www.grandonion.com, is open Monday through Friday 10:00 A.M. to 7:00 P.M., Saturday 10:00 A.M. to 5:00 P.M.; call for seasonal Sunday hours. Ask about getting on the store's e-mail list—weekly newsletters will keep you posted on new products, many of which can be mail ordered.

Yarborough Square carries the works of about 200 artists and craftspeople from the United States and Canada. A large collection of pottery, including stoneware, porcelain, and raku, is on display, as are metal sculptures and hand-crafted jewelry—everything from recycled glass to wrought-iron pieces, and candles. The gallery, which also represents several painters and numerous crafts people, is truly a North Country find. It's at 672 Bear Swamp Road, *Peru,* (518) 643–7057 and is open daily from 10:00 A.M. to 6:00 P.M.

The *Alice T. Miner Museum* was created in 1824 by Mrs. Miner, a pioneer in the colonial revival movement and wife of railroad industrialist and philanthropist William H. Miner. She worked for the next twenty-six years, until her death, to assemble the collection on exhibit in the fifteen-room museum. Included in the exhibit are period furniture; miniature furniture once toted about by traveling salesmen; a large collection of china, porcelain, and glass; early samplers; War of 1812 muskets; and other objects of early Americana.

The Alice T. Miner Museum, P.O. Box 628, 9618 Main Street, Route 9, *Chazy* 12921, (518) 846–7336, is open Tuesday through Saturday 10:00 A.M. to

4:00 P.M., with guided tours at 10:00 and 11: 30 A.M. and 1:00 and 2:30 P.M.; closed December 23 through January 31 and holidays. Admission is $3.00 for adults, $2.00 for seniors, and $1.00 for students. School groups are free.

If you've always wanted to try your hand at throwing or hand building pottery, consider a visit to the **West Chazy Pottery Studio.** Housed in a Pennsylvania Dutch carriage house, the studio has three electric wheels, spacious hand building tables, and electric and gas kilns for firing everything from low temperature terra-cotta to Raku. The studio hosts workshops in spring and fall, and students create their own painted tiles, hanging planters, mugs, bowls, goblets, or whatever else they may fancy. From May through October, the studio rents out a guest cottage for just $65 a night, including a continental breakfast (it can be rented with or without studio use). The studio is at 7695 Route 22, P.O. Box 75, West Chazy 12992, (518) 493–2217.

Western Adirondacks, Saint Lawrence Valley, and Thousand Islands

The **Akwesasne Cultural Center** is dedicated to preserving the past, present, and future of the Akwesasne Mohawk people, whose history in the area dates back thousands of years. The museum houses more than 3,000 artifacts and an extensive collection of black-ash splint basketry; it also offers classes in such traditional art forms as basketry, quillwork, and water drums. The library houses one of the largest Native American collections in northern New York and includes information on indigenous people throughout North America.

Akwesasne Cultural Center, Route 37 (R.R. 1, Box 14C), **Hogansburg,** (518) 358–2240, is open daily year-round except Sunday and major holidays. In July and August it is open Monday through Friday 8:30 A.M. to 4:30 P.M.; from September to June, Monday 12:30 to 5:30 P.M.; Tuesday through Thursday 8:30 A.M. to 8:30 P.M.; Friday 8:30 A.M. to 4:30 P.M.; and Saturday 11:00 A.M. to 3:00 P.M. Suggested museum contribution is $2.00 for adults and $1.00 for children ages 5 to 16.

New York State, as was mentioned in the introduction to this book, was somewhat of a staging area for America's westward expansion during the last century. It thus seems fitting that the greatest chronicler of the West in painting and sculpture was a New Yorker, who grew up in the town of Ogdensburg on the St. Lawrence River halfway between Massena and Lake Ontario. His name was Frederic Remington, and a splendid collection of his work and personal effects is today housed in the **Frederic Remington Art Museum** in that community.

Were There Civics Lessons?

Fifty years ago, the village of Mannsville, 21 miles south of Watertown, was the site of an unusual orphan asylum. The Klan Haven Home occupied a big frame house set on 300 acres, where boys could train in agriculture and the girls learned what was then called "domestic science." The curriculum probably also included a brand of social studies, because the home was run by the Ku Klux Klan for some thirty orphaned children of Klan members. It has long since ceased to operate.

Born in 1861, Remington quit Yale at the age of nineteen and went west, where he spent five years garnering the experiences and images that would come across so powerfully in his paintings and sculpture. Success as an illustrator and later as a fine artist came after 1885; when Remington died suddenly following an operation in 1909, he was still riding the crest of his popularity. His wife moved from the Remington home in Connecticut in 1915 and settled in the artist's boyhood home of **Ogdensburg,** in a rented house that had been built in 1810. Mrs. Remington willed her husband's art collection, along with those of his own works in his possession at the time of his death, to the Ogdensburg Public Library, and five years after her death in 1923, the museum exhibiting this collection was opened in the house where she had lived.

The Remington works housed in the museum include bronzes, oil paintings, watercolors, and several hundred pen-and-ink sketches. Selections of works from his own collection, among them paintings by Charles Dana Gibson and the American impressionist Childe Hassam, are also on display.

The Frederic Remington Art Museum, 303 Washington Street, Ogdensburg, (315) 393–2425, is open from May 1 through October 31, Monday through Saturday 10:00 A.M. to 5:00 P.M. and Sunday 1:00 to 5:00 P.M.; from November 1 to April 30, hours are Wednesday through Saturday 11:00 A.M. to 5:00 P.M. and Sunday 1:00 to 5:00 P.M. Closed legal holidays. Admission is $6.00 for adults, $5.00 for students ages 6 to 22 and senior citizens, and free for children 5 and under.

Around the turn of the century, when Frederic Remington looked west for artistic inspiration, hotel magnate George C. Boldt turned instead to his native Germany. Boldt's creativity wasn't a matter of putting paint to canvas or molding bronze, however. He was out to build the 120-room **Boldt Castle,** Rhineland-style, on one of the Thousand Islands in the St. Lawrence River.

Boldt, who owned the Waldorf-Astoria in New York and the Bellevue-Stratford Hotel in Philadelphia, bought his island at the turn of the century from a man named Hart, but that isn't why it is named Heart Island. The name derives from the fact that the hotelier had the island physically reshaped into the configuration of a heart, as a token of devotion to his wife, Louise, for whom the entire project was to be a monumental expression of his love.

Construction of the six-story castle and its numerous outbuildings began in 1900. Boldt hired masons, woodcarvers, landscapers, and other craftspeople from all over the world to execute details ranging from terra-cotta wall inlays and roof tiles to a huge, opalescent glass dome. He planned and built a smaller castle as a temporary residence and eventual playhouse, and he built an underground tunnel for bringing supplies from the docks to the main house. There were bowling alleys, a sauna, an indoor swimming pool—in short, it was to be the sort of place that would take years to finish and decades to enjoy.

But there weren't enough years left. Louise Boldt died suddenly in 1904, and George Boldt, heartbroken, wired his construction supervisors to stop all work. The walls and roof of the castle were by this time essentially finished, but crated fixtures such as mantels and statuary were left where they stood, and the bustling island fell silent. Boldt never again set foot in his empty castle, on which he had spent $2.5 million.

Boldt died in 1916, and two years later the island and its structures were purchased by Edward J. Noble, the inventor of Life Savers candy. Noble and his heirs ran the deteriorating castle as a tourist attraction until 1977, when it was given to the Thousand Islands Bridge Authority, which has, over the past twenty years, invested $11 million in rehabilitation efforts to preserve the historic structure.

Boldt Castle, Heart Island, Alexandria Bay, (315) 482–2520 or (800) 8–ISLAND, is accessible via water taxi from the upper and lower docks on James Street in *Alexandria Bay,* as well as to tour-boat patrons departing from both the American and the Canadian shores. The castle is open from Mother's Day to Columbus Day, Saturday and Sunday 10:00 A.M. to 6:30 P.M.; July and August, daily 10:00 A.M. to 6:30 P.M. For information call ahead, or write 1000 Islands International Council, P.O. Box 400, Alexandria Bay 13607. Admission is $5.25 for adults and $3.00 for children ages 6 to 12. Groups of twenty or more, senior citizens, and military personnel receive a discount.

When Boldt bought Heart Island it already had a house on it—if you can call an eighty-room "cottage" a house. It had been built in the late 1800s by Elizur Kirke Hart, who spared no expense in its construction. Boldt and his family summered here for several years before he decided the cottage didn't suit him. When he began construction of Boldt Castle, he had the cottage dismantled and skidded across the frozen St. Lawrence River to nearby *Wellesley Island,* where fifty of the original rooms were reconstructed. The Boldts used the renamed Wellesley House as their headquarters while the castle was being built, but in the 1950s the river cottage was torn down.

The remaining thirty rooms of Hart's original home were also erected on Wellesley Island and became the Thousand Islands Country Club, a place for ladies to sit over afternoon tea while the menfolk played a round of golf. In later years a newer clubhouse was built across the street, and the Hart House was renamed the Golf Course House.

In 1994 Rev. Dudley Danielson and his wife, Kathy, bought the now run-down thirty-room club house and have painstakingly converted it into the elegant **Hart House Inn.** Many of the dwelling's original features have been retained and renovated, including a massive pink granite fireplace in the lobby entrance. Each of the five beautifully decorated guest suites has a canopied bed, Italian ceramic tile whirlpool bath, views of the St. Lawrence, and fireplaces. Three rooms and suites in the older wing (open May through October) have private baths; the classic two-room Sunset Suite is perfect for a family of five, with library fireplace, two bedrooms, and deck with a great river view. A multi-course candlelit breakfast is served on the wraparound porch overlooking the golf course (in the winter, it's served in the fireplaced dining room).

Kathy is the granddaughter of a Hungarian innkeeper and takes great pride in her cooking. Reverend Danielson officiates at many weddings in his Grace Chapel; it also serves as a retreat for quiet contemplation.

The Hart House, P.O. Box 70, Wellesley Island 13640, (315) 482–LOVE or (888) 481–LOVE, is open year-round. Rates range from $135 for a classic room midweek to $315 for the stunning Kashmir Garden suite on a weekend. In winter, two-night packages feature an elegant fireside dinner. The chapel is available from May through November.

If you find the most appealing aspect of George Boldt's heyday to be the sleek mahogany runabouts

what'sinthewater?

The St. Lawrence River is renowned for game fishing. Among the most common: large- and smallmouth bass, Northern pike, yellow perch, and walleye.

and graceful skiffs that plied the waters of the Thousand Islands and other Gilded Age resorts, make sure you find your way to the **Antique Boat Museum** in **Clayton.** The museum is a freshwater boat-lover's dream, housing slender, mirror-finished launches; antique canoes; distinctive St. Lawrence River skiffs; handmade guideboats—about 200 historic small craft in all.

The Antique Boat Museum takes no sides in the eternal conflict between sailing purists and "stinkpotters," being broad enough in its philosophy to house a fine collection of antique outboard and inboard engines, including the oldest outboard known to exist. The one distinction rigidly adhered to pertains to construction material: All of the boats exhibited here are made of wood.

The Antique Boat Museum, 750 Mary Street, Clayton 13624, (315) 686–4104, is open from early May through mid-October, daily from 9:00 A.M. to 5:00 P.M. Admission is $8.00 for adults, $7.00 for seniors, AAA, and military personnel; $6.00 students; $4.00 ages 6 to 17; under 6 free.

When the ***Thousand Islands Inn*** opened in 1897, it was one of more than two dozen hotels serving visitors to the region. Today it is the last of the great hostelries that still offers guests all the amenities of a full-service establishment.

In addition to its distinction as a survivor, the inn has yet another claim to fame: Thousand Island salad dressing was first served to the dining public here in the early 1900s. The dressing was created by Sophia LaLonde for her husband, a guide, to serve to fishing parties as part of their shore dinners. One of his clients, a New York City stage actress named May Irwin, loved the dressing and gave it the name Thousand Island. She also gave the recipe to George C. Boldt, owner of Boldt Castle and New York's Waldorf-Astoria Hotel. He ordered his maître d', Oscar Tschirky, to put it on the hotel menu. But the Thousand Islands Inn had already made it into the record book: LaLonde had also given the recipe to Ella Bertrand, whose family owned the inn, then called the Herald Hotel.

Most of the rooms have a view of the St. Lawrence River and have been restored to re-create the flavor of the late 1800s, but with all modern conveniences. The inn's restaurant is a recipient of the Golden Fork Award of the Gourmet Diners Society of North America. It serves three meals daily.

The Thousand Islands Inn is at 335 Riverside Drive, Clayton, (315) 686–3030 or (800) 544–4241. Room rates range from $60.00 to $99.50, and several special packages are offered. The inn is open from mid-May until mid-September.

The Secret Recipe

Allen and Susan Benas, owners of the Thousand Islands Inn, sell their Thousand Island dressing, so they are naturally reluctant to give out the recipe. When we called to ask them about the one James Beard gives in his book, *American Cookery,* Allen said, "He's remotely on the right track, especially with the chili sauce—most people use catsup; but ours has several other ingredients." It's the closest we can come, so give it a try.

James Beard's recipe for Thousand Island dressing:

Blend ½ cup chili sauce, 1 finely chopped pimiento, 1 tablespoon grated onion, and 2 tablespoons finely chopped green pepper with 1 cup mayonnaise.

Shore to Please

You've been out on a charter fishing expedition all day and are ready to tuck into a traditional St. Lawrence River Shore dinner. Hope you're hungry: While your catch is being filleted by the crew, the meal begins with an appetizer of Thousand Islands–style bacon and tomato sandwiches, followed by a fresh garden salad topped with—what else?—Thousand Island dressing. The next course is a regional dish of salt potatoes and fresh corn on the cob (if it's in season). And then, the pièce de résistance, your fish (if you've come up empty-handed, don't worry; there's plenty on hand). Ready for dessert? How about some French toast browned in a cast iron pan over the fire, served piping hot with New York State maple syrup and captain's coffee (with a few secret ingredients)? After a meal like that, it may be best not to wander too close to the end of the pier.

Are you yearning to sail to a foreign land? *Horne's Ferry,* the only international auto/passenger ferry on the St. Lawrence River, crosses over to Wolfe Island, Ontario, Canada, in just ten minutes. The ferry makes hourly crossings from 8:00 A.M. to 7:30 P.M. daily from early May through late October. Rates are $8.00 each way for a car and driver, and $2.00 for additional passengers or pedestrians. For information write to P.O. Box 116, *Cape Vincent* 13618, (315) 783–0638.

The only place in the northeastern United States to see prairie smoke, a flower whose feathery plumes expand as it goes to seed, is in *Chaumont Barrens,* a unique "alvar" landscape characterized by a mosaic of austere, windswept vegetation.

Alvar sites lie scattered along an arc from here, through Ontario, to northern Michigan. Scientists hypothesize that the landscapes, distinguished by a linear pattern of vegetation, were formed during the retreat of the last glacier approximately 10,000 years ago, when a huge ice dam burst and a torrent swept away all surface debris and dissolved limestone bedrock along cracks and fissures.

The rare combination of extreme conditions at *Chaumont* have created a 2-mile landscape of exposed outcrops, fissures, moss gardens, patches of woods, shrub savannas, and open grasslands.

Chaumont Barrens, on Van Alstyne Road, Chaumont, is a property of the Nature Conservancy and is open daily from a half hour before sunrise until a half hour before sunset. For information call (585) 546–8030 or (315) 387–3600.

The international cooperation exemplified by the St. Lawrence Seaway and the peaceful coexistence that allows pleasurecraft to sail unimpeded along the boundary waters of the St. Lawrence River and Lake Ontario are things we take for granted today, but this state of affairs has hardly existed since time imme-memorial. Barely more than a century ago, the U.S. Navy kept an active installa-tion at **Sackets Harbor Battlefield**, on Lake Ontario's Black River Bay, against the possibility of war with Canada. And during the War of 1812, this small lakeport actually did see combat between American and British forces.

At the time the war began, **Sackets Harbor** was not yet a flourishing American naval port and the site of a busy shipyard and supply depot. It was from here, in April 1813, that the Americans launched their attack upon Toronto; a month later the tables were turned when the depleted American garrison at the harbor was beleaguered by a British attack upon the shipyard. The defenders repulsed the attack but lost most of their supplies to fire in the course of the struggle.

Today's visitor to Sackets Harbor can still see many of the facilities of the old naval base, including officers' homes and sites associated with the 1813 battle.

Sackets Harbor Battlefield State Historic Site, 504 West Main Street, Sackets Harbor, (315) 646–3634, is open from Memorial Day to Columbus Day; call for hours and for special off-season events. Admission charged for tours.

If you're going to set out on the 454-mile Seaway Trail—the state's only National Scenic Byway—plan to stop first at the **Seaway Trail Discovery Center,** housed in a three-story, 1817 limestone, Federal-style former hotel overlooking the lake. The New York State Office of Parks, Recreation and Preservation opened the facility to provide a "windshield" overview of the trail and its unique characteristics. Nine rooms of exhibits highlight the area's natu-ral history, recreation, agriculture, people, architecture, and maritime history.

The Seaway Trail Discovery Center, P.O. Box 660, Ray and West Main Streets, Sackets Harbor, (800) SEAWAY–T, is open year-round: daily May through October from 10:00 A.M. to 5:00 P.M.; November through April, Tuesday through Saturday from 10:00 A.M. to 5:00 P.M. Admission is $4.00 for adults, $2.00 for children.

The **American Maple Museum and Hall of Fame,** dedicated to pre-serving the history and evolution of the North American maple syrup industry, houses three floors of antique sugaring equipment, logging tools, and artifacts. There are replicas of a sugarhouse and a lumber camp kitchen, and a Hall of Fame. The museum hosts three all-you-can-eat pancake breakfasts a year—in February, May, and September—to raise funds. There is also an ice cream social around July 1, with entertainment and maple treats; a Maple Weekend in mid-March; and, in December, "Christmas in **Croghan,**" with hot chocolate and maple cream on crackers. Call for dates.

The American Maple Museum and Hall of Fame, Main Street, Route 812 (P.O. Box 81), Croghan, (315) 346–1107, is open Friday, Saturday, and Monday, 11:00 A.M. to 4:00 P.M. from Memorial Day to June 30; daily except Sunday, 11:00 A.M. to 4:00 P.M. from July 1 to early September. Admission is $4.00 for adults; $1.00 for children 5 to 14; $10 per family (two adults with two or more children).

The **North American Fiddler's Hall of Fame & Museum,** dedicated to "each and every fiddler who ever made hearts light and happy with his lilting music," preserves, perpetuates, and promotes the art of fiddling and the dances pertaining to the art. It displays artifacts and collects tapes of fiddlers, and since its inception in 1976, has inducted a new member (or members) into its Hall of Fame each year. The museum, across from Cedar Pines Restaurant, Motel, and Campground in Osceola, is open Sunday from 2:00 to 5:00 P.M. from Memorial Day through the first Sunday in October (except for the third weekend in September), during major events, and by appointment. Every Sunday afternoon from Memorial Day to the first Sunday in October there's also a free concert (donations are welcome). For information call (315) 599–7009.

In the latter part of the nineteenth century, Joseph and John Moser emigrated from Alsace-Lorraine to Kirschnerville. They cleared a plot of land, built a dwelling, purchased farm animals, and then brought the rest of their family from overseas. The Mosers were Mennonites, and three generations lived and worshiped here until the 1980s, when the farm was purchased by a group who wanted it to be preserved as a living history of the life and faith of the area's settlers.

Today the **Mennonite Heritage Farm,** under the auspices of the Adirondack Mennonite Heritage Association, tells of the life of the early Amish-Mennonite settlers. In addition to exhibits in the farmhouse, there is a Worship Room with the original benches (meetings were held in homes on a rotational basis until 1912, when the Croghan Mennonite Church was built). There are also a number of outbuildings, including a granary with a display of early tools and equipment.

On the first Saturday of July, the farm holds a special, day-long Zwanzigstein Fest, which features traditional Mennonite foods and crafts, a petting zoo, bread and butter and ice-cream making demonstrations, and horse-pulled wagon rides. The highlight of the day is the mini-auction of quilts, "comforts," and antiques.

The Mennonite Heritage Farm, P.O. Box 368, Erie Canal Road, Croghan 13327, (315) 346–1122; off-season, (315) 853–6879 or 376–8502, is open varying hours during July and August, or by appointment. Admission is charged only for the fest, but donations are gratefully accepted at any time.

The 2,100-acre **Whetstone Gulf State Park**, built in and around a 3-mile-long gorge cut in the eastern edge of the Tug Hill plateau, provides one of the most spectacular scenic vistas east of the Rocky Mountains. Mostly undeveloped, the park has sixty-two campsites, six of which are streamfront, a picnic area along Whetstone Creek, a man-made swimming area, and several hiking and cross-country ski trails (one circles the gorge). A 500-acre reservoir above the gorge provides canoeing and fishing (it's stocked with tiger muskies and largemouth bass).

Whetstone Gulf State Park, Route 26, **Lowville,** (315) 376–6630 or 482–2593, is open year-round, with admission charged during the summer months. Limited facilities are available in winter but the heated Beach Building has restrooms and is open from the second week in December until the first week of March. To reserve a campsite call the New York State Campsite and Cabin Reservation Program at (800) 456–CAMP. Admission is charged from two weeks before Memorial Day until two weeks after Labor Day.

The man who built **Constable Hall** was presented with a rather generous birthright: four million acres of Adirondack wilderness. His father, William Constable Sr., purchased the property with two other New York City capitalists/real-estate speculators and ultimately became the principal owner and chief developer. He sold large tracts to European and American land companies and families from New England, launching the settlement of the north country. In 1819 William Constable Jr. built a Georgian mansion patterned on a family-owned estate in Ireland, and five generations of the Constable family lived there until 1947, when the house became a museum. The original deed is just one of the family mementos displayed at the home, which still has many of its original furnishings.

Constable Hall, **Constableville,** (315) 397–2323, is open daily except Monday from June to October 15. Hours are Tuesday through Saturday 10:00 A.M. to 4:00 P.M., and Sunday 1:00 to 4:00 P.M. Admission is $3.00 for adults and $1.50 for children.

There are barely a dozen lighthouses in North America in which visitors can stay overnight. One is **Selkirk Lighthouse,** built in 1838, on Lake Ontario at the mouth of the Salmon River. Listed on the National Register of Historic Places, the lighthouse is heated, has four bedrooms (two single and four double beds), a kitchen, living room, and bathroom, and color cable TV with HBO. The rent per night is $125 on weeknights and $150 on weekends. Rates are for two people; for additional people, add $50 each. The lighthouse can be rented from April through early December and sleeps up to ten people. The lighthouse is part of a five-acre compound that includes a charter fishing fleet, cabins, boat rentals, and a launch ramp. For information contact Lighthouse Marina, Lake Road, P.O. Box 228, **Pulaski** 13142, (315) 298–6688, or check out their Web site: www.salmon-river.com.

Just north of Utica, in the foothills of the Adirondacks, you'll find **Steuben Memorial State Historic Site.** Frederick von Steuben was a Prussian officer who, at the age of forty-seven, emigrated to the United States in 1777 to help drill the soldiers of the Continental Army. His first assignment was a challenging one. He was sent to the American winter encampment at Valley Forge, where morale was flagging and discipline, in the face of elemental hardship such as hunger and bitter cold, was virtually nonexistent.

As might be expected of a good Prussian officer, von Steuben rose to the occasion. Washington's troops at Valley Forge might not have had boots, but they learned how to march in file, as well as proceed through the other elements of classic military drill and perform effectively with the eighteenth-century frontline weapon of choice, the bayonet. The German émigré even found time to write a masterful treatise on military training, *Regulations for the Order and Discipline of the Troops of the United States.*

Having served as inspector general of the Continental Army until the end of the war, von Steuben was richly rewarded by the nation of which he had lately become a citizen. Among his other rewards was a New York State grant of 16,000 acres of land. Allowed to pick his own site, he chose the area partially occupied today by the Steuben Memorial State Historic Site and built a simple two-room log house.

Steuben Memorial State Historic Site

In 1936 the state erected a replica of von Steuben's house on a site located within the fifty acres it had recently purchased as his memorial (the drillmaster is buried beneath an imposing monument not far from here, despite his wish that he lie in an unmarked grave). The cabin is open to visitors. Historical interpretations reflecting the military life of the Revolutionary War soldier are held at the memorial, and staff members are available to discuss the baron's life.

The Steuben Memorial State Historic Site, Starr Hill Road, *Remsen,* (315) 768–7224, is open from Memorial Day to Labor Day, Wednesday through Saturday 10:00 A.M. to 5:00 P.M., Sunday and Monday holidays 1:00 to 5:00 P.M. Guided tours are available; call ahead. Admission is free.

REGIONAL TOURIST INFORMATION— THE ADIRONDACKS

Adirondacks Regional Information,
(800) 487–6867 or (518) 846–8016
www.adk.com

Adirondacks Information Center,
Glens Falls between exits 17
and 18 off I-87,
(518) 792–2730

Town of Webb Visitor Center,
P.O. Box 68,
Old Forge 13420,
(315) 369–6983

**Lake George Regional Chamber
of Commerce,**
P.O. Box 272,
Lake George 12845,
(518) 668–5755 or (800) 705–0059
www.lakegeorgechamber.com

**Lake Placid Essex County
Visitor Bureau,**
Olympic Center,
Lake Placid 12946,
(518) 523–2999 or (800) 447–5224

**Plattsburgh–North Country–Lake
Champlain Regional Visitors Center,**
P.O. Box 310,
Plattsburgh 12901,
(518) 563–1000

**Saranac Lake Chamber of
Commerce,**
39 Main Street,
Saranac Lake 12983,
(800) 347–1992
www.saranaclake.com

Saratoga County Tourism Department,
4394 Broadway,
Saratoga Springs 12866,
(800) 526–8970

**Whiteface Mountain Regional
Visitors Bureau,**
P.O. Box 277,
Whiteface Mountain 12997,
(518) 946–2255 or (888) WHITEFACE
www.whitefaceregion.com

Places to Stay in the Adirondacks

KEENE

Bark Eater Inn
Alstead Hill Road
(518) 576–2221

LAKE LUZERNE

Roaring Brook Ranch and Tennis Resort
Luzerne Road
(518) 668–5767

NORTH CREEK

Copperfield Inn
224 Main Street
(518) 251–2500

PAUL SMITHS

Hotel Saranac of Paul Smiths College
101 Main Street
(800) 937–0211

ROCK CITY FALLS

The Mansion
801 Route 29
(518) 885–1607

SARATOGA SPRINGS

Adelphi Hotel
365 Broadway
(518) 587–4688
(open mid-May to mid-October)

The Batcheller Mansion Inn
20 Circular Street
(800) 616–7012

Gideon Putnam
Saratoga Spa State Park
(800) 732–1560

Union Gables
55 Union Street
(800) 398–1558

UPPER SARANAC LAKE

The Wawbeek
553 Panther Mountain Road
(800) 953–2656

WARRENSBURG

Merrill Magee House
2 Hudson Street
(518) 623–2449

Places to Eat in the Adirondacks

LAKE CLEAR

Lodge at Lake Clear
Routes 30 and 186
(518) 891–1489
(German cuisine)

LAKE LUZERNE

Heritage Steak House
Northwoods Road
(518) 696–3733
(Italian cuisine)

LAKE PLACID

Mirror Lake Inn
5 Mirror Lake Drive
(518) 523–2544

SARATOGA SPRINGS

Eartha's
60 Court Street
(518) 583–0602

43 Phila Bistro
43 Phila Street
(518) 584–2720

Sperry's
30 Caroline Street
(518) 584–9618

WARRENSBURG

Grist Mill on the Schroon
100 River Street
(518) 623–8005

WHITEHALL

Silver Diner
Routes 4 and 22
(518) 499–0422

OTHER ATTRACTIONS WORTH SEEING IN THE ADIRONDACKS

Akwesasne Mohawk Casino,
Route 37,
Hogansburg,
(518) 358–2222 or (888) 622–1155

Almanzo Wilder Farm,
Stacy Road,
Burke,
(518) 483–1207

Ausable Chasm,
Route 9,
Ausable Chasm,
(800) 537–1211

Enchanted Forest/Water Safari,
3183 Route 38,
Old Forge,
(315) 369–6145

Gore Mountain,
Peaceful Valley Road,
North Creek,
(518) 251–2411 or (800) 342–1234

High Falls Gorge,
Route 86, Wilmington Notch,
Wilmington,
(518) 946–2278

Natural Stone Bridge and Caves,
555 Stone Bridge Road,
Pottersville,
(518) 494–2283

Plattsburgh State Art Museum,
SUNY, 101 Broad Street,
Plattsburgh,
(518) 563–7709

The Mohawk Valley

Drums along the Mohawk . . . Leatherstocking . . . "I had a mule and her name was Sal/Fifteen miles on the Erie Canal"—the lore of the Mohawk Valley has long been a part of the national consciousness. The reasons are plain: The valley has been an important highway between the East and the Great Lakes for centuries, and countless Americans have passed through here via Indian trails, the **Erie Canal,** Commodore Vanderbilt's "Water Level Route" of the New York Central railroad, and today's New York State Thruway. Here was where Jesuit missionaries met their end at the hands of the Iroquois, where **James Fenimore Cooper's** Deerslayer stalked, and where those who were to homestead the Midwest struck out along a water-filled ditch, in barges pulled by draft animals. Surely, this is one of the most storied corridors of the republic.

Yet between Albany and Syracuse, there are plenty of places where people settled down to make things . . . guns in Ilion, pots and pans in Rome, gloves, as you might suspect, in Gloversville. They nevertheless left no shortage of open land, as you can see when you crest one of the gently rolling hills in the dairy country near Cooperstown. If you are coming from the East, what you see here is a harbinger of the next 1,500

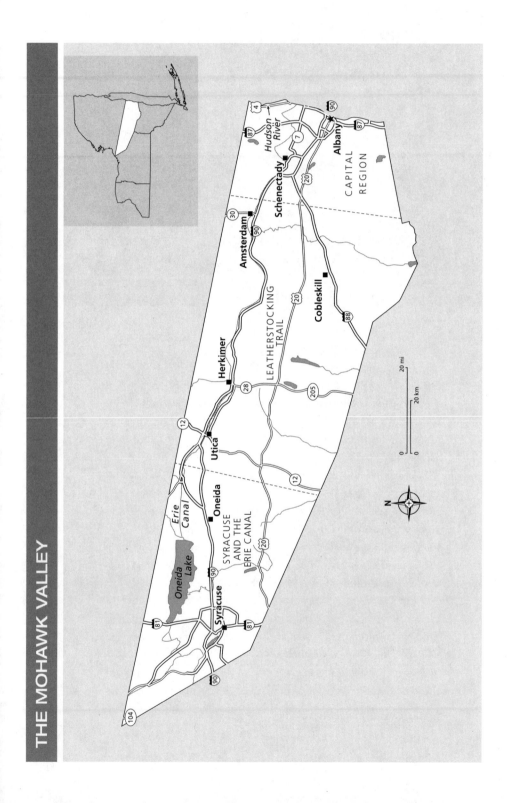

miles. It isn't prairie yet, but the land is opening up, and the horizon is growing more distant. This is where Midwestern vistas begin.

This chapter begins in *Albany,* very much an Eastern city and the capital of New York State. From here the direction followed is east to west, corresponding closely to the route of the Mohawk River itself and, conveniently, the New York State Thruway.

Capital Region

The conventional, foursquare approach to Albany is by way of the public facade it presents—the massively beautiful and ornate State Capitol building, partly designed by H.H. Richardson, or the four monolithic, marble-clad state office towers so closely associated with the grandiose visions of the late Nelson Rockefeller. But in order to see a subtler side of the city and surrounding area and to learn more of its antecedents and historic persona than is revealed by those gargantuan examples of power frozen in masonry, visit the *Albany Institute of History and Art.* Descended from lyceums and art galleries that date back to 1791, the institute has followed an acquisitions policy geared to collecting art, decorative arts, and historical artifacts related to the art, history, and culture of Albany and the upper Hudson River Valley from the seventeenth century to the present.

Hudson River art, of course, means the Hudson River School, which is well represented here with works by painters such as Cole, Durand, and Cropsey. But the institute possesses fine examples of an even older regional genre, the sometimes anonymous portraits of the Dutch burghers and their families who dictated the tone of Hudson Valley life during the seventeenth and eighteenth centuries. The Dutch in Holland had become the world masters of portraiture

AUTHORS' FAVORITES—MOHAWK VALLEY

Children's Museum

Fort Klock Historic Restoration

Iroquois Indian Museum

Mid-Lakes Navigation Company, Ltd.

The Petrified Creatures Museum of Natural History

Remington Arms Museum

Schoharie Crossing State Historic Site

Walter Elwood Museum

in the 1600s, as patrons and artists collaborated to compile a magnificent pictorial record of bourgeois life when the concept itself was still something new. It is fascinating to see how their New World counterparts worked a hundred years later. The experience is heightened by the institute's collection of early Hudson Valley furniture and silver, which formed the day-to-day surroundings of the people in the portraits.

The Albany Institute of History and Art, 125 Washington Avenue, Albany, (518) 463–4478, is open Wednesday through Saturday 10:00 A.M. to 5:00 P.M. and Sunday noon to 5:00 P.M. Admission is $7.00 for adults, $5.00 for senior citizens and students, and $3.00 for children ages 6 to 12.

The Schuylers were among the earliest of the Dutch settlers of the upper Hudson Valley and were involved throughout the colonial period in trading, agriculture, land development, and local politics. The most renowned member of the family was **Philip Schuyler** (1733–1804), whose manorial home is today preserved as the **Schuyler Mansion State Historic Site**.

Although Albany has grown up around the mansion and deprived it of its once-rural hillside setting, it stands as a monument not only to its talented and versatile builders but also to the best in eighteenth-century taste.

Philip Schuyler designed the mansion himself in the Georgian style, with rose-colored brick walls, graceful fenestration, and double-hipped roof (the awkward hexagonal brick entry vestibule is an 1818 addition), and furnished it largely with purchases he made during a 1761–62 trip to England.

After Schuyler died in 1804, his house and much of the family land in Albany were sold and used as a private residence and later an orphanage. The Schuyler Mansion was acquired by the state in 1912, restored, and opened to the public.

The Schuyler Mansion is as fine a place as New York State offers to learn about life as it was lived among the most fortunate levels of society in the mid-1700s. The mansion is an architectural gem, and it houses an excellent collection of colonial- and Federal-period furnishings.

The Schuyler Mansion State Historic Site, 32 Catherine Street, Albany, (518) 434–0834, is open April 15 through May 31 and September 7 through October 31, Wednesday through Sunday 11:00 A.M. to 5:00 P.M.; June 1 through September 6, Tuesday through Sunday 11:00 a.m. to 5:00 P.M.; November through April 14 by appointment. Also open on Memorial Day, Independence Day, and Labor Day. Admission is $4.00 for adults, $1.00 for children 5 to 12, and $3.00 for senior citizens and students.

In 1774 Mother Ann Lee, founder of the **Shakers,** left England with a small band of followers and came to New York City. A few years later the group established the country's first **Shaker settlement** in a town named Watervliet (now part of the town of **Colonie**).

Today the **Shaker Heritage Society** maintains a memorial to this historic settlement. Among the points of interest are a garden with some one hundred varieties of herbs (herbs were one of the early Shakers' major industries), the Ann Lee Pond nature preserve, and the Shaker Cemetery, where Ann Lee and other early Shakers are buried. The museum and gift shop are in the 1848 Shaker Meeting House, on the grounds of the Ann Lee Home.

The Shaker Heritage Society, Albany Shaker Road, Albany, (518) 456–7890, is open February to October Tuesday through Saturday 9:30 A.M. to 4:00 P.M.; November and December Monday through Saturday 10:00 A.M. to 4:00 P.M. A self-guided Walking Tour brochure is available for $1.00. Admission is $3.00 per person donation.

ANNUAL EVENTS IN THE MOHAWK VALLEY

MAY

Tulip Festival,
Albany,
(518) 434–2032 or (800) 258–3582

JUNE

Old Songs Festival of
Traditional Music,
Altamont,
(518) 765–2815

JULY

Hats off to Saratoga,
Saratoga Springs,
(518) 584–3255

New York State Blues Festival,
Syracuse,
(315) 435–2168

LATE JULY

Empire State Games,
Albany,
(518) 474–8889

AUGUST

New York State Fair,
Syracuse,
(800) 234–4797

Travers Festival Week,
Saratogo Springs,
(518) 584–3255

NOVEMBER

Christmas Parade,
Schenectady,
(518) 372–5656

DECEMBER

First Night,
Albany,
(518) 434–5132

One of Philip Schuyler's interests during his later years was the development of a canal and lock system in New York State. It was in the three decades after his death that canal building really hit its stride in the United States, turning formerly sleepy villages into canal boomtowns involved in the lucrative trade between New York City and points west. One such town is **Waterford**, located near Cohoes just upriver from Albany.

Founded by the Dutch as Halfmoon Point in the early 1620s at the point where the Mohawk River flows into the Hudson, Waterford was incorporated under its present name in 1794 and is today the oldest incorporated village in the United States. In 1799 it became the head of sloop navigation on the Hudson, but its glory days of commerce came later, in the 1820s, when the new Champlain and Erie canals made the town not merely a backcountry terminus but an important waystation and transfer point on a statewide transportation system.

Unfortunately for Waterford and many of its sister communities, not all major canal towns became major railroad towns after the iron horse ended the brief supremacy of the artificial waterways. Waterford did prosper as a small manufacturing center during the nineteenth century, however, and the legacy of this era is the village's lovely residential architecture, much of it in the regionally significant "Waterford" style characterized by Federal details and Dutch-inspired single-step gables. Such architectural distinctions have earned

shortandsteamy

The country's first railroad, with an 11-mile track, ran between Albany and Schenectady.

the village center inclusion on the National Register of Historic Places. The historic district is the subject of tours given during "Canalfest" the second Saturday of May each year. It features boat rides, hayrides, a boat show, a craft fair, food, and entertainment.

From April through October in the village center at Erie Canal Lock 2, a series of outdoor exhibits details the history of the 1823 canal and the present-day barge canal.

Waterford attractions outside the village center include the **Champlain Canal**, this section of which was dug in 1823 and is still filled with water; the **Waterford Flight**, a series of five locks on the still-operating New York State Barge Canal, whose 169-foot total rise is the highest in the world; a state park at **Lock 6**; and **Peebles Island State Park. Waterford Historical Museum and Cultural Center**, 2 Museum Lane (off Saratoga Avenue), Waterford, (518) 238–0809, is open from May 15 through October 1, Wednesday through Friday from 11:00 A.M. to 2:00 P.M., and Saturday and Sunday from 2:00 to 4:00 P.M.;

October 2 through October 24, Saturday and Sunday 2:00 to 4:00 P.M.; closed holiday weekends. Admission is free.

Leatherstocking Trail

The **Walter Elwood Museum,** in a former school, offers a wonderful overview of the area's history as well as an eclectic collection of historical and natural objects. It isn't one of those musty little spots with a collection of shaving brushes and pewter dishes; among the 20,000 artifacts, which include the fossilized footprint of a Tyrannosaurus rex, is the earliest television set (on permanent loan from the Edison Museum in Menlo Park, New Jersey) and an exhibit depicting life in the Victorian era—a life-size home with four completely furnished rooms.

The museum, one of the few and one of the largest public school–owned museums in the country, is named for a local teacher who opened a museum and bird sanctuary in 1940 so students could study nature and wildlife.

The Walter Elwood Museum, 300 Guy Park Avenue, **Amsterdam,** (518) 843–5151, is open July and August Monday through Thursday from 8:30 A.M. to 3:30 P.M. and Friday 8:30 A.M. to 1:00 P.M.; from September through June, Monday through Friday 8:30 A.M. to 4:00 P.M. Closed legal holidays and school holidays; open other times by appointment. Donations are welcome.

The Erie Canal and the feats of engineering that its building entailed are the focus of **Schoharie Crossing State Historic Site,** farther up the Mohawk, at Fort Hunter. Seven canal-related structures dating from three periods of the waterway's construction or expansion are preserved here and provided with interpretive displays that explain their use. The visitors' center has an exhibit on the **Erie Canal** and information on the site and surrounding area. **Putnam's Canal Store,** at Yankee Hill Lock 28 on Queen Anne's Road (2.2 miles east of the visitors' center), was built during the 1850s and served

What's in a Name?

The leather leggings worn by Yankees who settled in this area gave birth to the region's nickname, the Leatherstocking Trail. James Fenimore Cooper immortalized the name in his *Leatherstocking Tales*, which recounted the adventures of wilderness scout Natty Bumppo. Cooper is buried in the family plot in Cooperstown's Christ Church cemetery.

as a store along the enlarged Erie Canal for many years. It now houses an exhibit on Erie Canal stores.

Along the old canal towpath are views of modern-day barge traffic on the Mohawk River, the depth of which in this area allows it to be used as a link in the New York State barge canal system.

Schoharie Crossing State Historic Site, 129 Schoharie Street, P.O. Box 140, Fort Hunter 12069, (518) 829–7516, is open May through October 31 and Memorial Day, Independence Day, and Labor Day, Wednesday through Saturday 10:00 A.M. to 5:00 P.M. and Sunday 1:00 to 5:00 P.M. The grounds are open all year during daylight hours. Admission is free.

Long before there were canals or barges in this part of New York State, the waters of the Mohawk and its tributaries were plied by the canoes of the Iroquois. The Mohawk Valley was the heart of the empire of the Five Nations, one of which was the tribe that gave the river its name. In what is today the town of Auriesville stood the palisaded village of Mohawk longhouses called Ossernenon in the seventeenth century; here, in 1642, a raiding party of Indians returned with three French and twenty Huron captives in custody. Among the French were a Jesuit priest, Isaac Jogues, and his lay assistant, René Goupil.

Goupil was tomahawked to death when his attempt to teach a child the sign of the cross was interpreted as the casting of an evil spell. Jogues was rescued by the Dutch during a Mohawk trading foray to Fort Orange, and he returned to Europe and eventually Quebec. But he volunteered to go back to Ossernenon in May 1646, as part of a group attempting to ratify a peace treaty with the Mohawks, and was captured near the village by a faction of the tribe favoring a continuation of hostilities. Both he and a lay companion, Jean Lalande, were murdered by tomahawk-wielding braves in October of that year. Canonized by the Roman Catholic Church in 1930 along with five Jesuit missionaries martyred in Canada, Jogues, Goupil, and Lalande are honored at the **_National Shrine of the North American Martyrs_** in Auriesville.

The shrine, which occupies the hilltop site of the original Mohawk village of Ossernenon amid 600 verdant acres, is maintained by the New York Province of the Society of Jesus, the same Jesuit order to which Isaac Jogues belonged. Founded in 1885, the shrine accommodates 40,000 to 50,000 visitors each year during a season lasting from the first Sunday in May to the last Sunday in October. Mass is celebrated in the vast "Coliseum," the central altar of which is built to suggest the palisades of a Mohawk village; there are also a Martyrs' Museum, rustic chapels, and a retreat house.

For information on the schedule of observances at the National Shrine of the North American Martyrs, Noeltner Road, **_Auriesville,_** call (518) 853–3033.

The shrine is open from the first Sunday in May to the last Sunday in October, daily 10:00 A.M. to 4:00 P.M.

The French Catholic missionaries working among the Indians in the seventeenth century were not without their successes. The most famous name among Mohawk converts of that era is **Kateri Tekakwitha,** the "Lily of the Mohawks," born at Ossernenon and baptized at what is now the village of Fonda, where the **Fonda National Shrine of Blessed Kateri Tekakwitha** is located. Maintained by the Conventual Franciscan Order, the shrine commemorates the life of the saintly Indian girl who lived half of her life here, before moving to the community of converted Indians established by the French at Caughnawaga, near Montreal, where she died in 1680 at the age of twenty-four. (In 1980, on the tercentenary of her death, Pope John Paul II announced the beatification of Kateri Tekakwitha, which is the last step before canonization in the Catholic Church.)

Aside from its religious connections, the **Fonda** site of the Tekakwitha shrine is interesting because of its identification by archaeologists as the location of a Mohawk village, also called Caughnawaga. Artifacts dug from the village site are exhibited in the shrine's Native American Exhibit, located on the ground floor of a revolutionary-era Dutch barn that now serves as a chapel. Indian items from elsewhere in New York State and throughout the United States are also part of the exhibit.

The Fonda National Shrine of Blessed Kateri Tekakwitha, off Route 5, Fonda, (518) 853–3646, is open daily, May through October from 10:00 A.M. to 4:00 P.M. Admission is free.

Just north of Fonda and nearby Johnstown is **Gloversville,** home of the **Fulton County Museum.** Gloversville was originally called Kingsborough, but the townspeople adopted the present name in 1828 in homage to the linchpin of the local economy in those days—tanning and glove making. It is the glove industry that provides the Fulton County Museum with its most interesting

And We Don't Have to Tell You What They Fit Like

Daniel Storto is the last of a breed—he's the only custom glove maker left in Gloversville. Settling in the one-time glove capital of America in 2002, Storto set up shop to carry on his business of handcrafting gloves for clients such as Whoopi Goldberg, Diane Keaton, and Madonna.

exhibits, housed in the Glove and Leather Room. Here is the state's only glove-manufacturing display, a complete small glove factory of the last century, donated to the museum and reassembled in its original working format.

There is also a Weaving Room where craftspeople demonstrate the technique of turning raw flax into the finished product; an Old Country Kitchen; a nineteenth-century Lady's Room, complete with costumes and cosmetics; a Country Store; an old-time Candy Store; an Early Farm display; and a Country Schoolroom. Be sure not to miss the Indian Artifact exhibit on the first floor.

The Fulton County Museum, 237 Kingsboro Avenue, Gloversville, (518) 725–2203, is open May and June, Tuesday through Saturday noon to 4:00 P.M.; July and August, Tuesday through Saturday 10:00 A.M. to 4:00 P.M.; and September through mid-November, Tuesday through Saturday noon to 4:00 P.M. Admission is free.

Fate plays a capricious hand in deciding which industries a town will be noted for. Gloversville got gloves; *Canajoharie,* our next stop along the

If It Isn't Haunted, It Should Be

It isn't often that an individual house is unusual enough to make us stop in our tracks, park the car, and gawk, but that's just what happened one summer afternoon while we were driving through the small town of Palatine Bridge, just across the river from Canajoharie.

There it was, the archetype of the spooky, derelict Victorian mansion. An immense, three-and-a-half-story structure, rambling back from Grand Street for half a block, the house was a bold pastiche of just about every cliché of our own American Baroque, the Second Empire style of the 1870s: mansard roof, elaborately detailed dormers, tall entrance tower, and deep shady porches. It was very nearly in ruins. Great flotillas of bats, we could readily imagine, poured nightly out of gaps in the rotted eaves, completing the Charles Addams effect.

A weather-worn state historic marker told whose house it had been. Webster Wagner, a pioneer in the development of luxury railroad passenger cars, built the place in 1877. Nearly twenty years earlier, when he was depot master of the New York Central station at Palatine Bridge, Wagner had presented his plans for a sleeping car to his boss, Commodore Cornelius Vanderbilt. The Commodore liked the idea and helped bankroll what became the Wagner Palace Car Company. Wagner's firm was eventually taken over by George Pullman, of Pullman car fame.

By then, I knew, Webster Wagner had burned to death in one of his own sleepers, in an 1882 crash just north of New York City. If it were possible to make this once-proud pile on Grand Street even more melancholy, more grotesque, this recollection of its builder's horrible end certainly did the trick.

Mohawk, got chewing gum—specifically the Beech-Nut Packing Company, of which town native Bartlett Arkell was president in the 1920s. Because of Arkell and his success in business, Canajoharie also came into possession of the finest independent art gallery of any municipality its size in the United States: the *Canajoharie Library and Art Gallery.*

Arkell's beneficence to his hometown began with his donation of a new library in 1924. Two years later he donated the funds to build an art gallery wing on the library, and over the next few years he gave the community the magnificent collection of paintings that forms the bulk of the gallery's present holdings. Subsequent additions were made in 1964 and 1989.

This institution has become not merely an art gallery with a library attached, but an art gallery with a small town attached. The roster of American painters exhibited here is astounding, totally out of scale with what you would expect at a thruway exit between Albany and Utica. The Hudson River School is represented by Albert Bierstadt (*El Capitan*), John Kensett, and Thomas Doughty. There is a Gilbert Stuart portrait of George Washington. The Winslow Homer collection is the third largest in the United States. The eighteenth century is represented by John Singleton Copley; the nineteenth, by such luminaries as Thomas Eakins, George Inness (*Rainbow*), and James McNeill Whistler (*On the Thames*). Among twentieth-century painters are Charles Burchfield, Reginald Marsh, N.C. Wyeth and his son Andrew (*February 2nd*), Edward Hopper, Thomas Hart Benton, and even Grandma Moses. There is also a Frederic Remington bronze, *Bronco Buster.* Add a collection of eighty Korean and Japanese ceramics, the gift of the late Colonel John Fox, and you have all the more reason—as if more were needed—to regard Canajoharie as a destination in itself rather than a stop along the way.

The Canajoharie Library and Art Gallery, 2 Erie Boulevard, Canajoharie, (518) 673–2314, is open Monday through Wednesday 10:00 A.M. to 4:45 P.M., Thursday 10:00 A.M. to 8:30 P.M., Friday 10:00 A.M. to 4:45 P.M., Saturday 10:00 A.M. to 1:30 P.M.; closed Sunday. Admission is free.

Art played little part in the life of the Mohawk Valley in the year 1750, when Johannes Klock built the farmhouse-fortress preserved today as the *Fort Klock Historic Restoration.* Located above the river at *St. Johnsville,* Fort Klock is a reminder that the building of stout-walled outposts capable of being held defensively was by no means confined to the "Wild West" of the late 1800s. In 1750 the Mohawk Valley *was* the Wild West, and a man like Klock found it necessary to build a home that could serve just as easily as a fortress.

Like his neighbors at scattered sites along the river, Johannes Klock engaged in fur trading and farming. Canoes and bateaux could be tied up in the cove just below the house, yet the building itself stood on high enough ground and at a sufficient distance from the river to make it easily defensible should the waters of the Mohawk bring foes rather than friendly traders. The stone walls of Fort Klock are almost 2 feet thick and are dotted with "loop-holes" that enabled inhabitants to fire muskets from protected positions within.

Now restored and protected as a registered National Historic Landmark, Fort Klock and its outbuildings, including a restored Dutch barn, tell a good part of the story of the Mohawk Valley in the eighteenth century—a time when the hardships of homesteading were made even more difficult by the constant threat of the musket, the tomahawk, and the torch.

Fort Klock Historic Restoration, Route 5, St. Johnsville, (518) 568–7779, is open from mid-May through mid-October, Tuesday through Sunday 9:00 A.M. to 5:00 P.M. Admission is $1.00 for adults, 50 cents for children over 10.

The *Iroquois Indian Museum* is also devoted to the Iroquois Confederacy, but it specializes in researching the pre-Revolutionary Schoharie Mohawk who lived here. The museum's Archaeology Department is currently working with the State University of New York at Cobleskill to excavate and research a major 9,600-year-old Mohawk site discovered recently.

The museum traces the history of the Mohawk and other nations of the Confederacy; the building and exhibits, in presentation as well as in content, reflect the beliefs and traditions of traditional Iroquois. The main building at the museum resembles an Iroquois longhouse. (Visitors explore the museum in a counterclockwise direction, in the same way that longhouse dancers move.)

Two log homes at the edge of the museum's forty-five-acre nature park were moved from Canada's largest Iroquois community, the Six Nations Reserve. A Children's Iroquois Museum on the ground floor utilizes a hands-on approach to help interpret the adult museum for youngsters.

The Iroquois Indian Museum, P.O. Box 7, Caverns Road, *Howes Cave* 12092, (518) 296–8949, is open daily from July 1 through Labor Day weekend, Monday through Saturday 10:00 A.M. to 6:00 P.M. and Sunday noon to 6:00 P.M.; April, May, June, and Labor Day through December, open Tuesday through Saturday 10:00 A.M. to 5:00 P.M. and Sunday noon to 5:00 P.M. It is closed January through March. Admission is $7.00 for adults, $5.50 for senior citizens and students ages 13 to 17, and $4.00 for children ages 5 to 12.

"Believe it or not, we've even called New Zealand, and received a fax from England" boasts the literature for *Historic Throop Drugstore*. And indeed, it *is* hard for first-time visitors to believe when they first enter the oldest store in Schoharie County. The building was the site of Throop Drug Store from 1800 until 1934, and people filling prescriptions here today receive a huge dose of nostalgia along with their twenty-first-century pills.

The pharmacy is owned by David and Sarah Goodrich. David, a registered pharmacist, is also a history buff. The couple has restored the pharmacy to look much as Throop's did in the 1920s and 1930s, with antique druggists' bottles, past issues of *Life* magazine, and best of all, an old-fashioned soda fountain, where customers can order a milk shake (whipped up in a 1950s mixer), ice cream (including the house special Black Forest sundae), freshly baked Danish, or homemade soups, and then pull up an old ice-cream parlor chair and enjoy amid surroundings that predate cholesterol paranoia.

Historic Throop Drugstore, Main Street, Schoharie, (518) 295–7300, is open Monday through Friday 8:30 A.M. to 5:30 P.M.; Saturday the pharmacy is open from 9:00 A.M. to noon, and the soda fountain is open to "whenever"; closed Sunday.

Renovating a building takes a lot of effort; restoring an entire section of a town is a herculean undertaking, as visitors to **Sharon Springs** will immediately appreciate. The erstwhile resort community, whose waters were said to equal those of Germany's Baden-Baden in therapeutic value, thrived in the mid- to late-1800s when people came seeking cures for everything from "malarial difficulties" to "biliary derangements."

Don't miss the self-guided Historic Main Street Tour. Twenty plaques lining both sides of the historic district depict the village's golden era with stories, architectural facts, diary excerpts from the 1860s, and hundreds of photos from the nineteenth century.

Several lodgings in the historic district are opening as they are restored. Among them: the circa 1840 Greek Revival **Brimstonia Cottage** (518–284–2839) and Edgefield B&B (518–284–9771), an English-style inn. The restored, Spanish Colonial 1928 Adler Hotel and Spa (518–284–2285) has a pool, dining room, kosher kitchen, and sulphur baths.

The handsomely restored **American Hotel,** an 1847 National Register building, has nine rooms with private baths (rates start at $135 per night), a pub, and a restaurant with a good reputation. It serves lunch weekdays, dinner nightly in season, and Saturday and Sunday brunch. The American Hotel is located on Main Street in Sharon Springs; (518) 284–2105.

Although in far fewer numbers, people still come to Sharon Springs for the waters. They can drink the sulfurous brew at the octagonal beaux-arts White Sulphur Temple and have a facial splash in Blue Stone Spring, once used extensively as a "lotion for inflammatory conditions of the eye." In July and August, bathers can soak in the original tubs of the Imperial Baths. Each summer, the Sharon Springs Citizens Council of the Arts hosts a free Wednesday evening music and theater series in Chalybeate Park. During the summer, from 2:00 to

4:00 P.M. daily, the Sharon Historical Society opens its museum in a restored 1860 schoolhouse on Main Street. Be sure to sign the guest wall at the four-teen-room Cobbler & Company (518–284–2067) on Main Street, a combination museum/gift shop, which sells everything from English china to penny candy.

For information on Sharon Springs, look the town up at either of its Web sites: www.roseboro.com or www.sharonsprings.com.

Just out of town, **Clausen Farms** (Route 20, P.O. Box 395, Sharon Springs 13459, 518–284–2527; www.reu.com/clausen), an eighty-acre Victorian estate and llama farm, has four guest rooms in the main house, which dates to the late 1700s (open year-round) and seven in the Casino, a Victorian gentleman's guesthouse completed in 1892 (open April through October). The inn has great views of the Mohawk Valley, an 1892 swimming pool with a fountain, a 1911 bowling alley with original pins and balls, and cross-country skiing. Call for current rates.

Thirty miles south of the Mohawk River is the origin of another of America's great waterways, the Susquehanna River at Otsego Lake. The village of **Cooperstown** lies at the southern end of 9-mile-long "Glimmerglass," so named by James Fenimore Cooper, the American novelist whose family founded the village that is now synonymous with ultimate achievement in America's national pastime.

The National Baseball Hall of Fame is what initially brings most visitors to Cooperstown, but many miss the three-story **National Baseball Hall of Fame Library,** located in a separate building connected to the museum. It's a treasure trove of baseball: a collection of more than 2.5 million items including clippings, photographs, books, videos, movies, recordings—anything and everything you ever wanted to know about America's classic pastime. Established in 1939, the library is used by researchers but is open to visitors, who are invited to browse at their leisure. During your visit be sure to include the fifty-six-seat Bullpen Theater, where visitors can view the best in baseball highlight films and footage of the game's greatest plays.

The National Baseball Hall of Fame Library, Main Street, Cooperstown, (607) 547–0330, is open Monday through Friday 9:00 A.M. to 5:00 P.M., with half-hour tours throughout the day, during summer months. Museum visitors can enter the library from the museum at no additional charge. If you want to visit the library without touring the museum, call in advance and they'll leave your name at the admission booth so you won't be charged.

The **Fenimore Art Museum,** showcase for the New York State Historical Association, features changing exhibits of works largely from the eighteenth through early twentieth centuries, with an emphasis on paintings, early photographs, textiles, and other items relating to the American experience. Among the works are Hudson River School paintings by such luminaries as Thomas Cole and Asher B. Durand, folk art, and period furniture and paintings associated with Mr. Cooper.

The museum's $10-million, 18,000-square-foot new wing exhibits the Eugene and Clare Thaw Collection of American Indian Art, more than 700 masterpieces spanning 2,400 years that highlight the artistry of North America's indigenous peoples. The Great Hall features a selection of large-scale objects from regions throughout North America.

The museum, overlooking the lake, has a formal terrace garden and restaurant with outdoor seating that overlooks the lake.

Just across the street is the twenty-three-acre **Farmers' Museum,** a cluster of historic buildings where the trades, skills, and agricultural practices of nineteenth-century rural New York State come to life. The museum's 1845 Village Crossroads is made up of ten early-nineteenth-century buildings all built within 100 miles of Cooperstown and moved here as life-size working exhibits. Among the buildings are a tavern, blacksmith's shop, one-room schoolhouse, and print shop. All are furnished in period-style, and the museum interpreters perform the tasks appropriate to each building. Penny candy is sold at Todd's General Store. Lippitt Farmstead, a nineteenth-century house, barn, and outbuilding complex, presents farming practices of the day. The Herder's Cottage serves a light menu.

Be sure to include a visit to the fascinating **Seneca Log House,** at one time the home of a traditional Seneca family. At the site the daily life of a Seneca family in the 1840s is replicated as closely as possible. A docent demonstrates crafts of the period, including basketmaking, beadwork, and the making of tourist-related objects, and special seasonal events are held here throughout the year.

Among the special events are an old-time Fourth of July, the September Harvest Festival, and a Candlelight Evening at Christmastime that features sleigh rides and hot wassail.

The Farmers' Museum, Lake Road (607–547–1450) in Cooperstown, is open April, May, October and November, Tuesday through Sunday 10:00 A.M. to 4:00 P.M. June through September it's open daily 10:00 A.M. to 5:00 P.M. The Fenimore Art Museum, Lake Road (607–547–1400), is open April, May, and October through December, Tuesday through Sunday 10:00 A.M. to 4:00 P.M. and June through September, daily 10:00 A.M. to 5:00 P.M. A Cooperstown Discovery Pass, which provides admission to both museums as well as the National Baseball Hall of Fame, is available. Call (607) 547–1410 for information.

"When the building starts shaking, they've started making," says USA Today of **Fly Creek Cider Mill and Orchard,** a turn-of-the-century water-powered mill where visitors can watch apple cider being made as well as chow down on a host of cider-related products, including hot spiced cider, cider floats, and cider mill donuts. There's also a duck pond, tractorland kids' area, and gift shop selling everything from bagged cheese curds to home accessories. It's at 288 Gloose Street, Fly Creek , (607) 547–9692, and is open from early May until the day before Christmas, daily 9:00 A.M. to 6:00 P.M. Call for July and early August hours.

Hyde Hall, a New York State Historic Site, is fascinating because it's a work in progress that visitors can tour as it's being restored. Built in the early nineteenth century by one of the state's last great land-owning families, it's considered to be the finest example of a neoclassical country mansion north of the Mason-Dixon line.

The estate's builder, George Clarke, secretary and lieutenant governor of the British Province of New York from 1703 to 1743, wanted to build a home similar to the one he'd left behind in Cheshire, England. He retained Philip Hooker, one of America's foremost early nineteenth-century architects, and kept copious records of the house's construction, furnishing, and decoration, allowing today's restorers to replicate many of the original features as they work. Hyde Hall is a fascinating look into one man's vision, the damage time can render on a once-magnificent dwelling, and the dedication of a small group of people determined to restore the hall to its former glory.

Hyde Hall in *Springfield,* adjacent to Glimmerglass State Park and over-looking Otsego Lake, is open for tours May, June, September, and October, daily 10:00 A.M., noon, and 2:00 P.M., and weekends 10:00 A.M. to 5:00 P.M. (last tour at 4:00 P.M.) In July and August the daily and weekend tour hours are the same, except there is an additional daily tour at 4:00 P.M. Closed when there are events on site. Admission is $7.00 for adults, $6.00 for seniors, and $4.00 for ages 5 to 12. For information and events contact Friends of Hyde Hall, Inc., P.O. Box 721, Cooperstown 13326, (607) 547–5098, or check their Web site: www.hydehall.org.

Essential Elements offers a serene respite from the hurly-burly of down-town Cooperstown. Patrons listen to soothing music as they browse among books, CDs, aromatherapy, crafts, and jewelry. They're invited to enjoy lunch, teas, and desserts in the oak-paneled Tea Room or Secret Garden, and may also consult a local tarot card reader and astrologer while visiting the shop. Essential Elements Day Spa, on the second floor, offers a full range of services, including massage, facials, pedicures, and body wraps.

Essential Elements, 137 Main Street, Cooperstown, (607) 547–9432 or (800) 437–3265, is open daily July through October; call for off-season schedules.

Outstanding hospitality and gourmet breakfasts are the hallmarks of the **Landmark Inn,** an elegant 1856 mansion in the heart of Cooperstown. Innkeepers Jennifer and Pete Landers have nine rooms, all with private bath, cable TV, refrigerators, and air-conditioning at their smoke-free B&B. June through September, rates start at $160 per night. Weekends during the months of June through September require a two-night minimum stay, and kids are very welcome. The inn is at 64 Chestnut Street, Cooperstown, (607) 547–7225 or (866) 384–3466; www.landmarkbnb.com.

At one point in the nineteenth century, 80 percent of the hops produced in America came from within a 40-mile radius of Cooperstown. The **Brewery Ommegang,** on a 135-acre former hops farm alongside the Susquehanna River, is carrying on the region's proud tradition, using traditional Belgian brewing techniques, which include utilizing specialty malts, Syrian and Saaz hops, rare spices such as curaçao orange peel and paradise grain, and open fermentation, bottle-conditioning, and warm cellaring. Judge the result for yourself: The brewery is open for half-hour tours year-round, daily from noon to 5:00 P.M. A $4.00 tour fee is refunded with a purchase.

Brewery Ommegang is on County Route 33, paralleling Route 28 and midway between Cooperstown and Milford, (800) 544–1809 or (607) 544–1800.

Central New York's oldest museum, **The Petrified Creatures Museum of Natural History,** was established more than fifty years ago on land that the Devonian Sea covered 300 million years in the past. Today visitors are invited to climb on the backs of life-size purple and green dinosaurs, learn about life in prehistoric times, and dig for fossils to take home as free souvenirs (tools are provided by the museum). Don't miss the gift shop!

The Petrified Creatures Museum of Natural History, Route 20, **Richfield Springs,** (315) 858–2868, is open mid-May through mid-September, daily from 10:00 A.M. to 6:00 P.M. Admission is $8.00 adults and $4.00 children, under 5 free.

It was an environment very much like the one depicted at the Farmers' Museum's Village Crossroads that produced one of the great American toolmakers, inasmuch as dependable firearms were indispensable tools of frontier life and westward expansion. In 1816 **Eliphalet Remington** was twenty-four years old and in need of a new rifle. He made a barrel at his father's village forge and then walked into the Mohawk Valley town of Utica to have it rifled (rifling is the series of twisting grooves inside a gun barrel that give the bullet spin—and therefore accuracy—and distinguish it from the smoothbore muskets of earlier days). He may not have known it then, but gun making was to be his life's work and the Remington Arms Company his creation. You can learn the history of America's oldest gun maker at the **Remington Arms Museum** in

Antique Double Derringer,
Remington Arms Museum

Ilion, which houses an impressive collection of rifles, shotguns, and handguns dating back to Eliphalet Remington's earliest flintlocks. Here are examples of the first successful breech-loading rifles, for which Remington held the initial 1864 patents; rare presentation-grade guns; and company firsts including bolt-action and pump rifles, autoloading rifles and shotguns, and the Model 32 over-and-under shotgun of 1932.

Other displays include explanations of how firearms are built today, advertising posters and other firearms ephemera, and even antique Remington typewriters—yes, it was the same company.

The Remington Arms Museum, 14 Hoefler Avenue (off Route 5S), Ilion, (315) 895–3301 or (800) 243–9700, is open year-round, Monday through Friday from 9:00 A.M. to 5:00 P.M. and Saturday from 10:00 A.M. to 4:00 P.M. June, July, and August, tours are given Monday through Friday at 10:00 A.M. and 1:00 P.M. Admission is free. There's also a shop, which sells clothes and accessories.

"Herkimer diamonds," found just north of Ilion at *Middleville,* aren't really diamonds. Nor are they generally very valuable. But they're a load of fun to prospect for, and the *Ace of Diamonds Mine and Campground*—once known as the Tabor Estate, where the diamonds were first dug—can provide you with all the tools to begin your hunt.

The "diamonds" are really clear quartz crystals found in a rock formation called dolomite, buried ages ago. Surface water containing silicon seeped down through the earth and was trapped in pockets in the dolomite. Tremendous heat and pressure caused the crystals to form, and over the years erosion, weathering, and water have exposed the strata. The crystals at the Ace of Diamonds are found in pockets in the rock and in soil surrounding the weathered rock. They're primarily used for mineral specimens, but ones of gem quality are used in arts and jewelry.

Ace of Diamonds Mine and Campground, Route 28, Middleville, (315) 891–3855 or 891–3896, is open April 1 through October 31 daily from 9:00 A.M. to 5:00 P.M. There is a digging fee of $7.00 per adult and $2.00 for children 7 and under.

From Ilion it's just a short hop down the thruway to *Utica* and a pair of worthwhile museums. The *Munson-Williams-Proctor Arts Institute* is the sort of thing small cities do well, given farsighted founders and the right endowment. The institute is a multifaceted operation that places a good deal of emphasis on community accessibility and service, with free group tours, a speakers' bureau, and children's art programs, as well as free admission and a modestly priced performing arts series (some performances take place at the nearby Stanley Performing Arts Center). But you don't have to be a Utica resident to enjoy the major holdings, which include a collection of paintings strong in nineteenth-century genre work and the Hudson River School, as well as such moderns as Calder, Picasso, Kandinsky, and Pollock; comprehensive art and music libraries; a sculpture garden; and even a children's room where patrons can leave their kids for supervised play while they enjoy the museum. Also on the grounds of the institute is **Fountain Elms,** a beautifully restored 1850 home in the Italianate Victorian style, which was once the home of the philanthropic Williams family. Four period rooms on the ground floor exemplify Victorian tastes. At Christmastime the house is resplendent with Victorian ornamentation.

The Munson-Williams-Proctor Arts Institute, 310 Genesee Street, Utica, (315) 797–0000, is open Tuesday through Saturday 10:00 A.M. to 5:00 P.M. and Sunday 1:00 to 5:00 P.M., closed major holidays. Admission is free.

Having retrieved your little ones from the children's room at the institute, take them next to a museum of their own. Outside of New York City, Utica's **Children's Museum** is now the largest such institution just for kids in the state, having grown like Topsy since its founding by the city's Junior League. Since 1980 it has occupied its own five-story, 30,000-square-foot building, which it keeps chock-full of participatory and hands-on exhibits concentrating on natural history, the history of New York State, and technology. Installations designed for children ages two to twelve and their families include a Dino Den; Childspace, for children from infant to twelve; an Iroquois longhouse and artifacts; a natural history center; and bubbles, architecture, and dress-up areas. The museum also offers special exhibitions on a monthly basis and special programs for children and their families on Saturdays beginning at 2:00 P.M., from October through July. Portions of the permanent Railroad Exhibit, which includes a Santa Fe dining car and diesel locomotive, are on display next to the museum.

The Children's Museum, 311 Main Street, Utica, (315) 724–6129 (What's Up Line, 724–6128), is open year-round, Monday, Tuesday, Thursday, Friday, and Saturday from 9:45 A.M. to 3:45 P.M., and Sunday noon to 4:30 P.M. The museum is closed on most major holidays but open when school is closed. Admission is $4.00 per person; children under age one are admitted free.

In 1888 German-born F. X. Matt II opened a brewery in West Utica. Today the **Matt Brewing Company** is the second-oldest family-owned brewery—and twelfth largest—in the country. In addition to the Saranac family of beers, it also produces numerous specialty microbrews, including New Amsterdam and Harpoon.

You can tour the brewery and then sample the wares for free in the 1888 Tavern (the brewery makes an 1888 Tavern Root Beer for kids and teetotalers). The tour includes a visit to the seven-story brew house, the fermenting and aging cellars, and the packaging plant.

The Matt Brewing Company (now also known as Saranac Brewery), 830 Varick Street, Utica, (315) 732–0022 or (800) 765–6288, is open for tours year-round. June 1 through Labor Day, tours are given Monday through Saturday from 1:00 to 4:00 P.M., every hour on the hour. On Sunday tours are given at 1:00 and 3:00 P.M. The rest of the year, tours are given Friday and Saturday at 1:00 and 3:00 P.M. (closed major holidays). Advance reservations are recommended. Admission is $3.00 for adults and $1.00 for children ages 6 to 12. Free parking is available in the Tour Center Concourse at the corner of Court and Varick Streets.

Syracuse and the Erie Canal

Hop aboard a horse-drawn canal boat at *Erie Canal Village,* which opened in Rome in 1973 near the site where the first spadeful of dirt for the Erie Canal was dug on Independence Day in 1817. The short-lived canal era may have been only a prologue to the age of the railroad, but in the 1820s New Yorkers thought the Erie Canal was one of the wonders of the world.

The *Chief Engineer,* which keeps to a regular schedule of thirty-five-minute trips on the restored section of the original canal at the village, was built of Mohawk Valley oak to the same specifications as the passenger-carrying packet boats of the canal's early years. The Harden Carriage Museum displays a varied collection of horse-drawn vehicles used on roads and snow. Other buildings in the village—nearly all more than a hundred years old and moved here from other communities in the area—include a tavern, church, smithy, canal store, settler's house, barn, and the New York State Museum of Cheese. The Erie Canal Museum explains the technological and social importance of the Erie Canal. Fort Bull, dating from the French and Indian Wars, is also on the premises.

The village presents historical craft demonstrations, interpretive programs, and seasonal festivals, with the primary focus on canal and harvest activities.

Erie Canal Village, 5789 New London Road, Routes 49 and 46, **Rome,** (315) 337–3999 or (888) 374–3226, is open daily from Memorial Day weekend through Labor Day, Wednesday through Saturday from 10:00 A.M. to 5:00 P.M. and Sunday noon to 5:00 P.M. Admission is $4.00 for adults, $3.00 for seniors and students, and $2.00 for children 4 to 17. Boat and train rides are an additional $5.00 per person. If you purchase a boat ticket with admission, you'll save 50 cents.

Back before the Erie Canal was built, this part of New York State was the western frontier, ripe for settlement, agriculture, and the development of manufacturing. During those first decades of American independence, land development companies operated much as they had in colonial times, securing rights to vast sections of virgin territory and undertaking to bring in settlers and get them started. One such outfit was the Holland Land Company, which in 1790 sent its young agent John Lincklaen to America to scout investment possibilities. Two years later he reached the area around *Cazenovia Lake,* between present-day Rome and Syracuse, and his enthusiasm for the area's prospects led his firm to invest in 120,000 acres here. A village, farms, and small businesses soon thrived, with Lincklaen remaining in a patriarchal and entrepreneurial role that demanded the establishment of a comfortable family seat. The result was Lincklaen's 1807 building of his magnificent Federal mansion, Lorenzo, today preserved at the *Lorenzo State Historic Site*.

The little fiefdom of Lorenzo offers an instructive glimpse into why New York is called the Empire State. Lincklaen and the descendants of his adopted family, who lived here until 1968 (the same year that the house, with its contents, was deeded to the state), were involved with many of the enterprises that led to the state's phenomenal growth during the nineteenth century—road building, canals, railroads, and industrial development.

The mansion, surrounded by twenty acres of lawns and formal gardens, sits on the shores of a 4-mile-long lake. It is rich in Federal-era furnishings and the accumulated possessions of a century and a half of Lincklaens. The southwest

Lorenzo

And Not a Drop of Acid Rain

The first commercial wind farm east of the Mississippi stands on a 120-acre site along a ridge in Madison County, not far from Cazenovia. Seven 220-foot-high windmills with 100-foot blades each produce 1.65 megawatts of electricity—collectively, enough to power 10,000 homes when operating at full capacity.

bedroom was wallpapered with a reproduction of the original Jeffrey and Company of London paper, first hung in the room at the turn of the twentieth century. In the latest renovations Zuber & Cie, in business in Rixheim, France, since the eighteenth century, used their original printing blocks to reproduce an 1870 paper originally hung in Lorenzo in 1901. These projects are part of an ongoing process to fully restore the site to its turn-of-the-century beauty. There is a fine selection of Hudson River School artworks in the dining room.

Lorenzo State Historic Site, Route 13, Cazenovia, (315) 655–3200, is open from early May through October 31, Wednesday, Thursday, and Saturday, and Monday holidays 10:00 A.M. to 5:00 P.M., Sunday 1:00 to 5:00 P.M. The grounds are open all year, 8:00 A.M. to dusk. Admission is $3.00 for adults, $2.00 for seniors, and $1.00 for children.

Around the turn of the century, the aesthetic revolution called the Arts and Crafts Movement swept America. Its proponents rejected the superfluous ornamentation found in the popular Victorian furniture, advocating instead a return to simple ideas, honest craftsmanship, and sturdy construction. Gustav and Leopold Stickley, followers of the movement, began making Craftsman—also known as Mission—furniture.

Today Mission furniture is all the rage again, and cheap knockoffs can be found at discount stores throughout the country. But to see what the Stickleys had in mind, visit the company that continues to craft the same fine pieces that the brothers did at the turn of the century.

L. & J. G. Stickley, Inc., Stickley Drive, Manlius, (315) 682–5500, offers free tours Tuesday at 10:00 A.M. Tours take 1½ hours, and children under 12 are not permitted.

The state's largest antiques event—the *Madison-Bouckville Outdoor Antiques Show*—is held the third weekend in August in *Bouckville.* More than 1,000 dealers from the United States and Canada sell antiques and collectibles at stalls spread over ninety acres of farmland. A Dixieland band is on hand to provide entertainment, and a shuttle provides transportation to and from the parking lots. For information call (315) 824–2462 or check the Web site: www.bouckvilleantiquesshows.com.

At the beginning of the nineteenth century, a swamp northwest of **Manlius** became the site of Syracuse, which would be lifted to prominence by the salt industry and the Erie Canal, and which today contains the last of the "weighlock" buildings that once dotted the waterway. Built in 1850 in Greek Revival style, this weigh station for canal boats today houses the **Erie Canal Museum.**

Exhibits in the Weighlock Building, which houses the museum, include a 65-foot replica of a canal boat. The *Frank Buchanan Thomson,* named after a late museum director, offers a look at a typical Erie Canal vessel's crew quarters, immigrant accommodations, and cargo storage. Immigration along the canal is a special focus of the museum's exhibits, particularly with regard to its effects on Syracuse. The museum experience also includes a hands-on display of canal equipment and explanations of the engineering involved in connecting Albany and Buffalo by means of a 363-mile artificial waterway, with eighty-three locks and eighteen aqueducts. The job wasn't easy, but the result was the longest and most successful canal in the world.

The Erie Canal Museum, 318 Erie Boulevard East, Syracuse, (315) 471–0593, is open daily from 10:00 A.M. to 5:00 P.M.; closed major holidays. Admission is free.

Having passed through the stages from swamp to canal boomtown to major commercial and industrial center by the end of the nineteenth century, Syracuse was ready for an art museum. The **Everson Museum of Art** was founded by George Fisk Comfort, a lion of the American art establishment who had been instrumental in establishing New York City's Metropolitan Museum and served as founder and dean of the College of Fine Arts at Syracuse University. Comfort organized the museum as the Syracuse Museum of Fine Arts, and in 1900 the first exhibition took place. A progressive policy toward

onebigoldtree

In Camillus Forest Unique Area, in the town of Camillus just west of Syracuse, a sugar maple tree believed to be nearly 300 years old has achieved a diameter of 42 inches. The sugar maple is New York State's Official Tree.

acquisitions was in evidence even at that early date, with the initial show featuring, among older and more recognized masters, the work of impressionists such as Monet, Sisley, and Pissarro.

Renamed the Everson Museum in 1959 following a large bequest from the estate of Syracuse philanthropist Helen Everson, the museum moved in 1968 into its present quarters, a massive, modernist concrete structure that was architect I. M. Pei's first museum building. Its three exhibition levels contain nine galleries and a 50-foot-square two-story sculpture court.

Give Them the Dickens

Charles Dickens visited Syracuse, once also known as "Salt City," in 1869 to give a reading in the Weiting Opera House. He stayed in the Syracuse Hotel and wrote:

"I am here in a most wonderful out-of-the-world place, which looks as if it had begun to be built yesterday, and were going to be imperfectly knocked together with a nail or two the day after tomorrow. I am in the worst inn that ever was seen, and outside is a thaw that places the whole country under water . . .

"We had an old buffalo for supper and an old pig for breakfast and we are going to have I don't know what for dinner at 6. In the public room downstairs, a number of men (speechless) with their feet against window frames, staring out the window and spitting dolefully at intervals . . . And yet we have taken in considerably over 300 pounds for tomorrow night."

The Everson's holdings include anonymous colonial portraits (and one very famous and not so anonymous one of George Washington), the works of nineteenth-century genre and luminist painters, and paintings by twentieth-century names such as Robert Henri, John Sloan, Grandma Moses, Maxfield Parrish, Reginald Marsh, and Grant Wood. The museum possesses a good graphic-art collection and a small but comprehensive photography section.

The emphasis at the Everson is heavily American. The museum's Syracuse China Center for the Study of American Ceramics houses the nation's premier collection in this field, with holdings dating from A.D. 1000 to the present. Here are pre-Columbian Native American vessels, colonial and nineteenth-century pieces, and contemporary functional and art pottery, as well as some 1,200 examples of ceramic craftsmanship from cultures outside the Western Hemisphere.

The Everson Museum of Art, 401 Harrison Street, Syracuse, (315) 474–6064, is open Tuesday through Friday noon to 5:00 P.M., Saturday 10:00 A.M. to 5:00 P.M., and Sunday noon to 5:00 P.M. Closed holidays. Admission is free, although a suggested donation of $5.00 is welcome.

At **Clark's Ale House,** 122 West Jefferson Street, (315) 479–9859, you may be in a quandary about what to drink: It carries thirty-two draughts from around the world, including the house beer, Armory Ale, from Middle Ages Brewery just up the road. But eating is a breeze: The specialty is hot roast beef on an onion roll. The pub is in the Landmark Theatre building and is open Monday through Wednesday 11:00 to 1:00 A.M., Thursday through Saturday until 2:00 A.M.

If you've always wondered where salt comes from, visit the **Salt Museum** near Syracuse—"The City That Salt Built." At one time the area supplied the entire nation with the "white gold." The museum, constructed of timbers from former salt warehouses, explains the method of turning brine into salt, a process that ended in the 1920s.

The Salt Museum, in Onondaga Lake Park, Route 370, Onondaga Lake Parkway, *Liverpool,* (315) 453–6712, is open May through mid-October, daily 11:00 A.M. to 4:00 P.M. Admission is free.

Bed & Breakfast Wellington, a National Historic Landmark designed by Ward Wellington Ward, is a 1914 Arts and Crafts brick and stucco Tudor-style home with canvas flooring, an arched foyer, leaded glass windows, and tile insets. Rates for the five guest rooms (including a housekeeping suite) range from $75 to $125, including private bath and breakfast. The B&B is at 707 Danforth Street in Syracuse, (315) 474–3641 or (800) 724–5006; www.bbwell ington.com.

If your curiosity about canals has not yet been sated, you might want to sign on for a grand tour—a two-, three-, or four-day journey down the Cayuga-Seneca, the Oswego, the Champlain, and the Erie Canals. *Mid-Lakes Naviga-tion Company, Ltd.,* offers escorted, navigated, and catered cruises, with departures from Buffalo, Syracuse, and Albany. During the day passengers travel and dine aboard *Emita II,* a reconverted passenger ferry. At night the boat ties up on shore, and passengers check into a local hotel. It's a perfect blending of the nineteenth and twentieth centuries.

The company also runs weeklong bare-boat charters from Syracuse aboard European-style Lockmaster hireboats, as well as daily cruises on the Erie Canal and Skaneateles Lake.

Mid-Lakes Navigation Company, Ltd., is headquartered at 11 Jordan Street, P.O. Box 61, *Skaneateles* 13152, (315) 685–8500 or (800) 545–4318; www.mid lakesnav.com .

Lockmaster Hireboat, Mid-Lakes Navigation Company, Ltd.

Places to Stay in the Mohawk Valley

ALBANY

The Morgan State House
393 State Street
(518) 427–6063
(888) 427–6063

Desmond Hotel
660 Albany-Shaker Road
(518) 869–8100

Albany Mansion Hill Inn & Restaurant
115 Philips Street
(518) 465–2038

ALTAMONT

Appel Inn
590 Route 146
(518) 861–6557

COOPERSTOWN

The Otesaga
60 Lake Street
P.O. Box 311
Cooperstown 13326
(800) 348–6222

LITTLE FALLS

Gansevoort House
42 West Gansevoort Street
(315) 823–3969

Overlook Mansion
1 Overlook Lane
(315) 823–4222

ROTTERDAM

Mallozzi's Belevedere Hotel
1930 Curry Road
(518) 630–4020

SCHENECTADY

Parker Inn
424 State Street
(518) 688–1001

SCOTIA

The Glen Sanders Mansion
1 Glen Avenue
(518) 374–7262

REGIONAL TOURIST INFORMATION— THE MOHAWK VALLEY

Regional Information,
(800) 732–8259
(Capital-Saratoga)
www.capital-saratoga.com

Albany County Convention & Visitors Bureau,
25 Quackenbush Square,
Albany 12207,
(518) 434–1217 or (800) 258–3582
www.albany.org

Fulton County Gateway to the Adirondacks,
2 North Main Street,
Gloversville 12078,
(800) 676–3858
www.fultoncountyny.org

Schenectady County Chamber of Commerce,
306 State Street,
Schenectady 12305,
(800) 962–8007
www.schenectadychamber.org

Syracuse Convention & Visitors Bureau,
572 South Salina Street,
Syracuse 13202,
(800) 234–4797 or (315) 470–1910

OTHER ATTRACTIONS WORTH SEEING IN THE MOHAWK VALLEY

Historic Cherry Hill,
523½ South Pearl Street,
Albany,
(518) 434–4791

Howe Caverns,
Caverns Road,
Howes Cave,
(518) 296–8990

New York State Capitol,
Albany,
(518) 474–2418

New York State Museum,
Empire State Plaza,
Albany,
(518) 474–5877

Proctor's Theater,
432 State Street,
Schenectady,
(518) 382–3884 or (518) 346–2604

Schenectady Stockade Area,
Front Street,
Schenectady,
(518) 372–5656 or (800) 962–8007

Ten Broeck Mansion,
9 Ten Broeck Place,
Albany,
(518) 436–9826

Places to Eat in the Mohawk Valley

ALBANY

Jack's Oyster House
42 State Street
(518) 465–8854

Nicole's Bistro
351 Broadway
(518) 465–1111

Miss Albany Diner
893 Broadway
(518) 465–9148

COOPERSTOWN

Black Bart BbQue
64 Main Street
(607) 547–5656

Tunnicliff Inn Tap Room
34 Pioneer Street
(607) 547–9860

SCHENECTADY

Bourbon Street Bar & Grill
2209 Cemtral Avenue
(518) 382–1110

Center Stage Deli at Proctor's
432 State Street
(518) 377–5401

Royal Palace (Indian)
2788 Hamburg Street
(518) 355–9495

SCOTIA

Glen Sanders Mansion
One Glen Avenue
(518) 374–7262

The Finger Lakes

Here, between New York's "northern seaboard" along Lake Ontario and the Pennsylvania border, lies the region that many visitors consider to be the most beautiful part of the state. South of the Lake Ontario plain, the land appears to have been furrowed on a vast scale, with hilly farmland descending toward each of the Finger Lakes only to rise again before the next. The aptly named elongated lakes extend roughly north and south across an 80-mile swath of the state, offering vistas so reminiscent of parts of Switzerland that it's no wonder the city at the northern end of Seneca Lake was named Geneva.

Another distinctly European aspect of the Finger Lakes area is its status as New York State's premier wine-growing region. No longer limited only to the cultivation of native grape varieties, New York's vintners have come a long way, as visits to individual vineyards and the wine museum described in this section will demonstrate.

Scenes of well-tended vines in rows along steep hillsides may put you in mind of Europe, but the Finger Lakes region is rich in Americana. Here are museums of coverlets, Victorian dolls, and horse-drawn carriages. You'll even find Mark Twain's study and a museum devoted to Memorial Day.

THE FINGER LAKES

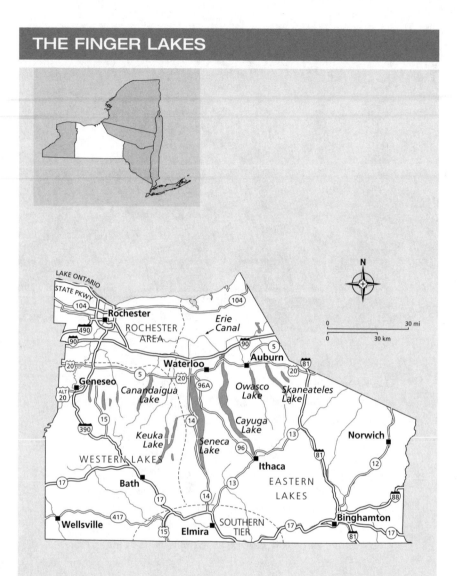

LAKE ONTARIO
STATE PKWY
104 Rochester
ROCHESTER AREA
Erie Canal
104
490
90
90 Auburn
5
20
Waterloo
81
5
20
Geneseo
96A
Owasco Lake
Skaneateles Lake
20
Canandaigua Lake
20
ALT 20
15
14
Cayuga Lake
13
Norwich
390
Keuka Lake
Seneca Lake
96
WESTERN LAKES
13
Ithaca
12
17
Bath
14
13
EASTERN LAKES
81
417
17
88
Wellsville
15
Elmira
SOUTHERN TIER
17
Binghamton
81
17

N

0 .... 30 mi
0 .... 30 km

We'll approach this area from the south, beginning near the Pennsylvania border and continuing up toward Rochester, then heading east along the New York State Thruway and the northern Finger Lakes.

The Southern Tier

In the city of **Elmira,** there is a site with significant associations in the life of **Mark Twain** but one that many Americans—including Twain aficionados familiar with his haunts in Hannibal, Missouri, and Hartford, Connecticut— know little about. This is the **Mark Twain Study,** a charming little summer house on the campus of Elmira College.

Mark Twain married an Elmira woman named Olivia Langdon in 1870, and for many years the author and his family took leave of their palatial Hartford home to spend summers outside Elmira with Olivia's sister, Mrs. Theodore Crane. Mrs. Crane and her husband lived on a farm, where in 1874 they built Twain a freestanding octagonal study, with windows on all sides and a massive stone fireplace. Here Twain wrote *Tom Sawyer* and completed sections of *Huckleberry Finn, Life on the Mississippi, A Connecticut Yankee in King Arthur's Court*, and other works. It was, he said, "the loveliest study you ever saw."

Twain spent his last summer in Elmira in 1903 and returned the following year for his wife's funeral. The author himself was buried in Woodlawn Cemetery, on Walnut Street in Elmira, in 1910.

Difficult to maintain and protect from vandalism, the study was donated to Elmira College by the Langdon family in 1952, whereupon it was removed to its present site on the campus.

The Mark Twain Study, on the Elmira College Campus off Main Street, Elmira, (607) 735–1941, is open from mid-June to Labor Day, Monday through

AUTHORS' FAVORITES—FINGER LAKES

House of Guitars

Letchworth State Park

Mark Twain Study

National Soaring Museum

Paleontological Research Institution

Pat Mitchell's Homemade Ice Cream

Rockwell Museum of Western Art

Schein-Joseph International Museum of Ceramic Art

Watkins Glen State Park (Timespell)

Willard Memorial Chapel

If You Hear Heavenly Music . . .

Mark Twain's son-in-law, Ossip Gabrilowitsch, studied piano in his hometown of St. Petersburg, Russia, and, at the age of sixteen, won the much-vaunted Rubinstein prize. He came to New York in 1900, was appointed conductor of the Detroit Symphony Orchestra, and married Twain's daughter Clara in 1909. He is interred, along with his father-in-law, in the Langdon plot at Elmira's Woodlawn Cemetery.

Saturday 9:00 A.M. to 5:00 P.M. and Sunday noon to 5:00 P.M. To arrange off-season visits write The Center for Mark Twain Studies, Quarry Farm, Box 900, Elmira College, Elmira 14901.

Head up Jerusalem Hill Road in Elmira to the ***Hill Top Inn Restaurant***'s outdoor terrace for a great view of the Chemung Valley along with satisfying traditional American cuisine. The Sullivan family has been greeting and feeding patrons since 1933. Their menu ranges from American staples such as steak, broiled seafood, and lamb, to Italian dishes including veal Marsala; homemade desserts are a specialty. The Hill Top Inn Restaurant is open for dinner Monday through Saturday beginning at 5:00 P.M., and in June, July, and August from 4:00 to 8:00 P.M. Closed some holidays. Reservations are recommended. Call (607) 732–6728 or (888) 4–HILL–TOP.

The three-story Italianate mansion ***Lindenwald Haus,*** with its twenty-one renovated Victorian guest rooms, has been a popular place to stay for more than 115 years since it was built to house widows of the Civil War. There are nine rooms with private bath, ten with shared bath. The five-acre grounds are dotted with fruit trees; guests are welcome to walk, bike, or swim.

Lindenwald Haus, 1526 Grand Central Avenue, Elmira, (607) 733–8753 or (800) 440–4287, is open year-round. Rates range from $75 to $125 for a deluxe suite and include a full breakfast.

When Mark Twain's study was at its original site on the Quarry Farm belonging to his in-laws, it commanded a lovely view of the undulating hills along the Chemung River Valley. Little did Twain suspect that within a few decades after his death, these same hills would attract recreationists content not merely to walk the trails and pastures but instead to soar quietly far above them. By the 1930s Harris Hill, outside Elmira, had become the "Soaring Capital of America." The science and sport of motorless flight is today kept vigorously alive at the ***National Soaring Museum***, which offers visitors earthbound exhibits and the opportunity to go aloft in sailplanes piloted by experienced professionals.

Regardless of whether you agree with the museum's philosophy that soaring is "flying as nature intended," a visit to the facility offers a good introduction to this often overlooked aspect of modern aviation. The museum houses the world's largest exhibit of contemporary and historic sailplanes, along with displays explaining the development of soaring and its relation to the parallel fields of meteorology and aerodynamics. You can even climb into a cockpit simulator, similar to those used to teach soaring, and learn what the experience of controlling a motorless plane is like.

Well, almost. To really understand soaring, you have to get off the ground. This can easily be arranged at the museum or at the Harris Hill Soaring Corp. Visitors' Center, which has a staff of competent pilots licensed by the FAA. Just check in at the Harris Hill Gliderport—the rides are available all summer long and on weekends throughout the year, weather permitting. Even if you don't go up yourself, it's fun to watch the graceful, silent flights and landings of the sleek sailplanes.

The National Soaring Museum, Harris Hill, RD 3, Elmira, (607) 734–3128 (office) or 734–0641 (glider field), is open daily from 10:00 A.M. to 5:00 P.M. (closed some holidays). Admission is $6.50 for adults, $5.50 for seniors, and $5.00 for children ages 6 to 17. Call regarding schedules and cost of sailplane flights.

Upstream along the Chemung River is ***Corning,*** indelibly associated in most travelers' awareness with the Corning Glass Company and its Corning Glass Center and Museum and Steuben Glass Factory. If you'd prefer a more intimate environment in which to watch magnificent glass pieces being created by traditional glassblowing techniques, visit ***Vitrix Hot Glass Studio*** in Corning's historic Market Street district. Since 1959 Vitrix has been turning out some of the country's finest handblown glass pieces.

Vitrix Hot Glass Studio, 77 West Market Street, Corning, (607) 936–8707, is open Monday through Friday 10:00 A.M. to 6:00 P.M., Saturday 10:00 A.M. to 8:00 P.M., and Sunday noon to 5:00 P.M. Glassblowers are at work on weekends only.

The aptly named ***Glass Menagerie*** is one of the world's largest dealers in kaleidoscopes. The shop represents more than 100 scope artists, inventories at

As in Life, So in Death

Elmira's Woodlawn Cemetery, burial place of Mark Twain, also contains the graves of Union and Confederate Civil War soldiers. The Confederates are facing south, and the Union graves surround them—exactly as the Union soldiers surrounded their prisoners of war when all died in a nearby railroad accident during the war.

least 200 examples of their work at all times, and hosts annual summer kaleidoscope shows. But the store has a much broader scope: It also carries leaded glass guardian angels made by Carl Goeller, a huge selection of mouth-blown hand-painted Christopher Radko limited edition Christmas ornaments, and unique paperweights. Also for sale: glass animals, perfume bottles, and glass and ceramic menorahs. One of the owners, Dick Pope, is a professional magician and often gives impromptu performances when he's around. Take time to

ANNUAL EVENTS IN THE FINGER LAKES

MARCH

Central New York Maple Festival,
Marathon,
(607) 849–3278

MAY

Lilac Festival,
Rochester,
(585) 256–4960

JUNE

Ithaca Festival,
Ithaca,
(800) 273–3646

Strawberry Festival,
Owego,
(607) 687–2556

Waterfront Festival and
Cardboard Regatta,
Watkins Glen,
(607) 535–3003

JULY

Hill Cumorah Pageant,
Palmyra,
(315) 597–5851

Finger Lakes Grassroots Festival,
Trumansburg,
(607) 387–5144

AUGUST

Empire Farm Days,
Seneca Falls,
(585) 526–5356

Monroe County Fair,
Henrietta,
(585) 334–4000

New York State Fair,
Syracuse,
(800) 475–FAIR

SEPTEMBER

Grand Prix Festival,
Watkins Glen,
(607) 535–3003

Golden Harvest Festival,
Baldwinsville,
(315) 638–2519

Great Grape Festival,
Naples,
(585) 374–2240

OCTOBER

Letchworth Arts Festival,
Mt. Morris,
(585) 493–3600 or (585) 237–3517

duck upstairs to **Books of Marvel.** The antiquarian enterprise has one of the world's largest collections of old and rare juvenile series fiction.

The Glass Menagerie, 37 East Market Street, Corning, (607) 962–6300, is open year-round. During the summer the shop is open daily from 9:30 A.M. to 9:30 P.M. Call for hours the rest of the year.

The **West End Gallery,** 12 West Market Street, (607) 936–2011, displays the works of more than forty artists, some nationally known and some emerging. The gallery is open Monday through Wednesday 10:30 A.M. to 5:30 P.M.; Thursday and Friday 10:00 A.M. to 5:00 P.M.; Saturday 10:00 A.M. to 4:00 P.M.; and Sunday noon to 5:00 P.M.

The **Rockwell Museum of Western Art** is an institution that owes its existence almost entirely to the single individual whose collection it comprises. Robert F. Rockwell is an area native and former proprietor of a small department store chain whose interest in western art dates to his youth spent on a Colorado ranch. He began collecting seriously in the late 1950s, over the years acquiring works not only by universally recognized masters of "cowboy" art such as Charles M. Russell and Frederic Remington, but also by landscapists of the caliber of Albert Bierstadt and Thomas Hill and by animal artists A.F. Tait and Carl Rungius.

Rockwell's protean interests went beyond western art and sculpture to include an area dear to him as a Corning resident: the beautiful art glass created by Frederic Carder, cofounder of the Steuben Glass Works, which was later incorporated into Corning Glass Works, now Corning, Inc. Rockwell even collected antique toys.

By the beginning of the 1980s, Rockwell's collections, particularly of western art and Carder Steuben glass, were too extensive to be casually shown in his department stores and as part of exhibitions loaned to other institutions. He needed a museum, and one arrived in the form of Corning's old city hall, a Romanesque Revival structure built in 1893. The Corning Company acquired the building from the city for $1.00, renovations were undertaken, and in 1982 the Rockwell Museum opened. At present it houses the largest collection of western art on the East Coast, more than 2,000 pieces of Carder Steuben glass, Navajo weavings, antique firearms, Indian artifacts, and the toy collection as well.

The Rockwell Museum of Western Art, 111 Cedar Street at Denison Parkway, Corning, (607) 937–5386, is open May, June, and Labor Day through October, Monday through Saturday 9:00 A.M. to 5:00 P.M. and Sunday 11:00 A.M. to 5:00 P.M. During the rest of the year, hours are daily 10:00 A.M. to 4:00 P.M., except July through Labor Day when hours are Monday through Saturday 9:00 A.M. to 8:00 P.M. and Sunday 11:00 A.M. to 8:00 P.M. The museum is closed Thanksgiving, Christmas Eve, Christmas Day, and New Year's. Admission is

$6.50 for adults, $5.50 for senior citizens, and a family rate of $20.00, with a two-adult maximum. Students 17 and under are free.

Western Lakes

The southern Finger Lakes region is a tranquil, easy-paced corner of the world that nevertheless nurtured one of twentieth-century America's great speed demons. At **Hammondsport,** on the southern tip of Keuka Lake, the **Glenn H. Curtiss Museum** chronicles the lifework of this native son, who was also a serious pioneer in motorcycling and aviation.

Glenn Hammond Curtiss started out, as did the Wright brothers, in the bicycle business. He quickly turned to motorcycles, building a V-8–powered bike on which he sped more than 136 miles per hour in 1907. He also built engines that powered lighter-than-air craft, and in that same year he became involved with Dr. Alexander Graham Bell and other enthusiasts in the "Aerial Experiment Association." Curtiss's engineering helped lift the association's airplane *Red Wing* off the ice of Keuka Lake on the first public flight (as opposed to the Wrights' secret 1903 experiment) of a heavier-than-air craft in the United States.

Glenn Curtiss's accomplishments over the next twenty years dominated the adolescence of aeronautics. In 1910 he landed a plane on water for the first time, and in 1911 he became the first American to receive a pilot's license. In 1919 a Curtiss "flying boat" made the first transatlantic crossing by air. Meanwhile he had built his Curtiss Aeroplane and Motor Company into an industrial giant, employing 10,000 men at the peak of production during World War I. Sensing the traveling trends of the motor age, he even manufactured the first successful house trailers. Following a merger, the company became Curtiss-Wright, producer of World War II aircraft such as the Navy Helldiver and the P-40 of "Flying Tigers" fame. The museum, founded in 1960, houses seven historic aircraft and three reproductions; one of the latter is a flyable replica of the inventor's 1908 *June Bug*.

The Glenn H. Curtiss Museum, Route 54, ½ mile south of Hammondsport, (607) 569–2160, is open from May 1 through October 31, Monday through Saturday 9:00 A.M. to 5:00 P.M. and Sunday 11:00 A.M. to 5:00 P.M.; from November 1 through April 30, it is open Monday through Saturday 10:00 A.M. to 4:00 P.M. and Sunday noon to 5:00 P.M. Admission is $6.00 for adults, $4.50 for senior citizens, $3.50 for students, and free for children ages 6 and under.

The Finger Lakes region is New York's wine country, and the area around Keuka Lake is in many ways its heart. It was along the shores of Keuka Lake that the late Dr. Konstantin Frank established his Vinifera Vineyards and proved to the world that the European grapes could survive New York State winters when grafted to hardy American rootstocks. Keuka Lake is also the home of Bully Hill Vineyards and the **Taylor Wine Museum**, which recounts the story of a century and a half of wine making in New York State, particularly in the Finger Lakes area.

The Taylor Wine Museum, G.H. Taylor Memorial Drive, Hammondsport, (607) 868–3610, is open from mid-May through October 31, Monday through Saturday 9:00 A.M. to 5:00 P.M., Sunday noon to 5:00 P.M. The visitors' center offers wine tastings every half hour and tours every hour. Donations are welcome. A restaurant next door specializes in moderately priced homemade pasta and dishes prepared with wine. The Bully Hill Vineyards can also be visited for tours and tastings; call (607) 868–3610.

Want to spend the night on a train? Check into the **Caboose Motel,** 8620 State Route 415N, **Avoca,** (607) 566–2216. In addition to 18 standard units, the state's only caboose motel rents five N5 cars equipped with all modern amenities and a speaker that provides train sounds. One unit can accommodate six, the others up to five in upper and lower berths. The cabooses rent for $75 a night weekdays; $85 on weekends. There are also eighteen conventional rooms that rent for $51 a night. Smaller units are available for $48 weekdays, $52 weekends.

Although far less well known than southeastern Pennsylvania for its Amish and Mennonite populations, the Finger Lakes region long ago attracted members of these peaceful and industrious sects because of its rich farmland and relative isolation from modern big-city hubbub. One of the most valued and enduring of Amish and Mennonite traditions is quiltmaking, and at **The Quilt Room** in **Penn Yan,** more than 200 quilts and wall hangings reveal the meticulous artisanship of women from the surrounding area. In addition to the quilts on display—many of them one of a kind—The Quilt Room can engage quilters to create special-order goods based on any of several thousand traditional designs. Repair work is available as well.

The Quilt Room, 1870 Hoyt Road, Penn Yan, (315) 536–5964 or (877) 536–5964, www.quiltroom.org, is open year-round; call for hours.

The Victorian **Finton's Landing Bed & Breakfast** overlooking Keuka Lake—nicknamed "the American Rhine"—was built in the 1860s as a steamboat landing for loading grapes harvested in the area. Today the carefully restored, secluded inn, with a gazebo and L-shaped dock, has four guest rooms with private baths and queen-size beds, air conditioning, and handmade quilts; and a wraparound porch where a two-course breakfast is served (weather permitting). There's also a private beach.

Finton's Landing Bed & Breakfast, 661 East Lake Road, Penn Yan, (315) 536–3146, www.home.eznet.net/~tepperd, is open year-round. The rate ranges from $119 to $159 for a double and includes breakfast. The inn is smoke-free.

If you're looking for seclusion—and magnificent mountain views—check out the **Vagabond Inn.** The 7,000-square-foot inn stands in splendid isolation on top of a mountain in the **Bristol** range. Popular with honeymooners, the inn has a 60-foot-long Great Room with two massive fieldstone fireplaces, a Japanese garden, and an in-ground pool.

Don't be hasty in choosing a room: Each of the five has its special charms. For example, the Kimberly, which rents for $115 a night, has lots of windows that provide great views. The Bristol has its own fireplace, a Jacuzzi for two (with views of the mountains), and rents for $195. The Lodge, for $225, has a huge river-stone fireplace and hot-tub chamber. Rates include breakfast.

The Vagabond Inn, 3300 Sliter Road, Naples, (585) 554–6271, www.vagabondinn.com, is open all year.

If you're visiting the area in late September, you might be just in time to sample one of the region's most unusual delicacies—Naples Grape Pie. Local bakeries produce more than 10,000 grape pies six weeks of the year, beginning with the start of the Annual **Naples** Grape Festival. If you're there any other time of the year, stop in for a slice at **Arbor Hill.** They serve them up all year, along with their wines and other wine food products, in a restored eighteenth-century building that once served as the local post office. They also serve light

---

A Visit with Dr. Frank

In the summer of 1975, a couple of friends and I made the ten-hour drive from Boston to the Finger Lakes town of Hammondsport to seek out the legendary Dr. Konstantin Frank. Dr. Frank was the Ukrainian-born German vintner who introduced the cultivation of European vinifera grapes to New York State, thereby raising local wine production to a level of sophistication undreamed of in the old Concord grape days. We found the septuagenarian doctor at his winery, where he offered us samples of some of his delicious Rieslings. We had bought a few bottles of this year and that, when one of the women in our group asked if she could purchase a case of the afternoon's best offerings, a vintage dating back to somewhere in the late 1960s. Dr. Frank leaned toward her, frowning.

"I have only six cases of that left," he said. "Have you been married twenty-five years?"

"No," she said. "But I've been single thirty-five."

"Ja," he said, smiling, appreciating the fast comeback. "Then just give me ein kuss."

So with a chaste peck on the cheek—probably actionable, had it been thirty years later—a case of that spectacular Riesling was hers.

—Bill Scheller

barbecue-style lunches featuring wine soup, wine sausage, and—for dessert—hot grape sundaes. In summer and fall, the winery hosts several five-course gourmet dinners and buffets featuring its vintages.

Arbor Hill, 6461 Route 64, **Bristol Springs** (Naples), (800) 554–7553 or (585) 374–2406, is open daily from May through the first week in January, Monday through Saturday 10:00 A.M. to 5:00 P.M. and Sunday 11:00 A.M. to 5:00 P.M., open weekends only from January through May. For a dinner schedule, check www.thegrapery.com.

At the southeast corner of the **Alfred University** campus is the **Stull Observatory,** considered to be one of the finest teaching observatories in the Northeast. It exists largely through the efforts of John Stull, who built or rebuilt all of the telescopes and many of the buildings. There are five major telescopes at the observatory: a 9-inch refractor dating from 1863, a 16-inch Cassegrain reflector, and 14-, 20-, and 32-inch Newtonian reflectors.

The Stull Observatory at Alfred University, **Alfred,** (607) 871–2208, offers public viewings (weather permitting) at the following times: September, October, November, February, March, and April, Friday from 9:00 to 11:00 P.M.; May, June, and July, Thursday from 10:00 P.M. until midnight. Admission is free.

Nearly 8,000 ceramic and glass objects—from pottery shards left behind by ancient civilizations, to works that reflect the cutting edge of ceramic technology—are housed at the **Schein-Joseph International Museum of Ceramic Art.** The museum is a teaching and research arm of the New York State College of Ceramics at Alfred University. Among its permanent collections are tomb sculptures from the Neolithic period through the Yuan dynasty, Chinese funerary jars, and works by artists such as Charles Fergus Binns, Walter Ostrom, Mary Roettger, Rosanjin Kitaoji, and Bernard Leach.

The Schein-Joseph International Museum of Ceramic Art, New York State College of Ceramics, Alfred University, Alfred, (607) 871–2421, is just off Route 244. It is just across from the Horticulture Building on the second floor of the Ceramics Corridor Innovation Center. The museum is open Wednesday through Friday 10:00 A.M. to 4:00 P.M. Admission is free.

In July 1937 a freight train pulled into Alfred Station carrying thirty-five bells from Antwerp, Belgium. Eighteen of the bells, which weighed a total of 5,153 pounds (one, called the Bourdon, weighs about 3,850 pounds), were made in 1674 by Pieter Hemony, a famous Netherlands bellfounder. They were hung in a wooden tower overlooking the valley and, shortly after, the **Davis Memorial Carillon** rang out over the hills for the first time.

A carillon is a musical instrument consisting of twenty-three or more cast bronze cup-shaped bells, which are precisely tuned so that many bells can be sounded together to produce a harmonious effect (the bells are stationary, only the clappers move). And if you're lucky enough to be in the vicinity on one of the days that the carillonneur is performing, you can hear just how harmonious a sound the carillon (which now has forty-seven bells) can make. Recitals are given Saturday (except over Christmas break and in August) at 4:00 P.M. throughout the year (except January and August) and on Monday, Wednesday, and Friday from 12:30 to 12:45 P.M. during the academic year. In addition the Wingate Memorial Summer Carillon Recital Series brings guest recitalists to perform Tuesday evenings in the month of July.

For information contact the Alfred University Division of Performing Arts, Alfred, (607–871–2562; www.alfred.edu/map/carillon). There is no admission fee.

At the 14,350-acre **Letchworth State Park,** nicknamed the "Grand Canyon of the East," the Genesee River cascades down more than twenty waterfalls as it winds its way north through a series of beetling gorges, some almost 600 feet high. Visitors can drive through the park on a road that parallels the gorge or hike one of twenty hiking trails of varying difficulty and length.

Accommodations at the park include a campground, cabins, and the yellow-and-white Victorian **Glen Iris Inn** (585–493–2622; www.glenirisinn.com) overlooking Mid Falls, which offers clean, comfortable rooms starting at $80 (efficiency units a short distance from the inn also are available for $75). The most expensive accommodation, the cherry suite, has a private balcony over the falls and rents for $175 a night. The inn, the former home of William Pryor Letchworth, who began construction on the building in 1859 and deeded the building and grounds to the state in 1907, has welcomed guests since 1914. Glen Iris serves three meals a day, and offers a special picnic menu.

Just across from the inn, the **Letchworth Museum** is stuffed with exhibits relating to the park's history. On a hill in back of the museum is the grave of Mary Jemison, the "white woman of the Genesee." A prisoner of the Seneca from the age of fifteen, she eventually married a chief and later became a leader of her adopted people. Under the Big Tree Treaty of 1797, she was granted a large parcel of land along the river and lived there until she moved to Buffalo Creek Reservation. William Letchworth had her remains brought back and interred here in 1910.

Letchworth State Park, Genesee State Park and Recreation Region, 1 Letchworth State Park, Castile, (585) 493–3600, is open year-round. There is an admission fee of $6.00 per day per car on weekends off-season; daily Memorial Day weekend through October. The museum (585–493–2760) is open daily from May through October between 10:00 A.M. and 5:00 P.M. A $1.00 donation is requested.

For those who would rather float over the falls than drive alongside them, **Balloons Over Letchworth** offers flights in the *Gentle Giant*, a seven-story hot-air balloon. The voyages, which last approximately one hour (guests should plan on a total time of 2½ to 3 hours) end with a champagne celebration and cost $189 for one person or $179 each for three or more. There is a $10 surcharge per person during the month of October. The launch area is at the Middle/Upper Falls picnic area, a thousand feet south of the Glen Iris Inn. The office is at 6645 Denton Corners Road, Castile, (585) 493–3340.

While at the park, tour the $25-million **Mt. Morris Dam,** which in its first thirty-four years of operation has prevented flood damages estimated at $346 million. For information call (585) 658–4220.

Just west of Canandaigua Lake, the little town of Bristol has become renowned for pottery, hand-thrown and hand-decorated by "the Wizard of Clay," master potter Jim Kozlowski, and his assistants at **The Wizard of Clay Pottery.** Jim's production facilities and retail stores are housed in seven geodesic domes he designed himself.

The potter's wheel and eight kilns are in the workshop. All pieces are fired at a temperature of 2,265° F, which makes them extremely hard and durable, then treated with a specially formulated glaze that gives them a richly colored finish. The Wizard's most original pottery is decorated with delicate imprints from real leaves gathered from the Bristol hills.

The Wizard of Clay Pottery, 7851 Route 20A in Bristol, 3 miles east of Honeoye Lake (mailing address: 7851 Route 20A, Bloomfield 14469), (585) 229–2980, is open daily from 9:00 A.M. until 5:00 P.M.; closed major holidays.

The town of **Horseheads** got its name in 1789 when settlers coming into the valley came upon the bleached skulls of pack horses left behind by General John Sullivan after his battle against the Six Nations of the Iroquois. The **Horseheads Historical Society Museum,** in the former train depot at the corner of Broad and Curns Streets, exhibits cartoons and paintings by the nationally renowned humorist Eugene Zimmerman, better known as "Zim." He lived in a home he designed at the corner of Pine and West Mill Streets: It is maintained by Historical Tours and open for tours by appointment. Zim also designed the bandstand in Teal Park.

The Horseheads Historical Society Museum is at the Depot, 312 West Broad Street & Curns Street, Horseheads (607) 739–3938. Call for hours.

Wings of Eagles, formerly known as the National Warplane Museum, houses an impressive collection of aircraft dating from World War II to the present, as well as exhibits tracing the development of flight, ongoing special events, and a flight simulator in which visitors can experience virtual flight and gain an understanding of what it's like to fly in the cockpit of a warplane.

Wings of Eagles, Elmira-Corning Regional Airport, off Route 17 in Horseheads, (607) 739–8200, is open Monday through Friday 10:00 A.M. to 4:00 P.M.,

Saturday 9:00 A.M. to 5:00 P.M., and Sunday 11:00 A.M. to 5:00 P.M. Closed some major holidays. Admission is $7.00 for adults, $5.50 for senior citizens, $4.00 for children ages 6 to 17, and free for children under 6. A family admission is available for $18.00.

Rochester Area

"Spend a day in the nineteenth century," reads the **Genesee Country Village & Museum**'s invitation—but what's different about this reconstructed village in **Mumford,** on the southern outskirts of Rochester, is that the properties mean the *whole* nineteenth century, not just a small part of it. The fifty-plus buildings originally standing on, or relocated to, this site—all of them restored—represent virtually every stage of the development of upstate New York, from frontier days to late Victorian times, and is the state's largest living history museum, with the largest collection of historic buildings in the East.

The rail-fenced pioneer settlement reveals what rural living was like up near Lake Ontario around 1800. Just twenty-five years later the region had prospered to the extent that sumptuous Greek Revival homes such as Livingston Manor, also on the village grounds, could reflect the rapidly cultivated tastes of the upstate gentry. Turn the pages of another half-century, and you find the Victorian quirks and fussy comforts of the 1870 Octagon House, with its tidy cupola and broad verandas. Other village buildings include a carriage barn containing a collection of forty horse-drawn vehicles; a Gallery of Sporting Art, showcasing paintings and sculpture inspired by wildlife and the hunt; and the **George Eastman** birthplace, moved here in homage to the man who made nearby Rochester a "film capital" of an entirely different sort than Hollywood, California. The John L. Wehle Gallery of Wildlife and Sporting Art exhibits North America's premier collection of wildlife and sporting art.

On a Pedestal

In 1899 Theodore Roosevelt, governor of New York, came to Rochester to dedicate the country's first public statue to be erected to honor an African American, Frederick Douglass (1807–95). The escaped slave, abolitionist, and newspaper publisher lived here for seventeen years. His home on Alexander Street was a station on the Underground Railroad. The bronze statue is in Highland Park on Highland Avenue. Douglass is interred in Mt. Hope Cemetery along with other luminaries, including his friend, women's rights champion Susan B. Anthony.

The Genesee Country Village & Museum, 1410 Flint Road off Route 36 in Mumford (mailing address: P.O. Box 310, Mumford 14511), (585) 538–6822, is open July through Labor Day Tuesday through Sunday 10:00 A.M. to 5:00 P.M.; the rest of the year Tuesday through Friday 10:00 A.M. to 4:00 P.M. and weekends 10:00 A.M. to 5:00 P.M. Closed Mondays except on holidays. There is a nature center at the village open all year, and special programs are held throughout the year. Admission is $12.95 for adults, $9.95 for seniors and students with ID, and $7.50 for children ages 4 to 16; under 4, free. There is a separate admission for the nature center only; $3.50 for adults, $3.00 for seniors and students, and $2.50 for children.

Richard Greeve's *Kiowa*, Genesee Country Museum

If you picture a little girl in crinoline playing in the parlor of the Genesee Country Museum's Octagon House, you can well imagine the sort of dolls she might have for companions. Up near Rochester, in **North Chili,** Linda Greenfield has assembled a wonderful collection of these delicate and elaborately dressed playthings in her **Victorian Doll Museum.** The thousands of dolls at the museum not only reflect the tastes of the Victorian era but also show many types of doll construction that have faded from the picture in these days of molded plastic doll faces and bodies.

The Victorian Doll Museum premises are also the home of the **Chili Doll Hospital,** also run by Linda, who is an expert at doll restoration and repair. Antique dolls are appraised by appointment, and a collector's gift shop offers fine modern and period reproduction specimens.

The Victorian Doll Museum and Chili Doll Hospital, 4332 Buffalo Road, North Chili, (585) 247–0130, are open February through December, Tuesday through Saturday 10:00 A.M. to 4:30 P.M. Admission to the museum is $2.00 for adults and $1.00 for children ages 12 and under.

"Please touch, feel, and explore" is the motto at one of the state's most unusual—and fun—museums. **Strong Museum,** the legacy of buggy-whip heiress Margaret Woodbury Strong, explores American life and tastes since 1820 with a variety of imaginative permanent and changing exhibits. Among the more than 500,000 objects is the world's largest and most historically significant collection and dolls and the country's most comprehensive collection of homecrafts, souvenirs, and advertising materials. The Time Lab, a hands-on learning lab and interactive warehouse, exhibits thousands of items, such as lava lamps and political buttons, from different periods. Visitors can select a tune from their tabletop jukebox while they dine on burgers and fries at the vintage Skyline Diner or enjoy a sundae at Louie's Sweet Shoppe. Those who suffer from vertigo might want to take a spin on the 1918 Allan Herschell carousel *before* they eat.

The Strong Museum, One Manhattan Square, Rochester, (585) 263–2700 (Events Line: 585–263–2702), is open Monday through Thursday from 10:00 A.M. to 5:00 P.M., Friday 10:00 A.M. to 8:00 P.M., Saturday 10:00 A.M. to 5:00 P.M., Sunday from noon to 5:00 P.M. Closed Christmas and Thanksgiving. Admission is $7.00 for adults, $6.00 for senior citizens and students with school ID, and $5.00 for children ages 2 to 17.

nodistractions?

John D. Rockefeller Sr., Jay Gould, F. W. Woolworth, and George Eastman were among a host of nineteenth- and early twentieth-century tycoons who rose from the obscurity of small-town birthplaces in upstate New York.

The music emporium with the acronym HOG, which counts among its customers Metallica, Aerosmith, Motley Crue, Jon Bon Jovi, and Ozzy Osbourne, is actually a rambling complex of five warehouses "jam" packed with an array of "musicana" from guitars to amplifiers to concert T-shirts to a pair of Elvis Presley's leather pants.

The **House of Guitars** was established in 1964 by three brothers named Schaubroeck. Today the musical mecca in **Rochester's** suburbs calls itself the "World's Largest Music Store" and stocks just about every brand of instrument (if they don't have it, they'll order it), including more than 11,000 guitars ranging in price from $60 to $50,000. Potential customers are invited to test the merchandise in one of several small rooms set aside for that purpose.

Don't be surprised if you stop by and find throngs of people at HOG. Throughout the year the musical brothers Schaubroeck host promotions and in-store appearances, featuring unknown, rising, and well-known performers. The winner of one of their most successful events, the "World's Worst Guitar Player Contest," won a $400 guitar and amp, six free lessons, and a one-way bus ticket to Canada.

The House of Guitars, 645 Titus Avenue, Rochester, (585) 544–3500, is open Monday through Saturday from 10:00 A.M. to 9:00 P.M. and Sunday 1:00 to 5:00 P.M.

Chances are you've never thought of Rochester as an international port of call, but think again. Ever since spring 2004, the city has been the U.S. terminus for a new ferry service that whisks cars and pedestrians across Lake Ontario to Toronto, Canada's largest city and cultural and financial capital. The **Breeze,** which can carry 750 people, 220 cars, and 10 trucks or buses, boasts a business class section with wireless Internet service, a restaurant and a bar, lounges, two movie theaters, and a children's play area. The crossing takes about two hours and forty-five minutes, which cuts an hour or more from the typical driving time between the two cities.

One-way, walk-on fares on the *Breeze* are $25 per person; fares for most cars and light SUVs are $40. For reservations, call toll-free (877) 825–3774 or book online at www.thebreeze.com.

South and east of Rochester is a monument to another important development in the history of American popular culture: the shopping mall. Not the steel-and-glass malls of the 1950s, but a sturdy wooden structure erected in 1879, it was built by Levi Valentine as an all-purpose market and community center for the settlement he was developing. Thus it lays claim to being the first multistore "shopping center" in the United States. Today it houses the **Valentown Museum,** a collection of nineteenth-century small-town memorabilia that includes a reconstruction of the first railroad station in the Rochester area and a "Scientific Exhibition," which traveled around the country in a covered wagon from 1825 to 1880.

Valentown Hall, as Valentine called his "mall," had front doors opening into a general store, meat market, cobbler shop, barber shop, bakery, and harness shop. The upstairs contained a Grange lodge, rooms where classes in the arts and trades were held, and a community ballroom. The ambitious scheme lasted only thirty years, since the promised railroad connection never materialized (the

. . . and a Side of Bacon

If the 1960s counterculture had an official breakfast cereal: It was granola. But the crunchy mixture actually originated in the 1860s as something called "granula," at a health resort in Dansville, New York. Devised by Dr. James Caleb Jackson for sojourners at his Our Home on the Hillside Sanitarium, granula consisted of graham flour baked into sheets, then crumbled and baked again before being soaked overnight in milk. Soon another health spa proprietor copied Dr. Jackson's recipe, adding oats and other ingredients—and changing the name of the concoction to "granola" only after Jackson sued. The new entrepreneur's name was John Harvey Kellogg.

restored station interior belonged to an earlier rail operation). The building was saved from demolition and restored in 1940 by J. Sheldon Fisher, a member of the Fisher family that gave its name to the town of **Fishers,** in which the hall is located. Mr. Fisher still conducts tours but call ahead to make sure he'll be there. Contact him at the Valentown Museum, Valentown Square, Fishers, (585) 924–2645. Donations are welcome.

"Ganondagan . . . a city or village of bark, situated at the top of a mountain of earth, to which one rises by three terraces. It appeared to us, from a distance, to be crowned with round towers." This is how M. L'Abbe De Belmont described a major town of the Seneca people, one of the five original Indian nations that have inhabited central New York since prehistoric times. A short time later the governor general of New France led an army from Canada against the Seneca in an effort to eliminate them as competitors in the international fur trade.

The story of the Seneca people and the Iroquois (Haudenosaunee) Confederacy to which they belonged is recounted at **Ganondagan State Historic Site,** the state's largest Seneca community in the seventeenth century. The 522-acre National Historic Landmark encompasses the palisaded granary M. L'Abbe De Belmont described, a sacred burial ground, and a system of trails. A twenty-seven-minute video in the visitor center relates the history of Ganondagan. A reconstructed bark longhouse similar to ones lived in by the Seneca people is one of the site's high points.

The Visitors Center at Ganondagan State Historic Site, 1488 Victor-Holcomb Road, **Victor,** (585) 924–5848, is open Tuesday through Sunday 9:00 A.M. to 5:00 P.M. from mid-May through the first week in November. Interpretive trails are open year-round from 8:00 A.M. to sunset, weather permitting. The bark longhouse is open Tuesday through Sunday 10:00 A.M. to noon and 1:00 to 4:00 P.M. The trails are open all year. Admission is free except during special events.

Along with shopping malls, what could be more intrinsic to American civilization than the electronic media? The early days of our fascination with the vacuum tube (a device, young readers, that brought us our news, sports, and "Top 40" before the invention of the transistor) are chronicled in the Antique Wireless Association's **Electronic Communication Museum** south of the thruway in **East Bloomfield.** The museum's collections, housed in the handsome 1837 quarters of the East Bloomfield Historical Society, have been amassed by AWA members throughout the world. They include nineteenth-century telephones (in working order!), some of Marconi's original wireless apparatus, early shipboard wireless equipment, and the crystal radio sets that brought the first broadcast programs into American living rooms. A special attraction is a fully stocked replica of a circa 1925 radio store; another is wireless station W2AN, an actual broadcast operation staffed by AWA members.

The AWA Electronic Communication Museum, on the Village Green just off Routes 5 and 20, Bloomfield, (585) 657–6260, is open May 1 to October 31, Sunday 2:00 to 5:00 P.M.; also open Saturday 2:00 to 4:00 P.M. during July and August. Closed holidays. Admission is free.

Preserved Americana seems to be the order of the day in this part of upstate New York, and the theme is carried along nicely at the *Granger Homestead and Carriage Museum* in *Canandaigua.* "Homestead" is actually a bit too homespun a term for this grand Federal mansion, which must have been the talk of Canandaigua and all the farms around when it was built in 1816 by Gideon Granger, a lawyer who had served as postmaster general under Jefferson and Madison. Granger came here to live the life of a country squire in his retirement, and his descendants lived here until 1930, when they willed many of the furnishings to Rochester's Memorial Art Gallery. The furnishings have been returned to the house on loan since it reopened in 1948. Nine restored rooms contain the furniture of the nineteenth century, including Federal, Empire, and Victorian styles. Decorative objects, original artworks, and China Trade porcelain are also displayed.

A distinctive attraction of the Granger Homestead is the Carriage Museum, which exhibits more than fifty horse-drawn vehicles made or used in western New York. The sociological implications of the various conveyances on display are explained in an informative exhibit titled "Sleighs and Surreys and Signs and Symbols." Forty-five minute horse-drawn antique carriage rides through the town's historic neighborhoods are offered by reservation on Friday at noon, 1:00, 2:00, 3:00 and 4:00 P.M. through late October. Adults are $20; children 4 to 12 are $10; under 3 free. The carriage can hold up to three adults or two adults and three children. The museum also gives horse-drawn antique sleigh rides on Sunday from 1:00 to 3:00 P.M., mid-January to mid-March, weather permitting. Adults are $5.00, ages 4 to 12, $3.00. Call for conditions and availability.

The Granger Homestead and Carriage Museum, 295 North Main Street, Canandaigua, (585) 394–1472, is open May through October. Guided tours are offered on the hour Tuesday through Friday 1:00 to 5:00 P.M. and in May, September, and October, and in June, July, and August, Tuesday through Sunday 1:00 to 5:00 P.M. Admission is $5.00 for adults, $4.00 for seniors, and $1.00 for children.

Sonnenberg Gardens are part of an estate built around a mansion representative of a much bolder and more expressive architectural aesthetic than Granger's Federal style—this is a Gilded Age extravaganza, part Tudor Revival, part Queen Anne, built in 1887 by Frederick Ferris Thompson, who founded the First National Bank of the City of New York. The forty-room mansion is well worth a tour, but even more impressive than the heavily carved Victorian

The Rose Garden, Sonnenberg Gardens

furniture and fine Oriental rugs contained beneath the house's multicolor slate roof are the gardens themselves.

Frederick Thompson died in 1899, and in 1902 his widow, Mary Clark Thompson, began the extensive formal and informal plantings on the estate as a memorial to her husband. She worked at creating the gardens for the next fourteen years and held occasional "public days" so that her Canandaigua neighbors (she had spent her youth in the town) could enjoy them as well. Since 1973 the gardens have been undergoing restoration, and they appear today much as they did during the first decades of the century.

What sets Sonnenberg (German for "sunny hill") apart is the gardens' sheer eclecticism. While many estates of the turn-of-the-century period were planted in a single style, usually formal French or the more naturalistic English, the gardens here represent just about every major mode of horticultural expression. Included are a Japanese garden, a rock garden, an Italian garden, a sunken parterre display in a Versailles-inspired fleur-de-lis motif, an old-fashioned garden, a garden planted entirely in blue and white flowers, and a rose garden containing more than 2,600 magnificent bushes blossoming in red, white, and pink. Not to mention a Roman bath, a thirteen-house greenhouse complex with a domed palm house conservatory, and fountains and statuary everywhere. After a while the mansion itself almost seems like an afterthought.

The Peach House, an informal restaurant in the greenhouse, has indoor and outdoor seating and is open daily in season from noon to 3:30 P.M.

There is no fee to visit the Wine Center (585–394–9016) in Bay House, which sells gourmet foods and wines from the Finger Lakes region. At the tasting room, visitors can sample ten to fifteem different wimes and choose from more than one hundred.

Sonnenberg Gardens, 151 Charlotte Street off Route 21, Canandaigua, (585) 394–4922, is open daily until Memorial Day weekend, 9:30 A.M. to 4:00 P.M.; Memorial Day to September 1, 9:30 A.M. to 5:30 P.M.; and September 2 to mid-October, 9:30 A.M. to 4:00 P.M. Walking tours are offered weekdays at 1:00 P.M. and on weekends at 10:00 A.M. and 1:00 P.M. (no tours before Memorial Day or after Labor Day). Admission is $8.50 for adults, $7.50 for senior citizens, and $3.50 for children ages 6 to 16. A season pass is available for $20.00 if purchased after the gardens open, $17.00 if purchased before. A free tram provides transportation around the grounds.

The gracious 1810 ***Morgan Samuels Inn,*** nestled on forty-six acres of land, is an 1810 English-style stone mansion with five elegantly furnished bedrooms with fireplaces and one suite, three balconies, and a tennis court. Guests are served breakfast by candlelight. The Victorian porch is a delightful spot to relax and view the gardens. It's at 2920 Smith Road, Canandaigua, (585) 394–9232; www.morgansamuelsinn.com. Rates range from $149 to $395 a night, depending on season.

One never knows where the nation's largest collection of this or that is going to turn up, but when it comes to coverlets, the answer is ***Palmyra.***

The homespun coverlets displayed at the ***Alling Coverlet Museum,*** part of ***Historic Palmyra,*** were collected over thirty years by Mrs. Merle Alling of Rochester, and is the largest collection of its kind in the nation. Heirlooms all, they represent both the simple spreads hand-loomed by farmwives and the somewhat more sophisticated designs woven on multiple-harness looms by professionals during the nineteenth century. The collection also includes a number of handmade nineteenth-century quilts and antique spinning equipment.

The Alling Coverlet Museum (Historic Palmyra, Inc.), 122 William Street, Palmyra, (315) 597–6737, is open daily June through mid-September, 1:00 to 4:00 P.M. and by appointment. Admission is free, although donations are welcome.

Another facet of Historic Palmyra is the ***William Phelps General Store Museum.*** Erected in 1825, this commercial building was purchased by William Phelps in 1867 and remained in his family until 1977. Having remained virtually unchanged over the past 130 years, the store, along with its stock, furnishings, and business records, amounts to a virtual time capsule of nineteenth- and early twentieth-century Palmyra. An unusual note: The gaslight fixtures in the store and upstairs residential quarters were used by a Phelps family member until 1976, electricity never having been installed in the building.

The William Phelps General Store Museum, 140 Market Street, Palmyra, (315) 597–6981, is open June through mid-September, Wednesday, Thursday, and Saturday from 1:00 to 4:00 P.M. Open Saturday only in October. Admission is free.

Historic Palmyra, Inc.'s final holding is the **Palmyra Historical Museum,** which was erected about 1900 as a hotel. It is now a museum housing a unique display of elegant furniture, children's toys and dolls, household items, tools, gowns, and other artifacts of bygone ages.

The Palmyra Historical Museum, 132 Market Street, Palmyra, (315) 597–6981, is open June through October, Tuesday through Thursday and Saturday from 1:00 to 4:00 P.M. and by appointment. Admission is free.

Eastern Lakes

For a fabulous day of fishing, head for **Sodus Bay** on the shore of Lake Ontario. In season more than twenty-five charter boat companies offer their services in this small fishing paradise. Stop for a bite at **Papa Joe's Restaurant** on **Sodus Point.** The only restaurant open here year-round, it has a children's menu and entertainment on the deck on summer weekends. Lunch and dinner are served from 11:30 A.M. until 10:00 P.M. A two-bedroom apartment overlooking the bay is available for rent on a nightly basis. Call (315) 483–6372.

The lighthouse at **Sodus Bay Lighthouse Museum** (Sodus Point 14555, 315–483–4936) was built in 1871 and remained in use until 1901. Museum displays include ship models, dioramas, shipboard equipment, a lens repair shop, and other maritime exhibits. There's a wonderful view of the lake from the tower. It's open May 1 through October 31, Tuesday through Sunday 10:00 A.M. to 5:00 P.M. Donations are suggested.

The 1870 Victorian **Carriage House Inn** (corner of Ontario and Wickham Boulevard, 315–483–2100), charges from $85 to $140 for rooms and suites with a private bath, TV, and full breakfast. Rooms are also available in the stone carriage house, which overlooks the lake and lighthouse. Two efficiencies, which sleep up to four, have outdoor decks and picnic tables.

Bonnie Castle Farm Bed & Breakfast, on fifty acres of landscaped grounds overlooking Great Sodus Bay, is a three-story Victorian with private balconies and bilevel decks. Each of the eight rooms has its own bath; the Bonnie Castle Suite has a kitchen. If you need three bedrooms, there's also an 1890 Victorian summer home—the Aldrich Guest House—whose balcony and porch overlook the water. Locust Grove Cottage, overlooking the meadow, can accommodate three to six people.

Bonnie Castle Farm Bed & Breakfast, 6603 Bonnie Castle Road, **Wolcott,** (315) 587–2273, is open year-round. Rates range from $89 to $169 for rooms to $250 for the guest house and include a full breakfast buffet with such dishes as appleknocker sausages, seafood pasta, and Mexican frittatas. There's also a private beach.

Don't Be a Carrier

If you're planning to put a boat into any of the Finger Lakes, make sure the trailer, hull, and external motor or drive apparatus have been thoroughly cleaned—especially if the vessel has been in the Great Lakes, St. Lawrence River, Lake Champlain, or connected waters. Zebra mussels and the aquatic weed milfoil are invasive, non-native pests whose spread you can help prevent by scrubbing down hulls, motors, and trailers with hot water.

From coverlets to clocks . . . the northern Finger Lakes region seems to be New York State's attic, filled with interesting collections of things we might otherwise take for granted. In *Newark* the ***Hoffman Clock Museum*** comprises more than a hundred clocks and watches collected by local jeweler and watchmaker Augustus L. Hoffman. Housed in the Newark Public Library, the collection includes timepieces from Great Britain, Europe, and Japan, although the majority of the clocks and watches are of nineteenth-century American manufacture, with more than a dozen having been made in New York State. Each summer the museum's curator mounts a special exhibit devoted to a particular aspect of the horologist's art.

The Hoffman Clock Museum, Newark Public Library, 121 High Street, Newark, (315) 331–4370, is open Monday noon to 9:00 P.M., Tuesday through Friday 9:30 A.M. to 9:00 P.M., and Saturday 10:00 A.M. to 3:00 P.M.; closed Sunday and holidays. Admission is free.

If your interest in antiques extends beyond timepieces, head south a few miles to *Geneva* for a tour of ***Rose Hill Mansion,*** the Geneva Historical Society's National Historic landmark property overlooking the east shore of Seneca Lake. Built in 1839, the twenty-six-room mansion is one of the nation's premier examples of the Greek Revival style at its peak of refinement and popularity. Formal, symmetrical, and serene within its boxwood garden, Rose Hill Mansion has been exquisitely restored and furnished with as many pieces original to the house as it has been possible to collect. The twenty-one room tour highlights the dining room, with its 5-foot-long 1815 Portuguese crystal chandelier; the front parlor, containing a seven-piece Rococo rosewood ensemble; and the Green Bedroom, decorated in the Empire style that paralleled the Greek Revival architectural trend. Rose Hill's formality is offset by its airy, spacious character—all of its front windows open from the floor, making a seamless link between ground-floor rooms and the colonnaded front porch.

Rose Hill Mansion, Route 96A, Geneva; (315) 789–5151 is open May through October, Monday through Saturday 10:00 A.M. to 4:00 P.M.; Sunday 1:00

to 5:00 P.M. Admission is $3.00 for adults; $2.00 for students and seniors. Children under 10 are free.

Two of the Finger Lakes' most elegant inn-restaurants overlook its deepest lake, Seneca, in Geneva, the self-proclaimed "Trout Capital of the World."

It took fifty men more than four years to build the turreted red Medina stone **Belhurst Castle**, overlooking Seneca Lake. When it was finally completed in 1889, the cost of construction exceeded $475,000. Today the Richardsonian Romanesque inn, on the National Register of Historic Places, has a reputation as one of the finer places in the region at which to stay and/or dine.

There are 14 period mansion rooms in the castle (including one with a private balcony and one in the castle turret, with a widow's walk) and several houses on the grounds behind the castle. These include the Carriage House, with a four-poster bed and private patio, and the Ice House, with a loft bedroom; both of these offer more private accommodations. A three-bedroom ranch house adjacent to Belhurst is also available. Rates range from $105 to $315 in season; off-season rates are available.

The restaurant, with six dining rooms, offers dishes such as osso buco, filet mignon, and veal and spinach crepes. Dinner is served on the lakefront veranda, weather permitting. Sunday brunch features chef-carved meats, hot entrees, and omelets made to order. Reservations are recommended for all meals. A lunch buffet is served Monday through Saturday.

White Springs Manor, sister property to Belhurst Castle, was once owned by a wealthy lawyer and land baron. The imposing 1806 Georgian Revival mansion, perched on a hilltop in the middle of eighteen acres, affords guests a panoramic view of Seneca Lake and beyond. Each of the twelve guest rooms and the "playhouse" (a detached house) has a private bath, gas fireplace, and queen- or king-size bed. Belhurst's new Vinifera Inn, opened in summer 2004, offers rooms with lake views, opulent appoimntments, fireplaces, and two-person jacuzzis. Rates are $160 to $295.

Belhurst Castle, Lochland Road (Route 14), Geneva, (315) 781–0201; www .belhurst.com, is open year-round.

"An oasis, a little island of beauty, peace, and friendliness in a busy world" is how **Geneva On The Lake** describes itself. The inn, with its terra-cotta tile roof, Palladian windows, Ionic columns, classical sculptures, and magnificent formal gardens, was built in 1910 by Byron Nester, who was inspired by the summer residences around northern Italy's Lakes Garda and Maggiore. All rooms are suites and range in price, depending on time of year, from $104 to $770 for a night's stay. Rates include wine, fresh fruit and flowers, the *New York Times* delivered to your door, a wine and cheese party on Friday evening, and Continental breakfast, weather permitting, on the terrace overlooking the gardens and lake.

Lunch is served on the terrace daily except Sunday, from mid-June to early September; candlelight dinners with live musical entertainment are served each evening; and an elegant brunch is served Sunday.

Geneva On The Lake, 1001 Lochland Road, Route 14S, Geneva, (315) 789–7190; www.genevaonthelake.com, is open all year.

"To honor in perpetuity these women, citizens of the United States of America, whose contributions to the arts, athletics, business, education, government, the humanities, philanthropy and science have been the greatest value for the development of their country." Thus were the parameters for entry outlined when the women of *Seneca Falls* created the *National Women's Hall of Fame* in 1969, believing that the contributions of American women deserved a permanent home.

And, indeed, the list of members reads like a "Who's Who": Marian Anderson, Pearl S. Buck, Rachel Carson, Amelia Earhart, Billie Jean King, Sally Ride, Dorothea Dix, and a host of others who have left their mark on American history and the American psyche.

Exhibits, housed in the bank building in the heart of the Historic District II, include a panel celebrating Elizabeth Cady Stanton, who led the way to rights for women, and artifacts and mementos about the members, events, and activities significant to women's history.

The National Women's Hall of Fame, 76 Fall Street, Seneca Falls, (315) 568–8060, is open from May through September, Monday through Saturday from 10:00 A.M. to 4:00 P.M. and Sunday noon to 4:00 p.m.; October through April, Wednesday through Saturday 10:00 A.M. to 4:00 P.M. Closed Thanksgiving, Christmas, and the month of January. Admission is $3.00 for adults, $1.50 for senior citizens and students. There is a family rate of $7.00.

A Snake in the Grass

Just outside the town of Geneva is Bare Hill, sacred to the Seneca. According to legend, it was here the Creator opened up the earth and allowed their ancestors to enter into the world. But a giant serpent lay in wait, eating the newborns as they appeared. Finally, a warrior, acting upon a dream in which the Creator told him to fear not, slew the snake with a magic arrow, and the snake, in its death throes, disgorged all those he'd eaten.

Once a stop on the Underground Railroad, the **Hubbell House Bed &
Breakfast** overlooking Van Cleef Lake was built in the 1850s as a Gothic
Revival cottage and later enlarged and remodeled in the Second Empire style.
The result is a delightfully eccentric building with scrolled bargeboards,
wooden pinnacles, windows of all sizes, and a rear mansard roof with dia-
mond-shaped slate tiles. It's furnished with an eclectic mix of antiques, including an 1860s Eastlake dresser, armchair, and rocker, and has four guest rooms
(two with private bath). The wrap-around porch overlooks the lake.

Hubbell House Bed & Breakfast, 42 Cayuga Street, Seneca Falls, (315) 568–
9690, is open all year. Rates, which include a full breakfast, range from $105 to
$135 a night. Guests can swim and use paddleboats from the inn's private
dock. Check out its Web site: www.hubbellhouse.com.

For a small town **Waterloo** is large on preserving history and has two
museums well worth a visit. It was in the village of Waterloo, in the summer of
1865, that a patriotic businessman named Henry C. Welles put forward the idea
of honoring the soldiers who fell in the Civil War by placing flowers on their
graves on a specified day of observance. On May 5 of the following year,
thanks to the efforts of Welles and Civil War veteran General John B. Murray,
the village was draped in mourning, and a contingent of veterans and townspeople marched to the local cemeteries and, with appropriate ceremonies, decorated their comrades' graves. Thus Memorial Day was born.

In 1966 President Johnson signed a proclamation officially naming Waterloo the birthplace of Memorial Day. On May 29 of that same Memorial Day
centennial year, Waterloo's **Memorial Day Museum** was opened in a reclaimed
mansion in the heart of town. The twenty-room, once-derelict brick structure is
itself a local treasure, especially distinguished by the ornate ironwork on its
veranda. Although built in the early Italianate Revival era of 1836–50, the house
is being restored to its appearance circa 1860–70, the decade of the Civil War
and the first Memorial Day observances.

The museum's collections cover the Civil War and the lives and era of the
originators of the holiday, as well as memorabilia from all other U.S. wars.

The Memorial Day Museum, 35 East Main Street, Waterloo, (315) 539–0533,
is open Memorial Day weekend through mid-September; spring and fall, Friday
through Monday noon to 5:00 P.M., Tuesday through Saturday 1:00 to 4:00 P.M.
Admission is by donation. Tours are given by appointment.

Just a block from the Memorial Day Museum is the **Waterloo Terwilliger
Historical Museum,** where the "antique and elegant" combine with the "long-
lasting and functional" to tell the story of Waterloo and surrounding areas. The
collection includes everything from Native American artifacts to Roaring Twenties fashions. Authentic full-size vehicles and a replica of a general store offer

Whatever Happened to Sticks and Stones?

Although Amelia Jenks Bloomer didn't invent "bloomers" (they were invented by Elizabeth Smith Miller), she was instrumental in making them the uniform of nineteenth-century suffragists. The *New York Tribune* described Mrs. Bloomer's outfit: " . . . a kilt descended just below the knees, the skirt of which was trimmed with rows of black velvet. The pantaloons were of the same texture and trimmed in the same style. She wore gaiters. Her headdress was cherry and black. Her dress had a large open corsage with bands of velvet over the white chamesette in which was a diamond stud pin. She wore flowing sleeves, tight undersleeves, and black lace mitts. Her whole attire was rich and plain in appearance."

Mrs. Bloomer and her fellow suffragists abandoned their costume when they became objects of ridicule and children would follow them, chanting:

"Hi Ho,

In sleet and snow,

Mrs. Bloomer's all the go.

Twenty tailors to take the stitches,

Plenty of women to wear the britches."

a slice of life as it used to be; five rooms, decorated down to the last detail, each depict a specific era.

The Waterloo Terwilliger Historical Museum, 31 East William Street, Waterloo, (315) 539–0533, is open year-round, Tuesday through Friday 1:00 to 4:00 P.M. Admission is by donation. Tours are given by appointment.

Between 1942 and 1946, Sampson Naval Training Station prepared 411,429 sailors and Waves to serve in World War II. The *Sampson WW-2 Navy Museum,* established in the station's original Navy brig facility, is filled with military artifacts donated by members of the Sampson WW-2 Navy Veterans organization and the U.S. Navy Department. The museum, in Sampson State Park, Route 96A, *Romulus,* (315) 585–6392, is open from May 30 to Labor Day, Wednesday through Sunday 10:00 A.M. to 4:00 P.M. (last tour at 3:30 P.M.), and from Labor Day until Columbus Day on weekends only. Admission is free, but there is a park entrance fee of $7.00 per vehicle ($6.00 until mid-June) from mid-June through Labor Day.

Some institutions have a pinpoint focus; others follow a more eclectic pattern of acquisition and education. Occasionally, a small institution finds its focus as it matures, as is the case with the *Cayuga Museum* in Auburn, which is really two museums in one.

Founded in 1936 in the 1836 Willard-Case Mansion, the Cayuga Museum contains the rich history of both **Auburn,** "the village that touched the world," and Cayuga County. Exhibits include business timekeeping devices such as the "Thousand Year Clock," manufactured by Auburn's Bundy brothers, whose Binghamton, New York, operation evolved into IBM. There's also an exhibit on the early history of the now-giant corporation. Other notables from Cayuga County who are highlighted at the museum include President Millard Fillmore; E. S. Martin, founder of the original, pre-Luce *Life* magazine; prison reformer Thomas M. Osborne; and Ely Parker, the Seneca Indian who penned the surrender at Appomattox.

In the Stanton Gallery, which once served as the dining room in the Willard-Case mansion, the Dyckman Collection of period furnishings typifies the decor found in upper-class European and American homes in the mid- to late 1800s.

In 1911 Theodore W. Case proved that recording sound on film was possible, and in late 1922 he made it a reality with the assistance of E. I. Sponable. Restored in 1993 after being forgotten for sixty years, the **Case Research Lab Museum** opened its doors to the public on the second floor of the Cayuga Museum's carriage house in June of that year. Exhibits include the laboratory building, the soundstage, and many examples of the early history, inventions, and laboratory equipment developed to commercialize sound on film. One of the museum's newest acquisitions is a 1928 REO Speedwagon panel truck.

The Cayuga Museum and the Case Research Lab Museum, 203 West Genesee Street, Auburn, (315) 253–8051, are open February through December, Tuesday through Friday and Monday holidays 10:00 A.M. to 5:00 P.M.; Saturday and Sunday noon to 5:00 P.M.; closed Thanksgiving, Christmas, and New Year's Day. Admission to the museum and lab is free, but a donation is welcome. Admission to Case Research Lab is $2.50 per person.

The "Woman Called Moses" is remembered at the **Harriet Tubman Home** in Auburn, where she settled after making nineteen trips to the South to rescue more than 300 enslaved persons. A guided tour includes a visit to the Tubman House, the Home for the Aged, the ruins of the John Brown Infirmary, the former Thompson Memorial A.M.E. Zion Church building, and Mrs. Tubman's grave at Fort Hill Cemetery.

The Harriet Tubman Home is at 180 South Street (315) 252–2081 is open Tuesday through Friday 10:00 A.M. to 4:00 P.M. and Saturday by appointment. There are extended hours in February, Black History Month. Admission is $5.00 for adults, $3.00 for seniors, and $2.00 for children.

Experts believe that the **Willard Memorial Chapel**—all that remains of the Auburn Theological Seminary campus, which thrived here from 1818 to 1939—

is the only extant example of a complete **Louis Comfort Tiffany** interior. The handsome gray limestone and red sandstone Romanesque Revival building, designed by A. J. Warner of Rochester, has a magnificent interior designed and handcrafted by the Tiffany Glass and Decorating Company. Among the highlights: a three-paneled stained-glass window of "Christ Sustaining Peter on the Water," nine leaded-glass chandeliers, and fourteen opalescent nave windows.

"The Tiffany Treasure of the Finger Lakes" hosts numerous concerts throughout the year, including the Tiffany Summer Concert Series on Wednesdays at noon in July and August. Admission is by donation. For a complete concert schedule, contact the Community Preservation Committee, Inc., at the number below.

The Willard Memorial Chapel, 17 Nelson Street, Auburn, (315) 252–0339, is open Tuesday through Friday 10:00 A.M. to 4:00 P.M. or by appointment; closed holidays. Admission is $2.00 per person.

"Quando mangiate da Rosalie sembra mangiare in Italia" (When you eat at Rosalie's, it's like eating in Italy), proclaims the menu at **Rosalie's Cucina.** Patrons and critics agree: The food here is superb and superbly authentic. Most of the dishes are northern Italian, and many are family recipes, such as *pesce diavolo* (shrimp, scallops, mussels, and calamari in a spicy red sauce), and *pollo marsala* (chicken, mushrooms, and proscuitto in a marsala wine sauce). House specialties include rotisserie duck ($25) and cioppino ($29). Entrees average between $18 and $24, and there's a fine selection of Italian wines. The restaurant is at 841 West Genesee Street, Skaneateles, (315) 685–2200 and is open for dinner nightly. Reservations for six or more only, based on availability. Rosalie's bread, baked on the premises, can be purchased to take home.

Classic cars, historic race cars, and racing memorabilia are all exhibited at the **D.I.R.T. Motorsports Hall of Fame & Classic Car Museum,** along with a "Hall of Fame" of legendary race car drivers.

Among the classic cars on display are a 1926 Duesenberg, the 1929 Dodge Roadster that won first place in a cross-country race in 1993, and a 1969 Dodge Charger Hemi 4-speed. For stock car enthusiasts, there's the Buzzie Reutimann "00" coupe, which won the first two Schaefer 100s, and "Batmobile" #112 driven by Gary Balough in 1980. In the Jack Burgess Memorial Video Room, the "master of the microphone" recounts exciting racing events of the past. The Northeast Classic Motorsports Extravaganza is held each August.

Also here is Cayuga County Fair Speedway, home of Drivers Independent Race Tracks (D.I.R.T.), the second-largest race-sanctioning body in the nation (races every Sunday night May through September).

D.I.R.T. Motorsports Hall of Fame and Classic Car Museum, Cayuga County Fairgrounds, Route 31, **Weedsport,** (315) 834–6606, is open daily April through

December, Monday through Saturday 10:00 A.M. to 5:00 P.M. and Sunday noon to 7:00 P.M.; closed January through March. Admission is $4.00 for adults and $3.00 for children and senior citizens.

In England, Americans Victoria and Richard MacKenzie-Childs worked for a small pottery shop, taught art, and designed and made clothing for stage and street wear. When they returned here, they opened *MacKenzie-Childs, Ltd.,* a multifaceted design studio and factory where more than 150 workers turn out handcrafted, hand-painted giftware including Majolica, glassware, linens, and floorcloths—all done, according to the couple, "within the elegance of a gentlemanly nineteenth-century estate . . . in an atmosphere of ethics, order, and grace."

MacKenzie-Childs, Ltd., 3260 State Route 90, *Aurora,* (315) 364–7123, showroom and shop are open year-round, Monday through Saturday 10:00 A.M. to 5:00 P.M. Studio tours are given Monday through Friday at 1:15 P.M. The tour is $10.00 for adults; senior and children under 12, $6.00. Reservations are recommended. The Happy Eating Restaurant serves a light lunch Wednesday through Sunday.

Beaver Lake Nature Center is an Onondaga County park incorporating several different ecosystems, all connected by 9 miles of well-maintained hiking trails. A 200-acre lake, offering beautiful vistas but no recreational facilities, is a migration-time magnet for up to 30,000 Canada geese. Guided canoe tours of the lake are available during the summer; rental canoes are available for these tours, and you must preregister. The entire center is a great place for birders; more than 180 species have been sighted here over the years. The informative Beaver Lake Visitor Center is the starting point for a regular schedule of hour-long guided tours of the trails, given by professional naturalists each weekend.

Beaver Lake Nature Center, 8477 East Mud Lake Road, *Baldwinsville,* (315) 638–2519, is open all year, daily from 8:00 A.M. to dusk; closed Christmas. Admission is $1.00 per car and $10.00 per bus and is paid at the automated gate as you exit. Call ahead to register for guided group nature tours.

Ithaca, home to Cornell University, is also home of the *Paleontological Research Institution* (PRI), whose Museum of the Earth houses more than two million fossils, one of the premier collections in the Western Hemisphere, telling the story of the planet's 4.6-billion-year history, with a focus on the Northeast, through exhibits, hands-on activities, and audiovisual presentations. The institution, located in a former orphanage on the southwest shore of Cayuga Lake, was founded by Gilbert D. Harris, a professor of geology at the university from 1894 to 1934.

Among the fossils exhibited are single-celled microfossils, ancient plants, the remains of ancient vertebrates such as dinosaurs, whales, and woolly mammoths, and a magnificent 425-million-year-old trilobite. The Hyde Park Mastadon Fossil skeleton is one of the most complete in the world.

PRI, 1259 Trumansburg Road, Route 96, Ithaca, (607) 273–6623, is open from Labor Day through Memorial Day, Monday, Wednesday and Saturday 10:00 A.M. to 5:00 P.M., Sunday noon to 4:00 P.M. (closed duing school breaks), and after Memorial Day until Labor Day, Monday through Saturday, 11:00 A.M. to 4:00 P.M. Admission is $8.00 for adults, $5.00 for students and seniors, $3.00 for children.

New York's highly rated four-star country inn (AAA and Mobil) is known locally as "the house with the circular staircase." It took two years for one man to carve the staircase at the Italianate **Rose Inn**. Built of Honduras mahogany, it extends up two stories to a cupola on the roof. It's a fitting centerpiece for the elegant inn, which also has a reputation as one of the finest restaurants in the area.

Innkeepers Charles and Sherry Rosemann have been hard at work improving guest accommodations since they purchased the 1850 home in 1953. Today the inn has twelve handsomely appointed guest rooms with private baths and eleven suites with fireplaces and Jacuzzis for two.

The eclectic seasonal dinner menu might include such offerings as rack of lamb, honey almond duckling, or roulade of ostrich. There's a prix fixe dinner menu in winter, and live jazz on Friday and Saturday evenings.

Rates at the Rose Inn, 813 Auburn Road, Route 34, Ithaca, (607) 533–7905; www.roseinn.com, range from $155 to $340 per night and include a full breakfast. A two-night stay is required if it includes a Saturday evening between Easter and Thanksgiving.

Paleontological Research Institution

Thanks to a poor boy who grew up to be a wealthy shoe manufacturer and benefactor, six of approximately 170 carved wood **carousels** remaining in this country are located in **Broome County.** Between 1919 and 1934 George F. Johnson donated six carousels manufactured by the Allan Herschell Companies of North Tonawanda to the county. He placed one stipulation on the gift: Remembering his poor childhood, he felt that everyone should be able to ride and insisted that the municipalities never charge a fee.

Today, gorilla chariots, pigs, and horses with lions hidden in saddle blankets transport riders on their backs to magical realms. And at two of the carousels—Recreation and Ross Parks—the animals twirl to the sounds of the original Wurlitzer band organs. Riders who take a spin on all six merry-go-rounds receive a special button.

The carousels are located at C. Fred Johnson Park, Johnson City (607–797–9098); George W. Johnson Park, Endicott (607–757–2427); West Endicott Park, Endicott (607–754–5595); Recreation Park, Binghamton (607–722–9166 or 662–7017); Ross Park, Binghamton (607–724–5461); and Highland Park, Endwell (607–754–5595). They operate from Memorial Day to Labor Day, and riders are asked to donate a piece of litter collected along the way. An exhibit at Ross Park explores the history of carousel making. For general information contact the Broome County Chamber of Commerce at (800) 836–6740.

Stand on a ledge deep inside **Watkins Glen** Gorge as state-of-the-art technology—laser images, panoramic sounds, and special effects—transport you from the gorge's beginnings 4.5 billion years ago, through the ice age, to the arrival of the people of the Seneca Nation.

The dramatic outdoor sound and light show, **Timespell,** is held in **Watkins Glen State Park** on weekends in June, September, and October at 8:00 P.M., and July through Labor Day at 9:00 P.M. nightly.

Admission for *Timespell,* in Watkins Glen State Park, Watkins Glen, (607) 535–8888, is $6.50 for adults, and $5.50 for seniors and children ages 5 to 12. Note: The route to the show area is not wheelchair accessible.

Seneca Lake lies at the heart of New York's Finger Lakes wine country, now the second-largest wine-producing region in the United States. The **Seneca Lake Wine Trail** has been planned to help visitors make the most of a ramble among the region's vineyards and related attractions, linking twenty-six wineries and tasting rooms along the shores of the big lake. Here you'll discover the setting, the soil, and the remarkably dedicated people responsible for the area's superb Rieslings and Cabernet Francs, along with other European viniferas, French-American hybrids, and native grape varieties. The wineries are never far from tidy villages, cozy inns and bed and breakfasts, casual bistros and elegant restaurants, and art galleries and antiques shops—all tucked amidst some of the loveliest scenery in the Northeast.

For a guide to the trail, visit or contact the Seneca Lake Wine Trail, 100 N. Franklin Street, Watkins Glen 14891; (877) 536–2717; www. senecalakewine.com.

For more than sixty years, Endicott has been home to ***Pat Mitchell's Homemade Ice Cream.*** Founded in 1920 by Joseph Travis, the store began to thrive in 1948 when Raymond "Pat" Mitchell bought the business and, using a vintage 1920s batch freezer, began making ice cream that has become legendary in these parts. Today's owners continue to make thousands of gallons, three gallons at a time, filling orders from coast to coast and around the globe.

What makes Pat Mitchell's ice cream so good? Everyone you ask has a different opinion. But what else would you expect when a store offers more than 250 flavors, with treats such as banana delight, made with fresh banana ice cream, cashews, and a chocolate weave; fresh cantaloupe; coconut almond fudge; and, of course, chocolate chip?

Pat Mitchell's Homemade Ice Cream shops are at 231 Vestal Avenue in Endicott, on Vestal Avenue in Binghamton, and on Route 434 in Apalachin. For information call (607) 785–3080 or 786–5501.

Places to Stay in the Finger Lakes

To receive a copy of the Finger Lakes Bed & Breakfast Association's brochure, write the organization c/o Finger Lakes Association, 309 Lake Street, Penn Yan 14527, (800) 695–5590.

BURDETT

The Red House Country Inn
4586 Picnic Area Road
(607) 546–8566

CANANDAIGUA LAKE

Canandaigua Inn on the Lake
Routes 5 and 20
(800) 228–2801

CAZENOVIA

Lincklaen House
79 Albany Street
(315) 655–3461

GROTON

Benn Conger Inn
206 West Cortland Street
(607) 898–5817

HAMMONDSPORT

Amity Rose Bed and Breakfast
11 William Street
(800) 982–8818

18 Vine Inn and Carriage House
18 Vine Street
(607) 569–3039

ITHACA

The Hound and Hare
1031 Hanshaw Road
(800) 652–2821

PENN YAN

The Fox Inn
158 Main Street
(800) 901–7997

SKANEATELES

Sherwood Inn
26 West Genesee Street
(800) 374–3796

WATKINS GLEN

Castel Grisch Estate Winery
Manor and Restaurant
3380 County Route 28
(607) 535–9614

Places to Eat in the Finger Lakes

CANANDAIGUA LAKE

Inn On the Twenty Restaurant and Wine Bar
3638 Main Street
(905) 562–7313

ELMIRA HEIGHTS

Pierce's 1894 Restaurant
228 Oakwood Avenue
(607) 734–2022

HAMMONDSPORT

Crooked Lake Ice Cream Parlor
Hammondsport Village Square
(607) 569–2751

Waterfront
648 West Lake Road
(607) 868–3455
All-you-can-eat crab legs

ITHACA

Ithaca Bakery
400 North Meadow Street
(607) 273–7110

John Thomas Steakhouse
1152 Danby Road
(Route 96B)
(607) 273–3464

Moosewood Restaurant
215 North Cayuga Street
DeWitt Mall
(607) 273–9610

Thai Cuisine
501 South Meadow Street
(607) 273–2031

LODI

Ginny Lee Cafe
Wagner Vineyards
9322 Route 414
(607) 582–6574

PENN YAN

Miller's Essenhaus
1300 State Route 14A
(315) 531–8260

PITTSFORD

Richardson's Canal House
1474 Marsh Road,
(585) 248–5000

ROMULUS

Three Seasons Restaurant at Knapp Vineyards
2770 Country Road
(607) 869–9271

SKANEATELES

Dougs' Fish Fry
8 Jordan Street
(315) 685–7343
(also at 3638 West Road, Cortland)

WATKINS GLEN

Wildflower Cafe
301 North Franklin Street
(607) 535–9797

REGIONAL TOURIST INFORMATION— THE FINGER LAKES

Finger Lakes Regional Association,
309 Lake Street,
Penn Yan 14527,
(800) 548–4386
www.fingerlakes.org

A Finger Lakes Visitors Connection (Ontario County),
20 Ontario Street,
Canandaigua 14424,
(877) 386–4669
www.visitfingerlakes.com

Greater Corning Area Chamber of Commerce,
42 East Market Street,
Corning 14830,
(607) 936–4686
www.corningny.com

Ithaca/Thompkins County Convention and Visitors Bureau,
904 East Shore Drive,
Ithaca 14850,
(800) 284–8422
www.visitithaca.com

OTHER ATTRACTIONS WORTH SEEING IN THE FINGER LAKES

Elizabeth Cady Stanton Home,
32 Washington Street,
Seneca Falls,
(315) 568–2991

George Eastman House/International Museum of Photography & Film,
900 East Avenue,
Rochester,
(585) 271–3361

Richardson-Bates House Museum,
135 East Third Street,
Oswego,
(315) 343–1342

Seward House,
33 South Street,
Auburn,
(315) 252–1283

Susan B. Anthony Home,
17 Madison Street,
Rochester,
(585) 235–6124

Watkins Glen International Raceway,
Route 16,
Watkins Glen,
(607) 535–2481

The Niagara-Allegany Region

Ever since the Erie Canal was opened a century and a half ago, New York City and Buffalo have assumed a front door–back door status in New York State. New York City became the Empire State's gateway to the world, a capital of international shipping and finance. The docksides and rail yards of Buffalo, meanwhile, were the portals through which the industrial output and raw materials of the Midwest flowed into the state. **Buffalo** became an important "border" city between the East Coast and the hinterlands, a center of manufacturing and flour milling whose fortunes have risen and fallen with the state of the nation's smokestack economy.

But don't write Buffalo off as an old lunch-bucket town that gets too much snow in the winter. Buffalo has some impressive architecture, from Louis Sullivan's splendid Prudential Building and the art deco City Hall downtown to the Frank Lloyd Wright houses described later in this section. South Park, with its conservatory, and Riverside Park on the Niagara offer welcome open spaces, and there are even culinary treasures like Buffalo chicken wings and beef on 'weck (hot sliced roast beef on a pretzel-salt–coated kimmelweck or kaiser roll).

The countryside at the western tip of New York provides further evidence as to why Niagara Falls isn't the only reason

THE NIAGARA-ALLEGANY REGION

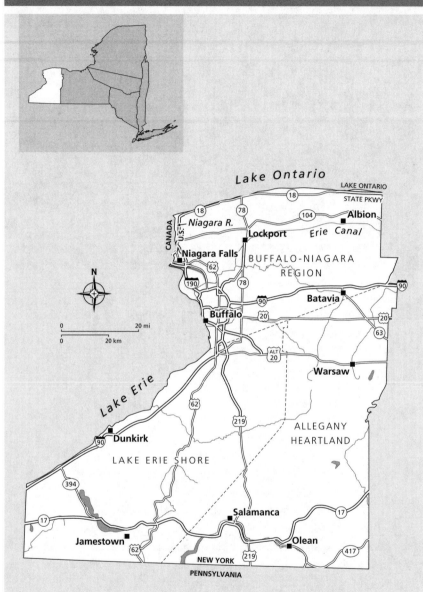

Lake Ontario

LAKE ONTARIO
STATE PKWY

18

Niagara R.

78

104

Albion

Lockport

Erie Canal

CANADA
U.S.

Niagara Falls

62

BUFFALO-NIAGARA
REGION

N

190

78

90

Batavia

90

Buffalo

20

20

63

0   20 mi
0   20 km

ALT
20

Warsaw

Lake Erie

62

219

ALLEGANY
HEARTLAND

Dunkirk

90

LAKE ERIE SHORE

394

17

Salamanca

17

Jamestown

62

219

Olean

417

NEW YORK
PENNSYLVANIA

to drive to the end of the thruway. The Pennsylvania border country boasts giant Allegany State Park, a hiking and camping paradise, and the byways along the Lake Erie shore wander through a picture-pretty territory dotted with vineyards, cherry orchards, and roadside stands selling delicious goat's milk fudge. Yes, goat's milk fudge. It's the little serendipities that make traveling fun.

Buffalo-Niagara Region

Just to mix things up a bit, we'll venture out into the sticks to begin our tour of the Niagara-Allegany region. Only 40 miles northeast of Buffalo is a pristine tract of some 19,000 acres, the core of which (11,000 acres) makes up the federal *Iroquois National Wildlife Refuge,* managed by the U.S. Fish and Wildlife Service. On either side of the refuge are the *Oak Orchard* (east) and *Tonawanda* (west) *Wildlife Management Areas,* operated by the state of New York's Department of Environmental Conservation.

Roughly two-thirds of Iroquois National Wildlife Refuge is made up of freshwater marshes and hardwood swamps that are fed by Oak Orchard Creek as it meanders east to west through the refuge. Forests, meadows, and fields slope up gently from the wetland's edge, attracting a wide variety of wildlife. The refuge maintains four scenic overlooks and three nature trails, which are open from sunrise to sunset year-round for self-guided visits and wildlife watching.

Both the Oak Orchard and the Tonawanda areas are primarily wetlands, with some grassland and forest habitat. The dikes surrounding the man-made impoundments, as well as several overlooks and parking areas, provide access that offers superb opportunities not only for hunters (during designated seasons) but for hikers and birders as well.

AUTHORS' FAVORITES— NIAGARA-ALLEGANY REGION

Burchfield-Penney Art Center	Q-R-S Music Rolls
Herschell Carrousel Factory Museum	Roger Tory Peterson Institute of Natural History
Luci-Desi Museum	The Roycroft Inn
Old Fort Niagara	Theodore Roosevelt Inaugural National Historic Site
Panama Rocks Scenic Park	
Pedaling History Bicycle Museum	

As the Twig Is Bent . . .

The handsome French Renaissance home at 484 Delaware Avenue in Buffalo was built in 1894 for S. Douglas Cornell, the successful owner of a lead foundry. Cornell, an avid amateur actor, had architect Edward A. Kent install a theater in the attic story of his new mansion. Here, he and his prominent Buffalo friends staged frequent performances. Among the amateur players' most enraptured fans was Cornell's little granddaughter, Katherine. Years later, when she was one of the great ladies of the American stage, Katherine Cornell credited those Delaware Avenue theatricals with kindling her ambition to become an actress.

The best time for birders to visit the area is from early March to mid-May. That's when more than 100,000 Canada geese, along with fewer numbers of ducks—black, pintail, mallard, American widgeon, teal, shoveler, and ring-necked—pause on their northward migration, with some staying to nest. The transitional habitat along the borders of the marsh attracts shore and wading birds and migrating spring warblers.

The Iroquois National Wildlife Refuge headquarters, 1101 Casey Road, **Basom,** (585) 948–5445, is open year-round Monday through Friday from 7:30 A.M. to 4:00 P.M., except holidays, and mid-March through May, Saturday and Sunday 9:00 A.M. to 5:00 P.M. Maps and other information are available here and on the Internet at http://iroquoisnwr.fws.gov. There are self-guided exhibits and an observation tower at the Oak Orchard Education Center on Knowlesville Road, just north of the town of Oakfield. The center is open daily from sunrise to sunset and is the starting point for four nature trails. For information about Oak Orchard and Tonawanda WMA contact the New York State Department of Environmental Conservation, P.O. Box 422, Basom 14013; (585) 948–5182.

The **Asa Ransom House** is an 1853 farmhouse on the site of one of the country's early gristmills. All but one of the nine guest rooms have fireplaces, and several have private front porches and balconies. The inn is also a full-service restaurant and serves a "country dinner" Sunday through Thursday, with specialties such as raspberry chicken and smoked corned beef with apple raisin sauce, and a five-course fixed-price dinner ($40) Friday and Saturday. Lunch is served Wednesday, and afternoon tea is served Tuesday, Thursday, and Saturday from 1:00 to 4:00 P.M. Dinner is served daily except Monday.

The Asa Ransom House (www.asaransom.com) is at 10529 Main Street, **Clarence,** (716) 759–2315 or (800) 841–2340. A double room, including full breakfast, ranges from $220 to $285 MAP (or Modified American Plan, i.e., with breakfast and dinner included in the rate) Friday and Saturday night; Sunday through Thursday a B&B rate of $98 to $155 is available, as well as an MAP rate of $150 to $205. Prices do not include service and tax.

Thirty Mile Point Lighthouse, more than 60 feet high, was built of hand-carved stone near the mouth of Golden Hill Creek in 1875 to warn vessels of the sandbar and shoals jutting out into Lake Ontario. Visitors can climb the circular steel staircase to the top of the tower for magnificent views of the lake and Canada. The lighthouse, now part of *Golden Hill State Park,* is free to those who pay a park entrance fee. It's open from July 4 to Labor Day, Friday through Sunday and holidays, 2:00 to 4:00 P.M. The park is on Lower Lake Road, *Barker,* (716) 795–3885.

It seems as if it isn't possible to tick off too many miles in this state without encountering one of the string of forts that once defended the thirteen colonies' northwestern frontier and played so prominent a role not only in the struggles between the British and the French for North American supremacy but in our own War of Independence as well. The westernmost of these (in New York, at least) is *Old Fort Niagara,* located in *Fort Niagara State Park* downstream from Niagara Falls at the point where the Niagara River flows into Lake Ontario.

Fort Niagara occupies what was, in the days of conventional warfare, one of the most strategic locations in all of the interior of North America. The great "French Castle" erected here in 1726 served as the core of Fort Niagara's defenses through nearly a century of intermittent warfare and was in use as officers' housing as recently as World War I. Now restored to its eighteenth-century appearance, it is the focal point of Old Fort Niagara.

Restored between the years 1927 and 1934, the older buildings of Fort Niagara are maintained by the non-profit, private Old Fort Niagara Association in cooperation with the State of New York. Beyond the silent military structures are broad vistas of Lake Ontario and, in clear weather, the rising mists of Niagara Falls 14 miles to the south.

Old Fort Niagara, Fort Niagara State Park, *Youngstown,* (716) 745–7611, is open year-round daily from 9:00 A.M. until sunset. Closed Thanksgiving, Christmas, and New Year's

Drummer at Old Fort Niagara

Day. During the summer there are frequent costumed reenactments of military drills, with musket and cannon firings. Admission is $8.00 for adults, $7.00 for senior citizens and AAA members, and $5.00 for children ages 6 to 12.

Scottish émigré Allan Herschell literally carved a place for himself in America's history when, in 1883, he produced the first steam-driven "riding gallery"—known today as a merry-go-round. By 1891, one machine a day was being shipped to places around the world; later the Herschell-Spillman Company became the world's largest producer of carousels and amusement park devices. And because merry-go-rounds need music, North Tonawanda also became a major producer of band organs.

The **Herschell Carrousel Factory Museum**, housed in a historic factory building, traces the history of Herschell, his hand-carved wooden animals, and the finished carousels. There are on-going woodcarving demonstrations, and best of all for all us kids, an antique, hand-carved wooden carousel to ride. "Super Sunday" family performances are held at 2:00 P.M. from mid-June through mid-September.

thegoatsweregot

According to legend, Goat Island is named for the only survivor of a herd that was left to winter there in 1779 by a settler named John Stedman.

The Herschell Carrousel Factory Museum, 180 Thompson Street, **North Tonawanda,** (716) 693–1885, is open April through mid-June, Wednesday through Sunday 1:00 to 5:00 P.M.; July and August, daily from 11:00 A.M. to 5:00 P.M.; and September through December, Wednesday through Sunday 1:00 to 5:00 P.M. Closed major holidays. Admission is $4.00 for adults and $2.00 for children ages 2 to 12 and includes one carousel ride. Extra rides cost just 50 cents.

Heading upriver (or more likely, down I–190) we come to Buffalo, the terminus town of the Erie Canal and gateway to the Midwest. For a quick introduction to this sprawling inland port, head downtown to reconnoiter the city and Lake Erie from the twenty-eighth-floor observatory of **City Hall** (open weekdays from 9:00 A.M. to 3:00 P.M.) and then visit the nearby historic neighborhood of **Allentown.**

The works of a number of important architects and the homes of several famous people are tucked into the compact Allentown neighborhood. Representative of the district's myriad building styles are the Kleinhans Music Hall on Symphony Circle, designed in 1938 by Eliel and Eero Saarinen; the 1869 Dorsheimer Mansion, 434 Delaware Avenue, an early work of the peerless Henry Hobson Richardson; Stanford White's 1899 Butler Mansion (672 Delaware) and 1895 Pratt Mansion (690 Delaware); and a lovely example of the Flemish Renaissance style at 267 North Street. As for the haunts of the famous, there are the childhood home of F. Scott Fitzgerald, 29 Irving Street; the home of artist Charles Burchfield (once a designer for a Buffalo wallpaper company) at 459 Franklin Street; and, at 472 Delaware Avenue, the carriage house belonging to the now-vanished house occupied circa 1870 by the editor and part-owner of the *Buffalo Morning Express*, a man who hated Buffalo—***Samuel Langborne Clemens,*** whom we met back in Elmira under the name of Mark Twain. For information call the Allentown Association at (716) 881–1024.

One house in the Allentown neighborhood stands above all others in historic importance. For fifty years the home of prominent Buffalo lawyer Ansley Wilcox, the Greek Revival house at 641 Delaware Avenue became part of American legend on September 14, 1901, when a vigorous young man who had just rushed from a vacation in the Adirondacks stepped into the library to take the oath of office as president of the United States. William McKinley was dead, the victim of an assassin; the era of Theodore Roosevelt was about to begin.

The story of that fateful day and the tragic event that preceded it is told at the ***Theodore Roosevelt Inaugural National Historic Site***, as the Wilcox House has been known since its restoration and opening to the public in 1971. Perhaps the most interesting aspect of the tale concerns the mad dash Roosevelt made from the Adirondacks to Buffalo. He had gone to the city and stayed for a few days at the Wilcox House after McKinley was shot by an anarchist at the Pan-American Exposition but had left to join his family at their mountain retreat after being assured by the president's doctors that his condition had stabilized. Notified several days later of McKinley's worsening state, the vice president made an overnight journey by horse and wagon to the nearest train station, where he learned that the president was dead. Roosevelt and his party then raced to Buffalo in a special train. Within two hours after his arrival, he was standing in Wilcox's library, wearing borrowed formal clothes as he took the oath of office as the nation's twenty-sixth president.

The Theodore Roosevelt Inaugural National Historic Site, 641 Delaware Avenue, Buffalo, (716) 884–0095, is open Monday through Friday 9:00 A.M. to

Assassination Location

On September 6, 1901, President McKinley was in Buffalo attending the Pan-American Exposition. While he was shaking hands with the public, Leon F. Czolgosz walked up and shot him with a revolver he had hidden under a handkerchief. Today the site where McKinley was assassinated is marked with a bronze plaque. It's on the traffic island on Fordham Drive between Elmwood Avenue and Lincoln Parkway. (Czolgosz was put to death the following October.)

5:00 P.M., weekends noon to 5:00 P.M. Closed New Year's Eve, New Year's Day, Easter, Memorial Day, Independence Day, Labor Day, Thanksgiving, Christmas Eve, and Christmas Day. Admission is $3.00 for adults, $2.00 seniors, and $1.00 for children 6 to 14.

The residential neighborhoods north of the downtown and Allentown areas of Buffalo boast five examples of the work of America's greatest architect, Frank Lloyd Wright. Wright's residential architecture is generally distributed within the central and upper Midwest, where he brought his "prairie style" to maturity. The fact that there exists a pocket of the master's work in Buffalo is due to his having designed a house in Oak Park, Illinois, for the brother of John D. Larkin, founder of the Larkin Soap Company of Buffalo. Larkin liked his brother's house and brought Wright to Buffalo to design the company headquarters. The Larkin Building, a light, airy masterpiece of commercial architecture, stood on Seneca Street from 1905 until it was unconscionably demolished in 1950. But fate was kinder to the five Buffalo houses built for Larkin Soap Company executives following Wright's arrival in town, all of which survive to this day. Here is a list of the **Frank Lloyd Wright houses** in Buffalo and their locations:

William Heath House, 76 Soldiers Place, corner of Bird Avenue, completed in 1906 and landscaped by Frederick Law Olmsted. (Private; not open to visitors.)

Darwin D. Martin House, 125 Jewett Parkway, corner of Summit Avenue. Also completed in 1906, this expansive home was unfortunately left vacant for seventeen years prior to the mid-1950s, during which time half of

Urban Renewal Strikes Again

When New York City's Pennsylvania Station was torn down, the Times editorialized that we would be remembered not for what we had built but for what we had destroyed.

I have an unusual paperweight that carries the same message. It is a brick from Buffalo's 1905 Larkin Building, a strikingly innovative five-story office structure designed by Frank Lloyd Wright and described by one guidebook as a "mountain peak" of modern architecture. In the best of all possible worlds, the brick would still be in the building, but the Larkin was torn down during that least historically sensitive American decade, the 1950s, to be replaced by a parking lot. I drove out Seneca Avenue when I was in Buffalo one day, and was surprised to find a few crumbling courses of the building's first-floor brickwork in a corner of the lot. I really should mark the thing, so my descendants don't throw it away.

—Bill Scheller

the original Wright windows were lost. It was restored in 1970 by the State University of New York at Buffalo, which uses it for offices. For information regarding tours contact the School of Architecture and Planning, Hayes Hall, 125 Jewett Parkway, Buffalo, (716) 856–3858. Tour schedules vary with seasons. Tours last one hour, except for two-hour in-depth tours offered on the fourth Saturday of each month at 11:00 A.M. Prices for tours are $10.00 for adults, $8.00 for students; in-depth tour charge is $18.00. The George Barton House is included in all tours.

George Barton House, 118 Summit Avenue, is a smaller brick structure with distinctive top-story casement windows and a broad roof overhang built in 1903–4.

Gardener's Cottage, Martin Estate, 285 Woodward Avenue. Constructed in 1906, the cottage is one of the few surviving service buildings of the Martin Estate. (Private; not open to visitors.)

Walter Davidson House, 57 Tillinghast Place. With the exception of Darwin Martin's 1926 summer house, built south of the city on a bluff above Lake Erie, the 1909 Davidson House is the last of Wright's Buffalo residences. (Private; not open to visitors.)

From what we know about Frank Lloyd Wright, we can surmise that if he ever caught a client putting a player piano in one of his houses, he would have rapped him across the knuckles with his walking stick. But the perennially old-fashioned machines began to flourish during the first decade of the twentieth century, when Wright was designing his radically modern houses, and they are with us still. Nowadays the most complete line of rolls for player pianos is manufactured and sold by a Buffalo institution called *Q-R-S Music Rolls.*

Q-R-S is one of the last (and oldest) manufacturers of player-piano rolls in the United States, having been founded in 1900 by Melville Clark, the man who perfected the player. During the heyday of the instrument in the 1920s, Q-R-S had plants in New York, Chicago, and San Francisco, but by 1966 only a small facility in the Bronx remained. A new owner bought the company and moved it to Buffalo, where subsequent ownership has kept it.

A piano-roll company like Q-R-S doesn't stay in business simply by cranking out reprints of "Sweet Adeline" and "You Are My Sunshine." Today you can buy rolls for Norah Jones' "Come Away With Me," or Toby Keith's "I Love This Bar," and other tunes penned long after your player was built.

But not all player pianos are antiques. The company is making a device that will enable any piano to play music programmed on special Q-R-S CDs. You can order a copy of the company's current catalog through the mail, but if you're in the area it's a lot more fun to stop in at the factory and make your purchase after taking a tour.

ANNUAL EVENTS IN THE NIAGARA-ALLEGANY REGION

APRIL

Buffalo in Bloom,
Buffalo and Erie County
Botanical Gardens
(716) 827–1574

MAY

G-gauge Train Races,
Holley,
(585) 638–6000

LATE JUNE TO EARLY JULY

Can-Am Arts Festival,
Niagara Falls,
(716) 473–2525

SEPTEMBER

**Niagara County "Fall Classic"
Fishing Derby,**
Lake Ontario,
(800) 338–7890

LATE NOVEMBER

International Festival of Lights,
Niagara Falls,
(716) 285–8484

Q-R-S Music Rolls, 1026 Niagara Street, Buffalo, (716) 885–4600, is open Monday through Friday 9:00 A.M. to 4:00 P.M., with tours at 10:00 A.M. and 2:00 P.M. Admission fees, refunded with a purchase, are $2.00 for adults and $1.00 for children.

Just minutes from downtown the *Buffalo Museum of Science* houses an extensive collection of natural science exhibits. The museum was built in the 1920s and features a blend of classic dioramas and modern museum exhibitry. A stunning glass-enclosed atrium connects the museum to the Charles R. Drew Science Magnet School, one of the first science magnet schools in the nation to be physically and programmatically linked to a museum.

The museum's main exhibit hall is filled with exciting temporary exhibitions. A visit to the permanent "Dinosaurs & Co." exhibit provides an exciting look at some of the favorite prehistoric giants. "Insect World" features insects six times life-size in two vastly different ecosystems—the cloud forest in the coastal Andean highlands of north central Venezuela and the Niagara frontier region of New York State. Two halls of space provide detailed information about our world and the worlds around us, and observatories provide views of stars, planets, and our sun. The museum also features exhibits on endangered species, zoology, flora and fauna, gems and minerals, and technology. "Camp

Wee Explorers," for kids 2 to 7, offers interactive exhibits focused on discovering the natural world.

The Buffalo Museum of Science is located at 1020 Humboldt Parkway (Best Street exit off the Kensington Expressway), Buffalo, (716) 896–5200. Open Thursday through Saturday, and on Monday of Presidents Day and Columbus Day weekends, from 10:00 A.M. to 5:00 P.M. and Sunday noon to 5:00 P.M. Closed January 1, July 4, Thanksgiving, and Christmas. Admission is $7.00 for adults, $6.00 for seniors, and $5.00 for students and children 3 to 18.

The Buffalo Museum of Science also operates *Tifft Nature Preserve* just 3 miles from downtown. Billed as an "Urban Nature Sanctuary," the preserve is a 264-acre habitat for animal and plant life, dedicated to environmental education and conservation. With miles of hiking trails, three boardwalks, and a self-guided nature trail, it's a wonderful place to spend the day hiking or fishing. For bird-watchers there's a 75-acre freshwater cattail marsh with viewing blinds. In winter the preserve rents snowshoes. "Wellness Walks" are offered on Thursday at 10:00 A.M. The Makowski Visitor Center has some wonderful exhibits on ecology, animals, and plant life.

The Tifft Nature Preserve, 1200 Fuhrmann Boulevard, Buffalo, (716) 825–6397 or 896–5200, is open daily from dawn to dusk; the Makowski Visitor Center is open November to April, Thursday through Saturday 10:00 A.M. to 4:00 P.M.; May to October, Wednesday through Saturday 9:00 A.M. to 4:00 P.M. Closed New Year's, Thanksgiving, Christmas Eve, and Christmas Day. There is no admission charge, but donations are appreciated.

The *Burchfield-Penney Art Center* exhibits the largest and most comprehensive collection of the works of Charles E. Burchfield, one of the country's foremost watercolorists, as well as the works of other western New York artists. The center, which serves the community as a multifaceted cultural and educational institution, also hosts numerous special exhibitions throughout the year.

One of the center's exhibits, "Access to Art," uses a unique assortment of interpretive tools such as hands-on art activities, interviews with artists, tactile works, and library resources to give visitors of all ages the skills to enjoy a museum without feeling intimidated.

The Burchfield-Penney Art Center, Rockwell Hall, Buffalo State College, 1300 Elmwood Avenue, Buffalo, (716) 878–6011, is open Tuesday through Saturday from 10:00 A.M. to 5:00 P.M. and Sunday from 1:00 to 5:00 P.M.; closed major holidays. Admission is $5.00 for adults, $4.00 for seniors, and $3.00 for students and children over age 3.

Cemeteries are not often thought of as places to go to for fun, but *Forest Lawn* is not a typical cemetery; it's more like a city park. The final resting place of prominent Buffalonians such as Red Jacket, the Seneca orator, and

Millard Fillmore, the country's thirteenth president, is also a nature sanctuary, with 6,000 trees and 157 species of birds.

At this cemetery you'll *know* for whom the bell tolls: Upon request, attendants will ring the 6-foot, 3,000-pound solid bronze Oishei bell cast in France. Other highlights include the Blocher monument, with life-size figures carved in Italian marble, and numerous unique monuments and mausoleums.

Sundays in June, July, and August, the staff offers free tours. Several of the interred, such as President Fillmore, make guest appearances during the hour-long bus and walking tours that relate the cemetery's history. (Tours are not given in inclement weather.) Advance reservations are required.

Forest Lawn Cemetery & Garden Mausoleums, 1411 Delaware Avenue at Delavan, Buffalo, (716) 885–1600, is open daily 8:30 A.M. to 6:00 P.M. in spring and summer; until 5:00 P.M. fall and winter.

Mark Twain aficionados will want to visit the **Buffalo & Erie County Public Library**'s Grosvenor Rare Book Room. Among the thousands of manuscripts and first editions dating back to the fifteenth century is the original manuscript of *The Adventures of Huckleberry Finn*. The room also contains other mementos of Twain, a one-time Buffalo resident.

Buffalo & Erie County Public Library, Lafayette Square, Buffalo, (716) 858–8900; call for hours.

Those buffalo-style chicken wings really were invented in Buffalo—at the **Anchor Bar and Restaurant,** which has been serving them up with celery and blue cheese dip since 1964. The restaurant has a reputation for good food, moderate prices, and large portions. It's at 1047 Main Street, (716) 886–8920.

Sample the city's other local specialty—beef on 'weck—at **Anderson's** or at **Charlie the Butcher;** both have several branches in the area.

More than 400 rare and unique bicycles and thousands of cycling-related collectibles span more than 185 years of bicycling history at the **Pedaling History Bicycle Museum,** the world's largest of its kind.

Among the exhibits are a reproduction of the very first bicycle (made in 1817), an Irish Mail four-wheel velocipede, some "boneshakers" dating back to the 1860s, a pneumatic highwheel safety American Star, an 1881 Marine bicycle and an electric bike from the year 2000. There are also extensive bicycle stein and lamp collections and ample photo opportunities.

The Pedaling History Bicycle Museum, 3943 North Buffalo Road (Routes 277 and 240), Orchard Park, (716) 662–3853, is open Monday through Saturday 11:00 A.M. to 5:00 P.M. and Sunday 1:30 to 5:00 P.M.; closed Tuesday through Thursday from January 15 to April 1. Admission is $6.00 for adults, $5.40 for seniors, $3.75 for children ages 7 to 15, and $17.50 for a family of up to four

It May Be the "Real Thing"

The Buffalo chicken wings recipe below is reputed to be the genuine Anchor Bar version—but only they know for sure, and they're not talking. In any event, it sure is good:

6 tablespoons Durkee's Hot Sauce

½ stick margarine

1 tablespoon white vinegar

⅛ teaspoon celery seed

⅛ to ¾ teaspoon cayenne pepper

¼ teaspoon Worcestershire sauce

1 to 2 teaspoons Tabasco sauce

dash of black pepper

Mix ingredients in a small saucepan over low heat until margarine melts, stirring occasionally.

Fry wings at 375° F for 12–15 minutes in vegetable or peanut oil.

Drain for a few minutes on a brown paper bag or paper towels, then put them in a bowl. Pour the sauce over them, cover the bowl, and shake it to coat the wings. (An option here is to put the wings on a baking sheet and bake a few minutes for an extra-crispy coating.) Serve with carrot and celery sticks and blue cheese dressing.

Here's a second "authentic" recipe:

1 tablespoon butter

¼ cup Durkee Red Hot Cayenne Pepper Sauce

Melt the butter and combine it with the hot sauce, then follow the directions above. This recipe, however, calls for baking the wings at 350° F for 11–12 minutes.

generations. Write or call for a listing of special free events, including antique bike parades on July 4 and other occasions.

Lake Erie Shore

The southwestern tip of New York State is packed with as eclectic a mix of off-the-beaten-path sights as can be found anywhere. Remember kazoos—those funny little musical instruments you could play just by humming into them? They're still being made in *Eden,* at the *The Original American Kazoo Company Factory, Museum, and Gift Shop.* Established in 1916, it's now the only metal kazoo factory in the world—and it's still making them the same way they were made in 1916. The company used to produce everything from toy flutes and fishing tackle boxes to metal dog beds and peanut vending machines, but in 1965 the demand for kazoos became so great that the firm stopped manufacturing everything else.

The "working museum" at The Original American Kazoo Company, Factory, Museum, and Gift Shop shows how "America's only original musical instrument" is made, chronicles kazoo history, and regales visitors with such fascinating trivia as "'Far, Far Away' is the most requested tune played on the kazoo."

The Original American Kazoo Company, Factory, Museum, and Gift Shop, 8703 South Main Street, Eden, (716) 992–3960 or (800) 978–3444, is open Monday through Saturday 10:00 A.M. to 5:00 P.M., Sunday noon to 5:00 P.M. Self-guided tours can be taken Monday through Thursday from 9:30 A.M. to 2:30 P.M. Closed Thanksgiving, Christmas, New Year's, Memorial Day, Easter, Fourth of July, and Labor Day. Admission is free.

Although it's now just a short hop off I–90, it's easy to imagine how isolated the **Dunkirk Historical Lighthouse** must have been when the lantern in the square, 61-foot tower first began guiding ships into Dunkirk Harbor in 1876. Today an automated light in the tower does the job, and the two-story stick-style keeper's dwelling has been converted into a **Veterans' Park Museum.**

Five of the museum's rooms are devoted to displays of each branch of the military; five are preserved to show how the lighthouse keeper used to live; one is a memorial to the Vietnam era. An exhibit of maritime history and lake freighters is on display in the souvenir store. A separate building displays artifacts from the submarine service and Coast Guard.

Displays on the grounds include a 45-foot lighthouse buoy tender, a 21-foot rescue boat, and Civil War cannons. Visitors can take a tour of the lighthouse tower. An admission fee is charged for grounds tours and tours of the museum.

Dunkirk Historical Lighthouse and Veterans' Park Museum, off Point Drive North, Dunkirk, (716) 366–5050, are open April through June and September through October, Monday, Tuesday, Thursday, Friday, and Saturday, from 10:00 A.M. to 2:00 P.M. with the last tour at 1:00 P.M. July and August the complex is open from 10:00 A.M. to 4:00 P.M., with the last tour at 2:30 P.M. Admission is $5.00 for adults and $2.00 for children ages 4 to 12.

Ready for a little beef on 'weck? Or perhaps a fancier lunch entree, like angel hair pasta with grilled chicken breast or tortellini Provençal? For dinner, how about Dijon-grilled salmon or a filet mignon preparation that might include bacon and smoked gouda? Stop at stately **White Inn** in **Fredonia.** Duncan Hines did, back in the 1930s, and was so taken with the food that he included it in his "Family of Fine Restaurants." Although the restaurant/inn has since undergone several transformations, it still proudly displays the Duncan Hines sign out front. And the building itself encompasses the original Victorian mansion built in 1868 and operated as an inn since 1919.

The White Inn, 52 East Main Street, Fredonia, (716) 672–2103 or (888) FREDONIA for reservations, is open daily year-round. Breakfast and lunch are served Monday through Saturday, and dinner is served nightly. Inn rates, from $69 to $179, include breakfast.

New owners John and Debra Zorazio and Jack and Marlene Gambino have made **Stockton Sales** one of Chautauqua County's favorite antiquing destinations. Casual browsers and serious antiques aficionados alike know that this is the place to look for items ranging from cobalt blue glassware to silver trays to Mikasa Japanese porcelain place settings. But fine tableware is by no means the only reason to cruise the aisles at Stockton Sales. "We've had everything from a harp to a 1930s wicker wheelchair," says John, "and our library is one of our biggest attractions. We've got hardcovers for $2.00, and paperbacks for $1.00, and we're always restocking." The proprietors also run monthly auctions with big lots of antique furniture. Call for dates.

Stockton Sales, 6 Mill Street, Stockton, (716) 595–3516, is open 10:00 A.M. to 6:00 P.M. daily.

Locals dubbed the sixteen-room mansion completed by James McClurg in 1820 "McClurg's Folly." He designed it, made and baked his own bricks, prepared local timber for the interior woodwork, and landscaped the spacious grounds with ornamental trees and shrubs and a water fountain stocked with goldfish.

Today the Chautauqua County Historical Society operates the restored frontier mansion as a museum and library and has filled it with furnishings, fine art, and local artifacts from its collection.

McClurg Museum, Village Park, Routes 20 and 394, **Westfield,** (716) 326–2977, is open Tuesday through Saturday from 10:00 A.M. to 4:00 P.M. Admission is $3.00 for adults, children free.

At the northern tip of Chautauqua Lake in **Mayville,** the people at **Webb's Candy Factory** have been making goat's milk fudge for more than sixty years. The goats are gone from out back now and the milk comes from cans, but the confection is just as rich and creamy as ever, and the chocolate fudge with pecans is a regional taste treat not to be missed. Webb's makes all its candies by hand, using the old-fashioned copper-kettle method, and has added a host of other treats to its repertoire, including "frogs," hard suckers, chocolate bars, divinity, and chocolate clusters. If you own a goat and want to start production, take a short tour of the candy factory between 10:00 A.M. and 4:00 P.M. Monday through Friday.

Webb's Candy Factory, Route 394, Mayville, (716) 753–2161, is open daily year-round. In summer the hours are 10:00 A.M. to 9:00 P.M.; in winter noon to 5:00 P.M. Call for holiday hours.

Chautauqua Lake is also the home of a 122-year-old enterprise that exemplifies the American penchant for self-improvement. The *Chautauqua Institution* gave its name to an endless array of itinerant tent-show lyceums around the turn of the century. A lot of us have forgotten, though, that the original institution is still thriving right where it was founded in 1874. Chautauqua's progenitors were Bishop John Heyl Vincent and the industrialist (and father-in-law of Thomas Edison) Lewis Miller, and their original modest goal was the establishment of a school for Sunday-school teachers. *Chautauqua* grew to become a village unto itself, offering not only religious instruction but a program of lectures and adult-education courses.

The largely secularized Chautauqua of today bears little resemblance to the Methodist camp meeting of a hundred years ago, although services in the major faiths are held daily. The Chautauqua emphasis on culture and mental and spiritual improvement has led to an extensive annual summer calendar of lectures, classical and popular concerts, dramatic performances, and long- and short-term courses in subjects ranging from foreign languages to tap dancing to creative writing. It has its own 30,000-volume library.

To put it simply, Chautauqua is a vast summer camp of self-improvement, a place where you can rock (in chairs) on broad verandas, walk tree-lined streets that have no cars, and listen in on a chamber music rehearsal on your way to lunch.

The season at Chautauqua lasts for nine weeks each summer, but admission is available on a daily, weekend, or weekly basis.

For complete information on facilities and programs, contact Chautauqua Institution, 1 Ames Street, Chautauqua, (716) 357–6200 or (800) 836–ARTS; www.ciweb.org.

Head south along the lake for a few miles to catch a ride on one of the last surviving modes of pioneer transport—the *Bemus Point–Stow Ferry.* The cable-drawn ferry has traversed the "narrows" of the lake at these points for more than 177 years. Unfortunately (or, for animal rights activists, fortunately), the oxen that once pulled the ferry with the aid of a treadmill and manila rope retired quite a while ago. But the pace and charm of the primitive open barge still remain. The six-minute ride debarks from North Harmony.

The Bemus Point–Stow Ferry, Stow (mailing address: 15 Water Street, Mayville 14757), (716) 753–2403, is open from 11:00 A.M. to 9:00 P.M. Saturday and Sunday in June and daily in July and August. Admission is $4.00 per car and $1.00 per person for walk-ons.

The same folks who run the Bemus Point–Stow ferry also offer tours on the **Chautauqua Belle,** one of only six authentic stern-wheel steamboats operating east of the Mississippi. The *Belle* cruises Chautauqua Lake daily from Memorial Day through Labor Day weekends, with departures at 11:00 A.M., 1:15 P.M., and 3:00 P.M. The trips last one-and-a-half hours. Fares are $14.00 for adults, $12.50 with AARP card, and $5.00 for ages 6 to 12; children under 6 are free. For information, call (716) 753–2403, or check the Web at www.chauta uquabelle.com.

Geologists believe that more than 300 million years ago **Panama Rocks**— reputed to be the world's most extensive outcropping of glacier-cut, ocean-quartz conglomerate rock—were islands of gravel and sand amid a vast inland sea that extended west toward what is now Utah. As layer after layer of these materials was deposited, the weight forced the water out, and a natural form of concrete called quartz conglomerate, or pudding stone, was created.

Approximately 165 million years ago, earthquakes and other geological upheavals raised what was to become Panama Rocks to its present altitude of 1,650 feet. The layers fractured, and water, carrying minerals such as iron and lead, seeped into the openings. A scant 10,000 years ago, during the last ice age, a passing glacier widened these fractures, creating thousands of crevices and alley passageways.

Today visitors can thread through these crevices and passageways along a mile-long trail that winds through a world of towering rocks, past cavernous dens and small caves. Most hikers take one-and-a-half hours to follow the route, although the more adventurous can leave the trail and explore at their own pace. Because there are no railings, adults are required to sign a waiver of liability and are warned that the upper part of the trail can be dangerous for children; the lower trail, which has the most dramatic scenery, is safer. Persons under the age of eighteen must be with an adult to enter the rock area. No pets are allowed.

Panama Rocks Scenic Park, 11 Rock Hill Road (County Route 10), **Panama,** (716) 782–2845, is open May 1 through late October, 10:00 A.M. to 5:00 P.M. Admission is $6.00 for adults, $4.00 for ages 13 through 17, $3.00 for children ages 6 to 12, and $4.00 for seniors. There is a picnic area with grills for guests. For more information check its Web site: www.panamarocks.com.

Jamestown, birthplace of one of the country's leading naturalists, is home to his **Roger Tory Peterson Institute of Natural History**, housed in a handsome wood and stone building designed by architect Robert A. M. Stern on twenty-seven acres of woods and meadows.

The institute's mission is to train educators to help children discover the natural world around them. Part of this program involves changing exhibitions of wildlife art and nature photography at the institute, and the public is invited to visit, hike the surrounding trails, and stop in the Butterfly Garden and gift shop.

The Roger Tory Peterson Institute of Natural History, 311 Curtis Street, Jamestown, (716) 665–2473 or (800) 758–6841, is open Tuesday through Saturday 10:00 A.M. to 4:00 P.M. and Sunday 1:00 to 5:00 P.M. Admission is $4.00 for adults, $3.00 for students, and $12.00 for families. The grounds are open daily dawn to dusk.

In *Jamestown,* expansion plans are in the works for a museum that pays homage to a local girl who made good and the husband who helped her rise to fame. The *Lucy-Desi Museum* stands in the heart of the city's theater district, between the Lucille Ball Little Theatre of Jamestown—the largest community theater in New York—and the former Palace Theater, where Lucy went with her grandfather to see vaudeville (it has been renamed the Reg Lenna Civic Center).

Among the exhibits are a computer program with Lucy trivia questions, an audio clip from the *My Favorite Husband* radio show, which preceded *I Love Lucy*, and exclusive clips from *Lucy and Desi: A Home Movie* produced by their daughter, Lucie. The gift shop carries over 600 *I Love Lucy* licensed products. When the expansion is completed, there will be a larger display of memorabilia about Lucy, her roots, and her life.

The Lucy-Desi Museum, 212 Pine Street, Jamestown, (877) LUCY FAN (582–9326) or (716) 484–0800, is open from May through October, Monday through Saturday 10:00 A.M. to 5:30 P.M. and Sunday 1:00 to 5:00 P.M.; November through April, it's open Saturday 10:00 A.M. to 5:30 P.M. and Sunday 1:00 to 5:00 P.M. or by appointment. Admission is $5.00 for adults and $3.50 for children ages 6 to 18 and seniors.

Jones Bakery, across the street from the museum, still makes the Swedish limpa bread that remained one of Lucy's favorites throughout her life. And if you're strolling through downtown Jamestown, look for the three outdoor wall murals depicting scenes from *I Love Lucy*—they're all within walking distance of the museum.

Great music at unbeatable prices draws lovers of gospel, bluegrass, and country to *The Mountain Depot.* Every Sunday between 2:00 and 7:00 P.M. from the end of April through October, families flock to the alcohol-free establishment on a hill above Ellington to hear The Mountain Railroad Band and guest musicians rock the halls. Admission is just $6.00 for adults and free for children under 12. The Depot is on Gerry-Ellington Road, Ellington, (716) 287–2316.

Ellington borders on *Amish Country,* which encompasses several towns to the north and east. The Amish first came to Cattaraugus County from Ohio in 1949. Although they prefer to keep quietly to themselves, they're friendly people who generally welcome questions about their way of life. (They do request, however, that you not photograph them.) There are a number of small shops on Route 62 in the town of **Conewango Valley** that offer products made by, or about, the Amish. **Franklin Graphics** sells Amish photos, books, and postcards. Stop at **Mueller's Valley View Cheese Factory** to sample Swiss cheese and forty other varieties made in Amish country. **Amish Country Fair** carries furniture and crafts.

Allegany Heartland

Salamanca is the only city in the United States located on a Native American reservation; it is also home to the largest park in the state's park system. The **Seneca-Iroquois National Museum** on the Allegany Indian Reservation traces the cultural and historical heritage of the Seneca, known as "Keeper of the Western Door of the Iroquois Confederacy." The museum exhibits collections of artifacts beginning with prehistoric times and re-creates the culture and history of the Seneca people.

The Seneca-Iroquois National Museum, Broad Street Extension, Salamanca, (716) 945–1738, is open November through March, except January, Monday through Friday 9:00 A.M. to 5:00 P.M.; call for hours between April and November. Admission is $4.00 for adults and $2.00 for children.

With 65,000 acres, two 100-acre lakes, and 80 miles of hiking trails, **Allegany State Park,** "the wilderness playground of western New York," is the largest of the state parks. It's a mecca for both summer and winter outdoor enthusiasts. There are lakes for boating and swimming, ballfields, tennis courts, picnic areas, playgrounds, bike paths, and miles of cross-country and snowmobile trails. Rowboats and paddleboats can be rented at the Red House boathouse; you will also find a tent and trailer area, and bicycle rental. The park has seasons for small game, turkey, and deer (archery only). There's an extensive campground as well as more than 370 cabins—163 winterized. Some are "turn-key," offering many amenities.

Allegany State Park, off Route 17, Salamanca, (716) 354–2182 or 354–9121, is open daily year-round. There is an entrance fee of $7.00 per car when the lake is open for swimming, and $6.00 per car when the lake is closed. The gate is closed weekdays off-season.

Before you leave Salamanca, stop at the **Salamanca Rail Museum,** a fully restored passenger depot constructed in 1912 by the Buffalo, Rochester, and Pittsburgh Railroad. The museum uses exhibits, artifacts, and video presentations to re-create an era when rail was the primary means of transportation from city to city.

Salamanca Rail Museum, 170 Main Street, Salamanca, (716) 945–3133, is open Monday through Saturday from 10:00 A.M. to 5:00 P.M. and Sunday from noon to 5:00 P.M.; closed January, February, and March; closed Monday in April, October, November, and December. Admission is free, but donations are welcomed.

It's the pleasant surprises that make traveling off the beaten path rewarding—like discovering that in addition to more than 260 species of rare and unusual trees and herbs and perennial gardens, *Nannen Arboretum* is home to Roanji Temple Stone Garden (an abstract garden of stone and sand) and Amano-Hashidate Bridge (bridge to heaven). The arboretum (716–699–2377 or 800–897–9189) is on Parkside Drive, directly behind Cornell Cooperative Extension, in Ellicottville. It is open daily from dawn to dusk. Donations are welcomed.

Head north on Route 219 a short distance to *Ashford Hollow* to see one of the most unconventional sculpture "gardens" ever. For more than thirty years, local sculptor Larry Griffis has been integrating his art with nature, placing his monumental abstract/representational creations throughout a 400-acre woodland setting/nature preserve. More than 200 of his pieces, most made of steel and between 20 and 30 feet high, are on exhibit at *Griffis Sculpture Park.*

Griffis Sculpture Park

Ten nudes ring a pond, sharing the banks with live swans and ducks. A towering mosquito awaits unwary hikers along one of the 10 miles of hiking trails. Giant toadstools grow in a field, waiting to be climbed on.

Griffis Sculpture Park, Route 219, Ahrens Road, Ashford Hollow (mailing address: 6902 Valley Road, East Otto 14729), (716) 667–2808, is open daily, May through October, from sunup to sundown; closed November through April. Admission to the Mill Valley Site is $5.00 for adults and $3.00 for seniors and students; admission to the Rohr Hill Site is free but donations are welcome. Tours are given by appointment.

About 320 million years ago, river and delta sediments were deposited on the eroded surface of

Devonian shoals. Crystalline igneous and metamorphic rocks with milky quartz veins were exposed, and long transportation of the sediments selectively weathered and eroded the nonquartz minerals.

What all this means is that **Rock City Park** is one of the world's largest exposures of quartz conglomerate (pudding stone), a place where you can wander through crevices and past towering, colorfully named formations like Fat Man's Squeeze, Tepee Rock, and Signal Rock, with its 1,000-square-mile view.

Rock City Park, 505A Route 16 South, **Olean,** (716) 372–7790, is open daily May through October from 9:00 A.M. to 6:00 P.M. Admission is $4.50 for all 12 years and older, $3.75 for seniors, and $2.50 for ages 6 to 12.

If you were heading off to a summer at Chautauqua three generations ago, you would have gotten there by rail—specifically by a steam-hauled train of the Erie, Pennsylvania, or New York Central Railroad. Of course, Amtrak can get you there today (nearest station: Erie, Pennsylvania), but if you want steam, you'll have to head to a nostalgia operation like the **Arcade and Attica Railroad,** headquartered just southeast of Buffalo in **Arcade.**

Maybe *nostalgia* isn't the right word, since the Arcade and Attica is a real working railroad with a healthy freight clientele. But the company's passenger operation is an unabashed throwback, relying for motive power on a pair of circa 1920 coal burners pulling old, open-window steel coaches that once belonged to the Delaware, Lackawanna, and Western. Arcade and Attica passengers enjoy a ninety-minute ride through some of upstate's loveliest farm country, ending right where they started by way of a trip back through time.

The Arcade and Attica Railroad, 278 Main Street, Arcade, (585) 492–3100, operates weekends from Memorial Day through the end of October, with Wednesday and Friday trips during July and August. Special excursions using a diesel engine, including an Easter Bunny run, a Santa Claus Express, and nature ride/hikes are scheduled off-season. Call for information. Tickets cost $10.00 for adults and $7.00 for children ages 3 through 11 and are available at the 278 Main Street office, or in advance by phone using a credit card.

Horse lovers can roll out of bed and onto a mount for a trail ride through the Colden Hills at **Pipe Creek Farm B&B,** a working equine farm. The four-bedroom inn has shared baths (private baths available on request) and an in-ground pool. Rates range from $50 to $125 and include a full country breakfast. In addition to trail rides, owners Phil and Kathy Crone give lessons in hunt seat, stock seat, and saddle seat. In the winter there are 200 acres of cross-country ski trails to enjoy.

Pipe Creek Farm B&B, 9303 Falls Road, **West Falls,** (716) 652–4868, is open all year-round.

One of the most interesting personalities of turn-of-the-century America was a self-made philosopher named **Elbert Hubbard.** In addition to writing a little "preachment" (as he called it) titled "A Message to Garcia" that dealt with the themes of loyalty and hard work, and publishing his views in a periodical called the *Philistine*, Hubbard was famous for having imported the design aesthetic and celebration of handcrafts fostered in England by the artist and poet William Morris. Elbert Hubbard became the chief American proponent of the Arts and Crafts movement, which touted the virtues of honest craftsmanship in the face of an increasing tendency in the late nineteenth century toward machine production of furniture, printed matter, and decorative and utilitarian household objects.

Visually, the style absorbed influences as diverse as art nouveau and American Indian crafts and is familiar to most of us in the form of solid, oaken, slat-sided Morris chairs and the simple "Mission" furniture of Gustav Stickley. Elbert Hubbard not only wrote about such stuff but also set up a community of craftspeople to turn it out—furniture, copper, leather, even printed books. He called his operation The Roycrofters, and it was headquartered on a "campus" in **East Aurora.**

There are several ways the modern traveler can savor the spirit of Elbert Hubbard in modern East Aurora. One is by visiting the **Roycroft Campus,** on South Grove Street. The campus grounds, now a National Historic Site, feature a gift shop, working pottery, art gallery, and several antiques dealers, all housed in Hubbard-era buildings. The site also includes the East Aurora Town Museum, housed in the Town Hall Building—the former Roycroft Campus chapel. For information contact the East Aurora Chamber of Commerce, 431 Main Street, East Aurora 14052, (716) 652–8444 or (800) 441–2881.

Another window on the Roycroft era is the **Elbert Hubbard–Roycroft Museum,** recently located in a 1910 bungalow built by Roycroft craftsmen and now on the National Register of Historic Places. Part of the furnishings, including the superb Arts and Crafts dining room, are original and were the property of centenarian Grace ScheideMantel when she turned the house over to the museum in 1985. (ScheideMantel's husband, George, once headed the Roycroft leather department.) Other Roycroft products on display at the house include a magnificent stained-glass lamp by Roycroft designer Dard Hunter and a saddle custom-made for Hubbard just prior to his death on the torpedoed *Lusitania* in 1915.

There is a wonderful period garden, complete with a sundial and a "gazing ball," maintained by "The Master Gardeners" of the Erie County Cooperative Extension Service.

The Elbert Hubbard–Roycroft Museum (ScheideMantel House), 363 Oakwood Avenue, East Aurora, (716) 652–4735, is open from June 1 to mid-October on Wednesday, Saturday, and Sunday 2:00 to 4:00 P.M.; by appointment the rest of the year. Admission is $5.00 for adults; free for children under 12. Private or group tours also can be arranged, year-round, by appointment.

Elbert Hubbard opened *The Roycroft Inn* in 1903 to accommodate the people who came to visit his Roycroft community of craftsmen. When Hubbard and his wife died in 1915, their son, Elbert II, assumed leadership of the Roycroft enterprises. Beginning in 1938, the ownership of the inn passed from the Hubbard family through a series of owners. In 1986 the inn was granted National Landmark status, and it reopened in 1995 after extensive restorations by the Margaret L. Wendt Foundation.

All of the inn's charm and history have been preserved. Although the suites have all of the modern-day amenities, each has been meticulously restored and furnished with historically accurate elements, including Stickley furniture, Roycroft lamps and wall sconces, and wallpaper in the style of William Morris.

The Roycroft Inn, 40 South Grove Street, East Aurora, (716) 652–5552 (for reservations only, 877–652–5552; www.roycroftinn.com), rents three-, four-, and five-room suites ranging from $120 to $230 a night, including continental breakfast. The restaurant is open for lunch Monday through Saturday, for dinner nightly, and for Sunday brunch.

Toy Town Museum is a must for anybody traveling with kids. The museum/children's activity center displays a large collection of antique toys (including many by local manufacturer Fisher-Price), as well as ToyWorks, a learning center for lots of "hands-on" fun. The museum hosts its annual three-day Toyfest at the end of August.

Toy Town Museum, 636 Girard Avenue, East Aurora, (716) 687–5151, is open Wednesday through Saturday 10:00 A.M. to 4:00 P.M. Donations are welcome.

Before taking leave of East Aurora, we should stop in at the home of one of our least-appreciated presidents, *Millard Fillmore.* Fillmore, who was born in the Finger Lakes town of Genoa in 1800, came to East Aurora to work as a lawyer in 1825. He built this house (the only presidential residence built by the president's own hands, and since moved to its present Shearer Avenue location) on Main Street in the same year and lived here with his wife until 1830. As restored and furnished by previous owners and the Aurora Historical Society, the *Millard Fillmore House National Landmark* contains country furnishings of Fillmore's era, as well as more refined pieces in the Greek Revival, or "Empire," style of the president's early years. A high desk to be used while standing was part of the furnishings in Fillmore's law office; the rear parlor, added in 1930, showcases furniture owned by the Fillmores in later years, when they lived in a Buffalo mansion. The large bookcase was used in the White House during the Fillmore presidency.

The Millard Fillmore House National Landmark (Aurora Historical Society), 24 Shearer Avenue, East Aurora, (716) 652–8875, is open the same times and at the same admission fees as the Elbert Hubbard–Roycroft Museum.

The village of **Wyoming,** settled in the early 1800s, has more than seventy buildings on the Historic Register. Gaslight Village Shops, in the historic landmark district, include the **Gaslight Christmas Shoppe, Silas Newell's Provisions, Eccentricities,** and **Carney's Antiques.** Stop for a cappuccino at the **Gaslight Village Cafe and Pub** or for lunch, dinner, or the night at Wyoming Inn B&B.

If you want to stay a bit out of town, **Hillside Inn,** on forty-eight acres of woods, streams, hills, and ravines, has twelve guest rooms. Built in 1851 as a health spa, the classic Greek Revival mansion serves an innovative American cuisine featuring entrees such as charred yellowfin tuna and sautéed tournedos of beef in a cabernet and black pepper sauce. All vegetables are grown in the inn's organic garden. Rates, which include a continental breakfast, begin at $100 for a room in Hollyhock Cottage and go up to $200 for a room with a whirlpool bath in the mansion. Water from the inn's mineral spring, in use since 1851 without even running dry, is used in whirlpools and for drinking throughout the property. Business customers are most welcome. Hillside Inn is located at 890 East Bethany Road, Wyoming, (585) 495–6800 or (800) 544–2249; www.hillsideinn.com.

We're sure you know in what town Jell-O was invented, but we bet you didn't know there is a museum dedicated to it, and that it's in the oldest house in town. In 1897 the village of **Le Roy** was already known as the Patent Medicine Capital of the world. But it was the gelatinous creation of P. B. Waite, which his wife named Jell-O, that earned it a place in history. Two years later, Mr. Waite sold his recipe to the Genesee Pure Food Company for $450, but it was not until 1964, when Jell-O was sold to the Postum Company (which later became General Foods), that Jell-O ceased being made in Le Roy.

Today, the **Jell-O Gallery,** in the Historic Society's Le Roy House, documents the creation and rise of Bill Cosby's—and America's—favorite dessert. Seven rooms of the 1823 building are furnished with period pieces of the nineteenth century, and there's an extensive exhibit of Morganville redware pottery made here by Fortunatus Gleason, Jr., in the nineteenth century.

The Jell-O Gallery, in the Le Roy House, 23 East Main Street, Le Roy , (585) 768–7433, is open May through October, daily 10:00 A.M. to 4:00 P.M.; November through April, Monday through Friday 10:00 A.M. to 4:00 P.M. Admission is $3.00 for those 12 years of age and older, and $1.50 for children 6 through 11.

Places to Stay in the Niagara-Allegany Region

ALBION

Tillman's Historic Village Inn
Corner Route 104
West & 98
(585) 589–9151

BUFFALO

Beau Fleuve
242 Linwood Avenue
(800) 278–0245

Lord Amherst Motor Hotel
500 Main Street
(800) 544–2200

CHAUTAUQUA

Brasted House B&B
4833 West Lake Road
(888) 753–6205

Athenaeum Hotel
Chautauqua Lake
(800) 821–1881

DUNKIRK

Ramada Four Points Hotel
30 Lakeshore Drive East
(800) 525–8350

ELLICOTTVILLE

Ellicottville Inn
8 Washington Street
(716) 699–2373

WESTFIELD

Westfield House
East Main Road
Route 20
(716) 326–6262

The William Seward Inn
6645 South Portage Road
Route 394
(800) 338–4151

Places to Eat in the Niagara-Allegany Region

BUFFALO

Just Pasta
307 Bryant Street
(716) 881–1888
(more than just pasta)

Il Fiorentino
1264 Hertel Avenue
(716) 447–8889

REGIONAL TOURIST INFORMATION— THE NIAGARA-ALLEGANY REGION

Buffalo-Niagra CVB,
617 Main Street,
Buffalo 14203,
(716) 852–0511
www.visitbuffaloniagara.com

Niagara County Tourism,
139 Niagara Street,
Lockport 14094,
(800) 338–7890
www.niagara-usa.com

Wyoming County Tourist Promotion Agency,
30 North Main Street,
P.O. Box 502,
Castile 13327,
(800) 839–3919

CHEEKTOWAGA

Pranzo
4243 Genesee Street
(Park Plaza Hotel)
(716) 634–2300

ELLICOTTVILLE

The Ellicottville Brewery
28-A Monroe Street
(716) 699–2537

JAMESTOWN

Mac Duff's
317 Pine Street
(716) 664–9414

KENMORE

Hourglass
981 Kenmore Avenue
(716) 877–8788

OLEAN

Old Library Restaurant
& Inn
116 South Union Street
(716) 372–2226

TONAWANDA

Saigon Bangkok
512 Niagara Falls
Boulevard
(716) 837–2115

WILLIAMSVILLE

Tandoori's
7740 Transit Road
(716) 632–1112

OTHER ATTRACTIONS WORTH SEEING IN THE NIAGARA-ALLEGANY REGION

Amherst Museum,
3755 Tonawanda Creek Road,
Amherst,
(716) 689–1440

Artpark,
South Fourth Street,
Lewiston,
(716) 754–9000

Broadway Market,
999 Broadway,
Buffalo,
(716) 893–0705

Colonel William Bond House,
143 Ontario Street,
Lockport,
(716) 434–7433

Davis Memorial Carillon,
Alfred University,
Saxon Drive,
Alfred,
(607) 871–2562

Fredonia Opera House,
9-11 Church Street,
Fredonia,
(716) 679–1891

Lily Dale Assembly,
5 Melrose Park,
Lily Dale 14752,
(716) 595–8721

Lockport Cave and Underground Boat Ride,
21 Main Street,
Lockport,
(716) 438–0174

Maid of the Mist Boat Tour,
151 Buffalo Avenue,
Niagara Falls,
(716) 284–4233
(in season) or 284–4122

Miss Buffalo, Niagara Clipper Cruise Boats,
Erie Basin Marina,
Buffalo,
(800) 244–8684

The Catskills

To many lifelong New York City residents for whom the Adirondacks might as well be the other side of the moon, the Catskills *are* upstate New York. At this point in our travels, we certainly know better—but nevertheless, if you had only a couple of days to get out of the city, the Catskills would be your best bet for a quick introduction to exurban New York.

The Catskills, of course, are "mountains" in the eastern rather than the western sense. Generally lower in elevation than the Adirondacks, these are old, worn peaks, part of the Appalachian Range. The higher elevations are to the north, where the larger ski areas are located. But some of the most dramatic Catskills scenery lies along the west shore of the Hudson, within 30 or 40 miles of the New York City line. Here are the majestic Palisades, brooding cliffs of volcanic basalt exposed by millions of years of water and weather; here also are Bear Mountain, Tallman, and Harriman State Parks, with their thick forests and panoramic views. Farther west are the abrupt cliffs of the Shawangunk Mountains, where some of the world's greatest rock climbers perfect their technique.

A place of mystery to the early Dutch settlers, and later a virtual synonym for a certain style of resort entertainment, the Catskill region has a history as varied as its terrain. We'll start

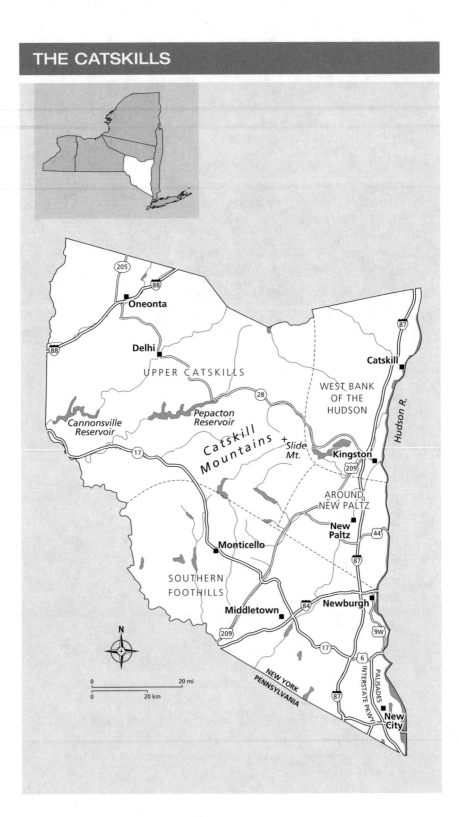

our exploration at the south, near the Hudson, and move north and then west toward the farther hills.

Southern Foothills

During World War II more than 1.3 million soldiers shipped out from Camp Shanks to battle in North Africa and Europe. In its heyday 2,500 buildings sprawled across 1,300 acres; today a small exhibit, vintage training films, and memorabilia at **Camp Shanks WWII Museum** tell the story of the men and women who were processed through here on their way to the front. The museum, on State Routes 303/340, Orangeburg, (845) 638–5419, is open Memorial Day to Labor Day, Saturday and Sunday 10:00 A.M. to 3:00 P.M.

The **Edward Hopper House,** birthplace and boyhood home of the realist painter famous for works such as *Night Hawk,* is now a New York State Historic Site. One room of the home, built in 1858, documents his life and work in Nyack. Three other rooms exhibit works by local artists. Jazz concerts are presented in the restored garden in the summer. The house and gallery, at 82 North Broadway, **Nyack,** (845) 358–0774, is open Thursday through Sunday from 1:00 to 5:00 P.M. in summer. There is a suggested donation of $1.00.

Just about everyone knows where West Point is, but how many Hudson Valley travelers or military buffs can locate Constitution Island? Geographic literalists might look for it in the first chapter of this book, since it's practically on the east shore of the Hudson, separated from the mainland only by marshes. But since visitors have to take a boat to get to the island, and since the boat leaves from West Point, we have it here among our Catskill sites.

Although **Constitution Island** never served any military purpose after the Revolutionary War, it had an important part to play in General Washington's

AUTHORS' FAVORITES—CATSKILLS

Catskill Corners Festival Marketplace

Catskill Fly Fishing Center and Museum

Gomez Mill House

Inn at Lake Joseph

Minnewaska State Park Preserve

Onteora, The Mountain House

Saugerties Lighthouse

Slabsides

Sugar Loaf Arts and Craft Village

West Point Washouts

Not everyone is cut out for the rigors of cadet life at West Point. In 1831, after eight months, Edgar Allan Poe was dismissed for insubordination. Artist James A. McNeill Whistler washed out in his third year when he failed chemistry. He later commented, "Had silicon been a gas, I would have been a major general."

strategy for keeping British naval traffic out of the upper Hudson River. During the earlier part of the war, the fortifications on the island were relatively ineffectual; begun in 1775, **Fort Constitution** was still unfinished when it was captured by the British two years later. Largely destroyed by its American defenders before they retreated, the fort was never rebuilt.

By the following year, however, the island was back in American hands and was more valuable than ever in view of its position opposite the new American defenses constructed at West Point. Here was a place where British ships could be stopped dead in the water, and the way to do it was to stretch an immense iron chain across the river from **West Point** to Constitution Island. The chain was forged of stout New Jersey iron (a portion of it can be seen at the state reservation at Ringwood, New Jersey), floated across the river on rafts of logs, and securely anchored at either shore. Three redoubts and a battery were constructed on Constitution Island to protect the eastern end of the chain.

The chain did its job, and Constitution Island saw no further hostilities throughout the remaining five years of the war.

Constitution gained fame in the nineteenth century as the home of the Warner sisters, Susan (1819–85) and Anna (1824–1915). Under pseudonyms the two sisters wrote a total of 106 books, collaborating on 18 of them. Part of the present-day tour of the island is a visit to the **Warner House,** fifteen rooms of which are furnished in the Victorian style of the Warner sisters' heyday.

Constitution Island is open to guided two-hour tours from late June through September. Boats leave West Point South Dock Wednesday and Thursday afternoons at 1:00 and 2:00 P.M., and reservations are required. Fare and admission to the house and fort are $10.00 for adults, senior citizens, students, and children 6 and over; $6.00 for children 3 to 5. For information contact the Constitution Island Association, Box 41, West Point 10996, (845) 446–8676.

You'll have to ask for directions for the abandoned **West Point Foundry** in **Cold Spring.** It's tucked well off the beaten path in a swath of woods bordering the eighty-five-acre Foundry Cove Historic Preserve, a fragile marsh environment owned by the Scenic Hudson Land Trust. But if you have a penchant for old, abandoned buildings with stories to tell, it's worth the search.

The foundry was opened here in 1816 to manufacture heavy ordnance for the government. But over the years other products were forged here as well, including the "Best Friend," the first railroad engine manufactured in the United States; and ornamental iron fronts for buildings in New York City and Troy. Robert P. Parrott, the foundry's superintendent, invented the Parrott gun while working here (there's a replica of it on the waterfront across from the Hudson House).

After the Depression the foundry floundered under a succession of owners, finally to close for good. Today efforts are underway to preserve the handsome, brick 1865 office building, "proudly wearing its cupola from which the Foundry bell regulated the lives of the residents of Cold Spring."

For insight into the foundry (and directions), visit the excellent ***Putnam Historical Society Museum,*** 63 Chestnut Street, Cold Spring, (845) 265–4010. It's open Tuesday through Thursday 10:00 A.M. to 4:00 P.M., and Saturday and Sunday 2:00 to 5:00 P.M.; closed January and February.

Manitoga, Algonquin for "Place of the Great Spirit," was the home of Russel Wright, one of the country's foremost designers of home furnishings and a proponent of American design. His designs reflected his love of natural, organic shapes, and he would extend this respect for the earth and nature to the grounds where he built his home, Dragon Rock.

When he bought the property for his home in 1942, it had been damaged by 150 years of logging and quarrying. Over the next 30 years, Mr. Wright worked to restore the land, designing a living theater—a carefully designed backdrop of native trees, ferns, mosses, and wildflowers that appears as if it grew naturally.

A Magnifico's Bequest

Harriman, the town, and Harriman State Park, a unit of the Palisades Interstate Park system, are now just names on the map to most travelers and New Yorkers alike—if anything, people tend to associate them with the late diplomat and one-time New York governor W. Averill Harriman. But the town and the park were named for the governor's father, E.H. Harriman, at one time the most powerful railroad baron in the United States. Edward Henry Harriman (1848–1909) controlled some 60,000 miles of American railways, including the Union Pacific. The present-day park consists of much of the 20,000-acre estate he acquired northwest of New City, and which he left to his wife with the intention that it would one day be transferred to state ownership.

ANNUAL EVENTS IN THE CATSKILLS

MAY

Irish Festival,
East Durham,
(800) 434–FEST

JULY

Peaceful Valley Bluegrass Festival,
Shinhopple,
(607) 363–2211 or 746–2281

AUGUST

Colonial Street Festival,
New Paltz,
(845) 255–1660

International Celtic Festival,
Hunter,
(518) 263–4223

Danial Nimham International Pow Wow,
Carmel,
(800) 470–4854

SEPTEMBER

Blues 2000 and Beyond Music Festival and Craft Fair,
Monticello,
(800) CONCORD

Great Catskill Mountain Quilt Show,
Windham,
(800) SKI–WINDHAM or (518) 734–4300

OCTOBER

Oktoberfest,
Hunter,
(518) 263–4223

A year before he died, the designer-naturalist opened his land to the public, and today programs at Manitoga teach ecology, science, art, and design. Visitors are invited to wander several one-way paths that Mr. Wright designed as journeys into the secrets of the forest. In building each, he would study the landscape and the land's natural contour to determine its direction. The main path passes by his home, designed to blend into the landscape of the quarry.

The grounds of Manitoga, P.O. Box 249, Route 9D, *Garrison* 10524, (845) 424–3812, are open from April through October, Monday through Friday 9:00 A.M. to 4:30 P.M. and Saturday and Sunday 10:00 A.M. to 6:00 P.M. The grounds are open the rest of the year on weekdays only. Ninety-minute tours of Dragon Rock, Mr. Wright's home built on the rock lege of an abandoned quarry, and of the woodland gardens, are given daily in season at 11:00 A.M. Visitors can take self-guided hikes on weekdays from 9:00 A.M. to 4:00 P.M.; and weekends from 10:00 A.M. to 6:00 P.M. April through October. A donation is requested if visitors hike the grounds. Admission for the tour is $15 (call for times).

In the 1830s John Jaques emigrated from Europe to the small town of *Washingtonville.* Trained as a shoe-and bootmaker, he planned to support himself with his trade. To augment his income he purchased ten acres of land on Main Street and planted grapes in the rich, loamy Hudson Valley soil to sell at market. When he became a church elder, he used some of his grapes to make sacramental wine.

Today **Brotherhood** is America's oldest winery, and the church where Mr. Jaques's wine was first served is the winery's gift shop. Brotherhood has been making wine continuously since 1839, having survived Prohibition by once again reverting to the sale of sacramental wine. Its vast underground cellars, comparable to those of famous European wineries, are the largest in the country and, in addition to sacramental wine, Brotherhood now makes specialty, table, dessert, and premium vintage wines, including Grand Monarque champagne. A tour of the winery includes a visit to the underground cellars and a sampling of a half-dozen wines.

Brotherhood, 100 Brotherhood Plaza, Washingtonville 10992, (845) 496–3661, offers guided half-hour wine-tasting tours daily at 1:00 P.M. and 3:00 P.M.; weekends only in January. The store is open from 11:00 A.M. to 5:00 P.M. Admission is $5.00 per person (free for those under 15). Call for a calendar of weekend events.

Orange County is known for its fine standardbred horses—the horses of the harness track. Hambletonian, sire of virtually all of today's trotters, was born here. For years it has been home to the Trotting Horse Museum, Home of the Hall of Fame of the Trotter, now officially the **Harness Racing Museum & Hall of Fame.**

Visitors to the museum can experience the thrill of harness racing—without the horse. Part of the museum's recent $3-million renovation included the

Harness Racing Museum & Hall of Fame

installation of the world's only "Thrill of Harness Racing 3-D Simulator." Participants sit on a twelve-seat motion-based platform (there are six stationary seats for those who want to see the film but not experience the motion) and watch a film that utilizes a variety of advanced techniques to create what amounts to a virtual harness race.

There are a host of other activities and exhibits, including the opportunity to call and judge a race, and a historic collection of photographs, ephemera, and fine art.

The Harness Racing Museum & Hall of Fame, 240 Main Street, **Goshen,** (845) 294–6330, is open daily from 10:00 A.M. to 6:00 P.M. except Christmas, Thanksgiving, and New Year's. Admission is $7.50 for adults, $6.50 for seniors, and $3.50 for children 6 to 12.

Across the way is *Goshen Historic Track,* the oldest active harness track in the country and the first sporting site in the nation to be designated a National Registered Historic Landmark by the National Park Service.

The hamlet of *Sugar Loaf* has enjoyed a reputation as a crafts community for more than 250 years. Today more than fifty artisans live and work in the original barns and buildings, creating a variety of goods ranging from stained glass to pottery to hand-tooled leather products. Visitors are invited to watch the artists at work in their studios and browse through a variety of specialty and gift shops peppered throughout the town.

There is an extensive program of concerts, festivals, and special events at *Sugar Loaf Arts and Craft Village* throughout the year. The 700-seat theater, Lycian Center (www.lycian.com/centre), offers a venue for performances by national and international touring companies in Broadway musicals, drama, dance, concerts, and children's shows.

Sugar Loaf Arts and Craft Village, Sugar Loaf Chamber of Commerce, Inc., P.O. Box 125, Sugar Loaf 10981, (845) 469–9181, is open year-round. Days and hours vary from shop to shop; request a brochure from the Chamber of Commerce or visit www.sugarloafartsvillage.com on the Internet.

The next time you eat an onion, consider this: It might well have been grown in black dirt formed 12,000 years ago in a glacial lake in an area now known as *Pine Island.* As the glaciers melted and the climate warmed, vegetation grew, died, and sank to the bottom of the lake. The lake area earned the nickname "the drowned lands" and remained a swamp until the early 1900s, when immigrants came, bought the land cheap, drained the lake by hand, built drainage ditches, and then planted onions in the rich black dirt. Today, with thousands of acres planted, the "black dirt" region is one of the country's leading producers of onions.

The cream of onion soup at *Ye Jolly Onion Inn* is made from Pine Island onions. So are the deep-fried onion blossoms, the onion rings, and the onion gravy on the Pine Island steak. And the vegetables on the salad bar are all from farms in the area (in season). After a visit to the "black dirt" region and Ye Jolly Onion Inn, you'll never again think lightly of the humble onion.

Ye Jolly Onion Inn, corner of Route 517, Pulaski Highway and Orange County Route 1, Pine Island, (845) 258–4277, is open Wednesday and Thursday 5:00 to 9:00 P.M., Friday and Saturday 5:00 to 10:00 P.M., and Sunday noon to 7:30 P.M.

If your interest in horses has been piqued by the Harness Racing Museum & Hall of Fame, head over to *New Hope Farms Equestrian Park* in *Port Jervis.* With eighty acres it's one of the largest equestrian facilities in the nation and features indoor and outdoor arenas and permanent stabling for one hundred horses. Visitors are invited to stop by at any time to watch thoroughbreds and warmbloods being trained for show jumping competitions.

Throughout the year there are events such as a tri-state rodeo, a family festival, polo matches, and a championship dressage; musical events are also presented. The indoor arena, which seats 2,500, is one of the largest in the country.

New Hope Farms Equestrian Park, 500 Neversink Drive, Port Jervis, (845) 856–8384, is open daily year-round from 8:00 A.M. to 5:00 P.M. From the end of January through March 15, most of the horses are moved south and there's very little activity. For a list of events, check www.webusers.warwick.net.

The *Inn at Lake Joseph* is a Victorian country estate high in the Catskill Mountains. It nestles against a 250-acre lake and is surrounded by thousands of acres of forest and wildlife preserve.

Built by Thomas Hunt Talmadge in the latter part of the nineteenth century, the estate served as a retreat for the Dominican Sisters, as a vacation home of Cardinals Hayes and Spellman of New York, and finally as a sumptuous inn.

What Next—Backward Baseball Caps?

Toward the end of the nineteenth century, in the community of millionaires' estates called Tuxedo Park in the Ramapo Mountains near the New Jersey border, daring young fashion plates scandalized their elders by abandoning traditional full evening dress with its cutaway tailcoats in favor of a shorter black jacket with the cut of an informal suit coat. Despite initial resistance the new style caught on, and the new semiformal uniform, complete with matching black trousers, came to be known as the tuxedo.

Rooms are available in the Manor, the Carriage House, and The Cottage. Several of the inn's ten guest rooms in the Manor have working fireplaces and whirlpool baths. If you yearn for even more privacy, request a room in the recently restored turn-of-the-century Adirondack-style Carriage House (where pets are welcome). Each has its own entrance, a working fireplace, and a whirlpool bath. Some have lofted ceilings and private sundecks. Pets are also welcome in The Cottage, which has three rustic, Adirondack–style guest rooms with stone fireplaces, full kitchens, whirlpool baths, and private sundecks. Meals are served, and there are plenty of outdoor sporting activities, including paddling around in a Victorian-style swimming pool. Lake Joseph has a reputation as one of the finest largemouth bass lakes in the state.

Inn at Lake Joseph, 400 St. Joseph Road, *Forestburgh,* (845) 791–9506, www.innatlakejoseph.com, is open year-round. Weekend rates range from $170 to $385. There is a $20-per-day fee for pets.

From December through March (eagle time), Sullivan County becomes home to a large concentration of migrant *bald eagles*—mostly from Canada. A few of their favorite nesting places include Mongaup Falls Reservoir and Rio Reservoir in Forestburgh and the Rondout Reservoir in Grahamsville. For an update and complete list of sites, contact the *Audubon Society of New York State,* P.O. Box 111, *Eldred* 12732, (845) 557–8025.

Getting from one place to another quickly and with panache is an American preoccupation. In the nineteenth century a fast trotting horse might have done the trick; in the twenty-first we have the option of zipping along on or off the ground. If you like the idea of slipping silently through the air and didn't get your chance at the National Soaring Museum in Elmira, you'll find another opportunity in the southern Catskills at *Wurtsboro Airport.*

Established in 1927, *Wurtsboro* bills itself as the oldest soaring site in the nation. The airport's Flight Service is the largest soaring school in the United States, offering lessons for people with no flight experience as well as for those licensed to fly power planes. For the casual visitor, however, the big attraction is the demonstration rides. After being towed aloft by a single-engine Cessna, you'll glide high above the Catskills with an FAA-rated commercial pilot at the stick. The demonstration ride lasts fifteen to twenty minutes and costs $50. For $10 more you can turn your joyride into an introductory lesson. Be sure to call in advance for a reservation.

Wurtsboro Airport and Flight Service, Route 209, Wurtsboro, (845) 888–2791, is open daily all year from 8:30 A.M. to 6:00 P.M. or dusk (weather permitting), whichever comes first. Closed major holidays.

According to the folks at *Memories,* buyers searched five states and three countries to fill their 20,000-square-foot building with more than 25,000 unique items covering every style and taste from the early 1800s to the 1950s. Stock includes furniture, lamps, clocks, rocking horses, decoys, glass, china, magazines, and, as they say, "who knows what's coming in?"

Memories, Route 17 Quickway, **Parksville,** (845) 292–4270, is open daily year-round from 10:00 A.M. to 5:00 P.M.

Many devotees of fly-fishing believe that, in North America, the sport began in the Catskills. And seeing the streams that run along the Beaverkill and Willowemoc Valleys, it's hard to imagine a more suitable birthplace—or a more suitable location for a center devoted to preserving the heritage and protecting the future of fly-fishing in the United States. That's the mission of the **Catskill Fly Fishing Center and Museum/Hall of Fame,** on the shores of the Willowemoc River between Roscoe and Livingston Manor.

Founded in 1891, the new facility, which opened in May 1995, illuminates the contributions and lives of the great names associated with the Catskill era—Gordon and Hewitt, Dette and Darbee, LaBranche and Flick—as well as Lee Wulff, Poul Jorgensen, and others from the world of fly-fishing. Interpretive exhibits on the evolution of the sport, as well as hundreds of meticulously crafted rods, flies, and reels are on display. Special guest fly tyers demonstrate their craft every Saturday afternoon throughout the season. The center offers a variety of educational and recreational programs year-round, including courses in stream ecology and angling, fly tying, and rod building.

Catskill Fly Fishing Center and Museum/Hall of Fame, 1031 Old Route 17, **Livingston Manor,** (845) 439–4810, is open daily 10:00 A.M. to 4:00 P.M. from April through October; Tuesday through Friday 10:00 A.M. to 1:00 P.M.; and Saturday 10:00 A.M. to 4:00 P.M. Call for off-season hours. Closed holidays. A $3.00 donation is requested.

Feeling stressed? Consider escaping for a peaceful weekend at **Dai Bosatsu Zendo,** a Zen Buddhist monastery on 1,400 acres in the Catskill Mountain Forest Preserve. All are welcome here, whether it be for a three-day weekend for novices who want to learn basics, such as sitting, breathing, and chanting; a longer stay for those steeped in the way of Rinzai Zen Buddhism; or even those just looking for an overnight retreat. The grounds are open to day visitors March through November.

As expected, accommodations are simple but comfortable and include three vegetarian meals a day. Rooms with private and shared baths are available. Rates for the three-day weekend begin at under $200.

Dai Bosatsu Zendo, 15 Beecher Lake Road, Livingston Manor 12758, (845) 439–4566, requests that guests reserve at least two weeks in advance. A schedule of programs is available on its Web site: www.daibosatsu.org.

More than one hundred varieties of cheese and fifty flavors of jelly beans make **The Cheese Barrel** a popular stop for kids of all ages. The shop specializes in gourmet goodies and breads from Bread Alone. The old stockroom has been turned into an ice-cream parlor, and the dining area serves continental breakfasts and light lunches with homemade soups, salads, and sandwiches. The latest innovation: an espresso bar.

The Cheese Barrel, corner of Main and Bridge Streets, *Margaretville,* (845) 586–4666, is open daily. The ice-cream parlor is open until 8:00 p.m.; later during the summer.

Around New Paltz

The 90,000-acre Northern Shawangunk mountain range, whose cliffs, summits, and plateaus are home to almost forty rare plant and animal species, has been designated a "Last Great Place on Earth" by the Nature Conservancy.

Minnewaska State Park Preserve, high in the Shawangunk Mountains, is an outdoor paradise of hiking trails, waterfalls, and scenic vistas. A network of carriageways accessible to bicyclists, hikers, and horseback riders links many of the park's major highlights. It will require a hike of approximately 3 miles, however, to reach one of the park's greatest draws: lovely Lake Awosting, a mile-long swimming lake rimmed by pine trees. Although it's a popular spot on a hot summer day (a lifeguard is on duty), those used to the crowds at ocean beaches will feel almost as if they're at a private party. For the less ambitious there's also swimming at the more accessible Lake Minnewaska, nestled amid white sandstone cliffs (it's easy to see why the Indians named it "floating waters").

Minnewaska State Park Preserve, off Route 44/55, New Paltz, (914) 255–0752, is open year-round. There is a $5.00 daily admission fee for cars from mid-June through Labor Day, and a $4.00 fee weekends and holidays off-season.

Not far from Minnewaska is a 4,600-acre tract of land that contains one of the world's best examples of a ridgetop dwarf pine barrens: *Sam's Point Dwarf Pine Ridge Preserve*. According to the Nature Conservancy, managers of the barrens, one of Earth's most endangered ecosystems thrives here for several reasons: "limited water during the growing season; exposure to direct sun and wind; shallow, highly erodible soils; and the regular occurrence of fires. All of these processes, and perhaps yet unknown factors, have historically worked together to shape the plant and animal communities that thrive there today."

Several trails wind through the preserve. One of the most popular, Verkeerderkill Falls/Long Path, meanders through the barrens to the falls and offers panoramic views to the southeast.

For information contact the Nature Conservancy, Eastern New York Chapter, 200 Broadway, Third Floor, Troy 12180, (518) 272–0195.

In 1714 Louis Moses Gomez, a refugee from the Spanish Inquisition, purchased 6,000 acres of land along the Hudson highlands and built a fieldstone blockhouse. Today the **Gomez Mill House** is the earliest surviving Jewish residence in North America.

Over the ensuing years subsequent owners of the house made changes to the original structure. The most famous twentieth-century owner was the Craftsman-era designer Dard Hunter, who rebuilt the old gristmill on "Jew's Creek" into a paper mill and then made paper by hand, cut and cast type, and hand-printed his own books.

Today the house, continuously inhabited for more than 280 years, is preserved by the Gomez Foundation for Mill House; the foundation is made up of friends and descendants of families who lived here.

The Gomez Mill House, Mill House Road, **Marlboro,** (845) 236–3126, is open from the Wednesday after Easter and Passover through October, Wednesday through Sunday 10:00 A.M. to 4:00 P.M., with tours at 10:00 and 11:30 A.M. and 1:00 and 2:30 P.M. Admission is $5.00 for adults, $3.50 for seniors, and $2.00 for students. On Sundays the museum sponsors a lecture series. Check its Web site for a calendar: www.gomez.org.

The gristmill at **Tuthilltown Gristmill & Country Store** has been grinding flour and meal without interruption since 1788! The historic landmark was grinding while Napoleon fought in Austria . . . grinding through the War of 1812 . . . grinding when Abraham Lincoln and John F. Kennedy were shot . . . grinding when this book went to press. . . . Little has changed over the years, but a store at the rear of the building now sells stone-ground flours and grains, pancake and waffle mixes, and a host of other baking ingredients and gift items.

Tuthilltown Gristmill & Country Store, 1020 Albany Post Road, Gardiner, (845) 255–5695, is open all year, Tuesday through Sunday 8:00 A.M. to 6:00 P.M.

Tuthilltown Gristmill & Country Store

Back in the old Hudson Valley town of New Paltz, we encounter one of those odd superlatives—something you might never have devoted a moment's curiosity to but that is nonetheless fascinating once discovered. This is **Huguenot Street,** the oldest street in America that still has its original houses. Think about it: Find a street where each building lot has had only one house upon it, and chances are you're in a modern subdivision. But the stone houses on Huguenot Street were built between 1692 and 1712, and they'll look good for at least another 300 years.

Persecuted by the Catholic majority in their native France and displaced by the incessant religious warfare of the seventeenth century, many Huguenots—peaceful members of a Protestant sect—came to southern New York in pursuit of freedom and tolerance. In 1677 twelve of their number purchased the lands around present-day New Paltz from the Esopus Indians and built log huts as their first habitations.

As the twelve pioneers and their families prospered, they decided to build more permanent dwellings. And permanent they were. Here are five perfectly preserved houses, with additions that were built by the settlers' descendants over the years. All of the houses are maintained by the Huguenot Historical Society, which gives tours Tuesday through Sunday from May 1 through October 31.

Tours of the houses are available for $10.00 for adults, $9.00 for students and seniors, $5.00 for ages 6 to 17; free for under 5. Family rate is $24.00. For information contact the Huguenot Society, 18 Broadhead Avenue, New Paltz, (845) 255–1660 or 255–1889.

Just north of New Paltz, at High Falls, is a museum dedicated to a great work of engineering brought about because of an energy crisis. No, this one had nothing to do with OPEC or Iranian crude—it was the crisis in coal supply brought about by America's 1812–14 war with Great Britain. Two Wurts brothers, Maurice and William, figured that a canal was the way to bring Pennsylvania anthracite (hard coal) from the mines to New York City and vicinity, thus avoiding future shortages brought about by depending on foreign suppliers.

The two men formed the Delaware and Hudson Canal Company in 1825, with the stated purpose of linking Honesdale, Pennsylvania, with the Hudson River port of Eddyville, New York. The surveying and engineering of the 108-mile route was handled by Benjamin Wright, chief engineer of the Erie Canal. The Delaware and Hudson Canal, completed in 1828, was the first million-dollar enterprise in America. Between 1847 and 1852 it was enlarged and deepened to accommodate heavier traffic. A lot of coal came down in barges along the old route, but the company that built it made a bold move in 1829 that would soon doom canals and the way of life they represented. In that year the company began to work its gravity-operated rail line between Honesdale and Carbondale, Pennsylvania, with a new English contraption called a steam locomotive. Except for a few weedy stretches, the canal is gone, but the Delaware and Hudson Railroad survives to this day as the oldest transportation company in the United States.

The **Delaware and Hudson Canal Museum** is a private institution established to tell the story of the old canal, and it does so not merely through glassed-in exhibits but by preserving the extant structures, channel, and locks in the **High Falls** vicinity. Visitors learn about the canal through sophisticated dioramas, photos, and technological exhibits, including models of a working lock and gravity railroad. There are five locks at High Falls. The Delaware and Hudson Canal Historical Society has done whatever restoration and preservation work is possible on them and has linked canal sites in the area with a system of hiking trails. Self-guided tours take in nearby canal segments as well as the remains of John Roebling's suspension aqueduct.

The Delaware and Hudson Canal Museum, Mohonk Road, High Falls (845) 687–9311, is open May through October, Thursday, Friday, Saturday, and Monday 11:00 A.M. to 5:00 P.M., and Sunday 1:00 to 5:00 P.M. Admission is $3.00 for adults, $1.00 for children.

Chef John Novi, heralded as "The Father of American Nouvelle Cuisine" by *Time Magazine,* prepares appetizers such as quail cutlet with hazelnut crust, and entrees such as rare venison medallions with maitake mushroom risotto and roast poussin with truffle mashed potato, in his restored, 1797 stone tavern on the Delaware and Hudson Canal.

Originally built to serve canal workers, the **Depuy Canal House** still has its original fireplaces and wooden floors, and diners are invited to watch meals being cooked from the second-floor balcony that overlooks the kitchen.

Chef Novi offers a variety of meal options, including an a la carte menu, a four-course dinner for $60, and a seven-course dinner for $75.

Those looking for a weekend getaway won't have to travel far after dinner: The **Locktender's Cottage** next to the restaurant offers a variety of comfortable accommodations, including the Chef's Quarters, with a Jacuzzi for two and a kitchenette.

The Depuy Canal House, Route 213, High Falls, (845) 687–7700, is open for dinner Thursday through Sunday and for Sunday brunch. Reservations are highly recommended.

The prodigious industrial expansion made possible by canals and railroads in the America of the nineteenth century was often accomplished at the expense of the natural environment, a phenomenon that persists in our own day. Fortunately the 1800s also produced great pioneers of the conservationist spirit, whose writings and example point the way for those who continue their struggle today. Among them, of course, are the Californian John Muir and his equally dedicated, near-contemporary John Burroughs, a native New Yorker who wrote twenty-five books on natural history and the philosophy of conservation. In 1895 Burroughs built a rustic log hideaway in the woods outside the village of **West Park,** barely 2 miles from the west bank of the Hudson. He called it *Slabsides,* and it is a National Historic Landmark today.

Burroughs, whose permanent home was only a mile and a half away, came to his little retreat to write and to quietly observe his natural surroundings. John Muir came here to talk with Burroughs, as did Theodore Roosevelt and Thomas Edison. They sat around the fire on log furniture of Burroughs's own manufacture, much of it still in the cabin.

Slabsides, which was deeded to the John Burroughs Association after the author's death in 1921, now stands within the 191-acre *John Burroughs Sanctuary,* a pleasant woodland tract that forms a most fitting living monument to his memory. The sanctuary is open all year; on the third Saturday in May and the first Saturday in October, the John Burroughs Association holds an open house from noon to 4:00 P.M. In addition to an opportunity to see the cabin, the special days include informal talks and nature walks. Admission is free. The sanctuary has 2½ miles of hiking trails open to the public daily from dawn to dusk. For further information write the association at 15 West Seventy-seventh Street, New York City 10024, or call (845) 384–6320 or (212) 769–5169.

Nestled in the heart of a 24,000-acre natural area in the Shawangunk Mountains, overlooking Lake Mohonk, is a sprawling Victorian castle resort called **Mohonk Mountain House.** Built in 1869, the castle is a National Historic Landmark whose facilities include 251 guest rooms, 5 guest cottages, 150 working fireplaces, and 200 balconies. Above the Mohonk Mountain House stands **Sky Top Tower**, an observation tower built in 1923 of Shawangunk conglomerate that was quarried at its base. From the top of Sky Top Tower, on a clear day, you can see forever—or at least as far as the Rondout and Wallkill valleys, New Jersey, Connecticut, Vermont, Pennsylvania, and Massachusetts. (The tower is also known as the Albert K. Smiley Memorial Tower in tribute to the cofounder of the Mohonk Mountain House.) Guests, of course, have use of the resort's spacious grounds and many amenities, but even if you're not an overnight guest, you can pay a day-visitor fee that will give you access to the tower; 85 miles of hiking trails, paths, and carriage roads; and the lovely landscaped grounds with their formal show gardens, herb garden, and new Victorian maze.

Day visitors are also invited to visit the **Barn Museum,** in one of the largest barns in the Northeast. Built in 1888, it houses more than fifty nineteenth-century horse-drawn vehicles and many working tools made more than one hundred years ago. The Barn Museum, (845) 255–1000, ext. 2447, is open Wednesday, Saturday, and Sunday during the winter and daily in summer and fall. In the winter, day visitors can cross-country ski on more than 35 miles of marked, maintained cross-country ski trails. In the summer and fall, a shuttle ($5.00 per person round-trip) runs to and from Picnic Lodge—the day-visitors' center, which serves sandwiches and pizza—and the parking lot.

Mohonk Mountain House, Lake Mohonk, New Paltz, (845) 255–1000 (for reservations, 800–772–6646). Overnight rates vary according to view and decor, but all include three meals. They range from $379 a night for a double in one of the traditional style rooms to $735 for a tower room. A day-visitor pass to the facilities and grounds (it does not permit entrance to the Mountain House or use of the lake and its facilities) is $10.00 for adults midweek and $14.00 weekends and holidays; $8.00 for children under 12 midweek and $10.00 weekends and holidays; and, for families with children under 12 (two adults and two children under 12), $28.00 midweek and $38.00 weekends and holidays. NOTE: If you have breakfast, lunch, or dinner in the resort's dining room, you get free access to the grounds for the day. Meal reservations are required and may be made by calling (845) 256–2056.

West Bank of the Hudson

When mayonnaise king Richard Hellmann was told, at the age of fifty-five, that he had only six months to live unless he moved to the country, he did what any sane millionaire would do. (No, he didn't go to the Mayo Clinic.) He built a magnificent estate on the side of Mount Ticetonyk overlooking the Esopus River valley, moved there with his family, and lived to be ninety-four.

Now a B&B, *Onteora, The Mountain House* (Onteora is the Mohican name for the Catskills, which translates to "the land and the sky") is surrounded by 225 acres of forest and features a magnificent multiwindowed 20- by 30-foot Great Room with a massive stone fireplace; a 40-foot covered dining porch with Adirondack-style tree-trunk columns and railings; and a new 60-foot southwest deck. All five guest rooms have private baths. The house is filled with an eclectic collection of antiques and Japanese and Korean art.

Onteora, The Mountain House, Piney Point Road, *Boiceville,* (845) 657–6233, www.onteora.com, is open year-round. Rates, which include a full breakfast (with items such as crepes with three fillings and Eggs Hellmann), range from $165 a weekday night to $240 a weekend night; there is a two-night minimum on weekends.

Totem Indian Trading Post, one of, if not *the* oldest trading post in the state, is a New York State Historic Site. It's also the site of numerous megalithic sculptures done by Emil Brunel, founder of the New York Institute of Photography, who died in Boiceville in 1944. The ashes of the man who perfected the one-hour film developing process seventy years before it became popular are interred in one of his cement pieces here.

Totem Indian Trading Post, Sacred Ground, Route 28, Boiceville, (845) 657–2531, is open Friday, Saturday, and Sunday from noon to 6:00 P.M.

Floating down Esopus Creek on a lazy afternoon as it winds through the Catskill Mountains is the ultimate vacation: relaxing, scenic, and fun. *The Town Tinker* rents tubes, helps chart your course, provides instruction as needed, and arranges transportation. There are separate 2½-mile routes for beginner and expert tubers. Each route takes approximately two hours, and transportation is provided by either Town Tinker Tube Taxis on weekdays or the Catskill Mountain Railroad on weekends.

The Town Tinker, Bridge Street (Route 28), *Phoenicia,* (845) 688–5553, is open daily mid-May through September from 9:00 A.M. to 6:00 P.M. (last rentals are at 4:00 P.M.). Basic inner tubes rent for $10.00 a day. There is an additional charge for other equipment. A full-gear package for $30.00 includes a tube with seat, life vest, wetsuit, and helmet as well as one-time transportation. Children must be 12 years old and good swimmers. Taxi transportation is $5.00 per trip.

On weekends and holidays *Catskill Mountain Railroad* transports novice tubers back to Phoenicia at the end of their run (one-way fare is $5.00). But if you'd rather tour Esopus Creek by rail, the railroad offers a 6-mile round-trip ride, stopping at Phoenicia at a circa 1900 train depot being restored by the Empire State Railway Museum.

Catskill Mountain Railroad Company, Route 28, *Mt. Pleasant,* (845) 688–7400, operates weekends and holidays Memorial Day weekend through early September with trains running hourly 11:00 A.M. to 5:00 P.M. Mid-September through mid-October, trains run weekends and holidays hourly from noon to 4:00 P.M. Fare is $8.00 round-trip for adults, $5.00 for children ages 4 to 11. Call ahead to verify schedules.

The *Marketplace at Catskill Corners* is home to *Kaleidoworld,* a collection of giant interactive kaleidoscopes that visitors can peer through, ride on, and manipulate. The 60-foot kaleidoscope housed in the silo of a nineteenth-century barn re-mains the world's largest—and the world's second largest is also on site. It's the Amazing Dondoakahedron, a giant kaleidoscopic starship with imagery from the Hubble Telescope. Kaleidoworld also features Tom's Crystal Palace, home to eighteen giant, hands-on kaleidoscopes, and the Gallery of Light and Magic, billed as the largest and most spectacular exhibit of light sculptures on the East Coast. Admission is $5.00 per person.

Daphne and Niles did it in a memorable episode of *Frasier.* Al Pacino's blind character did it with a stranger in *Scent of a Woman.* And every night, they do it all over Buenos Aires. Where you don't expect it, though, is in the rustic old Catskills.

What is it? The tango, of course. And it has indeed come to the Catskills, where "Tango at the Cat" sets a sultry tone in **Woodstock.** The "Cat" is the **Catamount Cafe,** where Rosa Collantes and Angel Garcia-Clemente offer classes in tango, emphasizing the basic moves

Kaleidoworld

along with musicality, close embrace exercises, and how to make the most of a crowded dance floor. Their offerings include a one-hour afternoon "Fundamentals for All" class ($20); and a one-and-a-half-hour Intermediate class ($25). The cost for a combination of both classes is $40, and couples discounts are available. Fees include admission to an evening *milonga,* a performance of tango and other traditional Argentine music at which Rosa and Angel demonstrate their own considerable skills. Admission to the *milonga* alone, including an introductory tango lesson, is $12; for $35, the Catamount throws in a pre-*milonga* champagne dinner.

The Catamount Cafe, Route 28, **Mt. Tremper,** (845) 246–1122, also offers dinner and dancing on the deck overlooking a stream, when the weather is nice; a bar and lounge; and a late bar menu. Overnight packages are available.

The Marketplace also hosts exhibits focusing on the history of the Catskill Region in the Longyear House, home of the founder of the Ulster & Delaware Railroad. The papers and writings of Catskill-born naturalist John Burroughs are exhibited in the 1841 Riseley Barn.

The Marketplace at Catskill Corners, Route 28, Mt. Tremper, (845) 688–2451 or (888) 303–3936, is open daily from 10:00 A.M. to 6:00 P.M. Individual tickets are available for each of the kaleidoscopes.

The **Lodge at Emerson Place** offers a variety of Adirondack-style accommodations including suites with wet bars and whirlpool baths. Rates for a standard double range in season (late May through mid-October) from $190 to $200. For information call (877) 688–2828.

Opened in June 2000, the **Emerson Inn and Spa** bills itself as "a show-place of refined elegance and exceptional style." Tucked deep in the Catskill Forest Preserve, the twenty-four-room hotel offers luxurious accommodations, fine dining, and an elegant spa with more than forty services. And, surprisingly, the inn is pet friendly.

Guest rooms are decorated in a variety of themes, including Persian, Victorian, West Indian, Colonial, African, and Asian. The featherbeds are wrapped in triple-sheeted Frette linens. Rates, which include breakfast, range from $489 to $1000 (for the duplex suite) weekdays; to $539 to $1100 weekends. The Modified American Plan (MAP), which includes breakfast, afternoon tea, and lunch, is available for an additional $75 per person, per day.

French cuisine, prepared with fresh regional ingredients, might include dishes such as an appetizer of pan-seared scallops with caramelized leeks in a champagne mussel broth, and an entree of roasted loin of lamb with a parsnip puree and port-glazed white asparagus. The three-course, prix-fixe dinner costs $70 per person. The dining room's award-winning wine list, with more than 5,000 bottles, is exceptional.

The Emerson Inn and Spa is at 146 Mt. Pleasant Road, Mount Tremper; (845) 688–7900; www.theemerson.com.

If you're looking for a different dining experience, **Catskill Rose** is an excellent option. How about appetizers such as smoked shrimp with ginger black beans and entrees like smoked duckling with apricot tamarind chutney? The restaurant, on Route 212 in Mt. Tremper, (845) 688–7100, begins serving dinner at 5:00 P.M. Thursday through Sunday. Reservations are appreciated.

One of the country's first art colonies was founded in **Woodstock** in 1903, and today Ulster County is still a haven for artists. The **Woodstock Guild,** a multiarts center, displays and sells works of some of the area's best. It's at 34 Tinker Street, Woodstock, (845) 679–2079, and is open Friday through Sunday from noon to 5:00 P.M.; closed January and February.

Andre Lefort, a third-generation Parisian oven builder, was brought over from France to craft the oven at **Bread Alone,** 22 Mill Hill Road, Woodstock, (845) 679–2108. Workers at the European-style bakery shape the breads by hand and then bake the loaves in the wood-fired ovens. Among the house specialties: brioche, challah, and sourdough current buns. The bakery, open daily from 7:00 A.M.. to 5:00 P.M. (Friday and Saturday until 6:00 P.M.), also has locations in Boiceville, Rhinebeck, and Kingston.

There are numerous excellent restaurants in Woodstock. Among the more unusual is **New World Home Cooking Company,** 1411 Route 212, Woodstock, (845) 246–0900, featuring "New Wave" cooking—an eclectic assortment of ethnic dishes often pepped up with hot peppers and Asian spices. House specialties include Jamaican jerk chicken, cajun-peppered shrimp, and *ropa vieja*. There's a lovely outdoor patio and a great selection of beers to extinguish the fire. Open for dinner nightly, and lunch Friday through Monday in fall and winter. Reservations are highly recommended.

For almost forty years Harvey Fite has been creating a monumental environmental sculpture out of an abandoned Saugerties bluestone quarry. *Opus 40,* made of hundreds of thousands of tons of finely fitted stone, covers more than six acres. Visitors can walk along its recessed lower pathways, around the pools and fountains, and up to the nine-ton monolith at the summit. To create his Opus, Fite worked with traditional tools that were used by quarrymen here. His *Quarryman's Museum* houses his collection of tools and artifacts.

Opus 40 and Quarryman's Museum, 7480 Fite Road, *Saugerties* 12477, (845) 246–3400, is open Memorial Day weekend through Columbus Day weekend, Friday, Saturday and Sunday and most Monday holidays (call in advance) noon to 5:00 P.M. Admission, which includes the museum, is $6.00 for adults, $5.00 for older students and senior citizens, and $3.00 for children in school.

If you've ever looked longingly at a distant lighthouse, wishing you could escape Wal-Mart, McDonald's, and the Internet for a bit, check into the *Saugerties Lighthouse,* a 130-year-old stone structure at the mouth of Esopus Creek on the Hudson River.

Deactivated by the U.S. Coast Guard in 1954, the lighthouse has since been restored by the Saugerties Lighthouse Conservancy, which operates it as a museum and inn. In 1990 the Coast Guard installed a fourth-order solar-powered light, and the lighthouse once again aids mariners.

Two second-floor bedrooms are for rent. Guests share a kitchen and bath. Guests get to the lighthouse via a half-mile nature trail (at low tide only) or by private boat. From April through November the rooms rent for $160 per night. November through March, the rate is $135. Reservations are essential.

The museum at Saugerties Lighthouse Conservancy, P.O. Box 654, Saugerties 12477, (845) 247–0656, is open Saturday, Sunday, and holidays from 3:00 to 5:00 P.M. Memorial Day through Columbus Day. There is a suggested donation of $3.00 for adults and $1.00 for children.

New York's highest waterfall, 3 miles east of *Tannersville,* is no broad Niagara but more a miniature version of Angel Falls in Venezuela. (As you drive on Route 23A up the winding road, watch for the vehicle pullout and park there. Follow the sign that says TRAIL back down the road a short distance to the bridge to view the falls.) *Kaaterskill Falls* leaps from a rock ledge as a narrow curtain of white water, plunging past a natural grotto to a second scooped-out shelf at which it gathers force to finish its plunge toward the floor of Kaaterskill Clove.

Now little celebrated outside of hikers' guidebooks, the falls was once the Catskills' most renowned natural wonder. Thomas Cole, founder of the Hudson River School of art, immortalized the falls in his painting *View of Kaaterskill Falls* in the early 1800s. Washington Irving described the clove as "wild, lonely, and shagged, the bottom filled with fragments from impending cliffs, and scarcely lighted by the reflected rays of the setting sun."

The path to the base of the falls is not particularly difficult, although in the spring, when its snow cover has melted and refrozen into glare ice, it requires a gingerly step. But it is a short trail, and it follows the ravine gouged by Kaaterskill Creek for less than a mile before reaching the base.

Now we're going to the Broncks. No, it's not the wrong chapter—or the wrong spelling. Bronck was the family name of one of the original clans of Swedish settlers in New Amsterdam and the Hudson Valley. The farmstead of Pieter Bronck, who settled on the west bank of the Hudson near what is now *Coxsackie,* today makes up the ***Bronck Museum.***

It is one thing to have a surviving seventeenth-century house, but it is the great good fortune of the Greene County Historical Society, owner of the Bronck Museum, to be in possession of an entire farm dating from those early years of settlement. The reason the Bronck property has come down virtually intact is that eight generations of the family lived there, working the farm, until Leonard Bronck Lampman willed the acreage and buildings to the historical society. Thus, we get to appreciate not only the oldest of the farm buildings but also all of the barns, utility buildings, and furnishings acquired over two centuries of prosperity and familial expansion. What it all amounts to is an object lesson in the changes in style, taste, and sophistication that took place between the seventeenth and nineteenth centuries.

The Bronck Museum, Pieter Bronck Road off Route 9W, (518) 731–6490, is open Memorial Day until mid-October, Tuesday through Saturday and holiday Mondays 10:00 A.M. to 4:00 P.M. and Sunday 1:00 to 5:00 P.M. Call for admission fees.

Upper Catskills

The clear, cold streams of the Catskills—Beaver Kill, Esopus Creek, the east and west branches of the Delaware River—are among the most hallowed waterways in the history of American trout fishing. Not surprisingly, the Catskills have a rich tradition of handcrafted trout flies. If you're headed up this way to do some fishing, be sure to stop in at Mary Dette's home, where she sells flies hand-tied by artisans from around the Catskills region. (Mary also ties some herself, but we hear the wait for these is up to a year.) ***Dette Trout Flies,*** a local institu-

The Bridges of Delaware County

Three historic covered bridges are among the rural attractions of Delaware County. The Hamden and Fitches Bridges span the west branch of the Delaware River, while the Downsville Bridge, crossing the Delaware's east branch, is at 174 feet the longest covered bridge still in use in New York State.

tion, is at 68 Cottage Street, Roscoe; (607) 498–4991. Look for the sign out front: DETTE TROUT FLIES: WALT, WINNIE, MARY. It's open daily from 8:00 A.M. until 8:00 P.M.

If you're heading west from the Hudson Valley into the upper Catskills, a stop at the **Durham Center Museum** in **East Durham** provides an instructive look at the things a small community finds important—in many ways this museum is archetypal of the "village attics" that dot the land, and travelers could do worse than to take an occasional poke into one of these institutions. At the museum, which is housed in a circa 1825 one-room schoolhouse and several newer adjacent buildings, the collections run to Indian artifacts, portions of local petrified trees, old farm tools, and mementos of the 1800 Susquehanna Turnpike and the 1832–40 Canajoharie-Catskill Railroad, both of which passed this way. There is also a collection of Rogers Groups, those plaster statuette tableaux that decorated Victorian parlors and played on bourgeois heartstrings before Norman Rockwell was born. Finally, don't miss the collection of bottled sand specimens from around the world, sent by friends of the museum. If you're planning a trip to some far-off spot not represented on these shelves, don't hesitate to send some sand.

The Durham Center Museum, Route 145, East Durham, (518) 239–8461, is open the third weekend in May through Columbus Day, Thursday through Sunday from 1:00 to 4:00 P.M. and Thursday from 7:00 to 9:00 P.M. (winter by appointment). Admission is $2.50 for adults and $1.00 for children under 12. Groups are welcome by appointment. Genealogical researchers are welcome year-round by appointment.

Two 1876 Queen Anne boarding houses were restored and joined to create **Albergo Allegria,** a luxurious sixteen-room inn with an elegant Victorian flavor and modern-day amenities. There is also a carriage house with five suites. Rates, which range from $73 for a weekday room in the inn to $244 (in summer) for the Millenium Suite, include afternoon tea (served alfresco on warm days) and a gourmet breakfast, with treats such as stuffed French toast, Belgian waffles, and honey-cured bacon. The B&B is on Route 296, Windham, (518) 734–5560; www.albergousa.com.

The Long Good Night

Literature's greatest snoozer, Rip Van Winkle, hailed from Palenville and took his twenty-year nap in a ravine halfway up Catskill Mountain. Hikers still search for the spot where Rip sat, drank from a keg offered to him by an old man with thick bushy hair and a grizzled beard, and watched odd-looking fellows playing ninepins before he drifted off.

In 1824 a young man named *Zadock Pratt* came to a settlement called Schoharie Kill to establish a tannery. He bought some land, surveyed it, and set up his factory. Over the next twenty years, more than 30,000 employees, using hides imported from South America, tanned a million sides of sole leather, which were shipped down the Hudson River to New York City. And in the meantime Mr. Pratt established *Prattsville,* one of the earliest planned communities in New York State.

Mr. Pratt went on to become a member of the U.S. Congress in 1836 and 1842. One of the bills he sponsored created the Smithsonian Institution, but one of the most enduring legacies he left behind was *Pratt Rocks Park* (518–299–3395), on Main Street, which he donated to the town in 1843. Carved into the park's cliffs are symbols of Mr. Pratt's life, including a huge bust of his son who was killed in the Civil War, a horse, a hemlock tree, an uplifted hand, his tannery, a wreath with the names of his children, and an unfinished tomb where Pratt was to be buried overlooking the village (he was buried in a conventional grave at the other end of town). There's also a grave site with a stone bearing the names of his favorite dogs and horses.

While you're in Prattsville, take time to visit the *Zadock Pratt Museum* (518–299–3395), located in Zadock Pratt's restored homestead in the center of town. The museum, on the National Register of Historic Places, is just a half

Breaking "Legs"

The tiny town of Acra was once home to one of Prohibition's most infamous criminals. Jack "Legs" Diamond heard about a potent applejack that the locals made from cider and decided to move in and "organize" the stills. He bought a farmhouse just north of the village for his gang headquarters and began calling on the mountain bootleggers. Unfortunately for "Legs," the locals didn't want to be organized, and he was gunned down. Wounded, he had the trunks of the trees around his house painted white to hinder a possible ambush and was eventually killed in an Albany rooming house.

mile from the rocks: It focuses on the history and culture of the northern Catskills in the mid-nineteenth century and is open Memorial Day to Columbus Day, Thursday through Monday 1:00 to 4:00 P.M. There is an admission fee. Nearby, the National Register **Reformed Dutch Church,** with its handsome three-tiered tower, was built in 1804.

Roxbury, New York, is where we again come into contact with the naturalist **John Burroughs.** He may have spent much of the last decades of his life at Slabsides, down on the Hudson, but it was here in Roxbury that he was born in 1837 and here where he spent the last ten summers of his life at Woodchuck Lodge. He was buried here, in a field adjacent to the lodge, on April 2, 1921. The grave site and the nearby "Boyhood Rock" that he had cherished as a lad are now part of **Burroughs Memorial State Historic Site.**

The Burroughs Memorial is unique among historic sites in that its chief feature (apart from the grave and the rock) is simply a field surrounded by forests and the rolling Catskill hills. This is as fine a memorial as one could possibly imagine for a man who once said about the Catskills, "Those hills comfort me as no other place in the world does—it is home there."

Burroughs Memorial State Historic Site, off Route 30 (take Hardscrabble Road to Burroughs Road), Roxbury, is open during daylight hours. Admission is free. For information call (518) 827–6111.

Many of John Burroughs's modern-day spiritual descendants use the term *appropriate technology* to refer to renewable, nonpolluting sources of energy. Over in the northwestern Catskills town of **East Meredith,** the **Hanford Mills Museum** celebrates one of the oldest of these so-called alternative-energy sources, the power of running water harnessed to a wheel. Kortright Creek at East Meredith has been the site of waterpowered mills since the beginning of the nineteenth century, and the main building on the museum site today was built in 1846.

The old mill became the Hanford Mills in 1860, when David Josiah Hanford bought the operation. During the eighty-five years in which it owned the mill, the Hanford family expanded its output to include feed milling and the manufacture of utilitarian woodenware for farms and small industries. The mill complex grew to incorporate more than ten buildings on ten acres, all clustered around the millpond. The mill continued in operation until 1967.

Much of the original nineteenth-century equipment at Hanford Mills is still in place and in good working order. Today's visitors can watch lumber being cut on a big circular saw and shaped with smaller tools, all powered by the waters of Kortright Creek. At the heart of the operation is a 10-by-12-foot waterwheel, doing what waterwheels have done for more than 2,000 years. Visitors may explore at their leisure, or take a guided tour.

OTHER ATTRACTIONS WORTH SEEING IN THE CATSKILLS

Byrdcliffe Historic District,
c/o Woodstock Guild,
34 Tinker Street,
Woodstock,
(845) 679-2079

Catskill Game Farm,
400 Game Farm Road,
Catskill,
(518) 678-9595

Fort Delaware Museum of Colonial History,
Route 97,
Narrowsburg,
(845) 252-6660

Hudson River Cruises,
Rondout Landing,
Kingston,
(845) 340-4700 or (800) 843-7472

Hunter Mountain Skyride,
Route 23A,
Hunter,
(518) 263-4223

Knox's Headquarters State Historic Site,
Forge Hill Road, Route 94,
Vails Gate,
(845) 561-5498

Last Encampment of the Continental Army,
Route 300,
Vails Gate,
(845) 561-5073

Museum Village in Orange County,
Route 17M, Museum Village Road,
Monroe,
(845) 782-8247

New Windsor Cantonment State Historic Site,
Temple Hill Road, Route 300,
Vails Gate,
(845) 561-1765

Rondout Lighthouse,
One Rondout Landing,
Kingston,
(845) 338-0071

Thomas Cole House,
218 Spring Street,
Catskill,
(518) 943-7465

Tomsco Falls,
Mountaindale,
(845) 434-6065

Trolley Museum,
Route 89 East Strand,
Kingston,
(845) 331-3399

U.S. Military Academy,
West Point,
(845) 938-2638

Washington's Headquarters State Historic Site,
84 Liberty Street,
Newburgh,
(845) 562-1195

West Point Museum,
Main Street,
USMA Visitor Center,
West Point,
(845) 938-3590

The Hanford Mills Museum, intersection of County Routes 10 and 12, East Meredith, (607) 278–5744 or (800) 295–4992, is open May 1 to October 31, daily 10:00 A.M. to 5:00 P.M. Admission is $6.00 for adults, $5.00 for senior citizens, and $3.00 for children. Group rates are available.

Places to Stay in the Catskills

GREENVILLE

Greenville Arms 1889 Inn
South Street
(518) 966–5219

HIGH FALLS

Capt. Schoonmaker's 1760 House
RD #2, Box 37
High Falls 12440
(518) 687–7946

MONROE

Roscoe House
45 Lakes Road
(845) 782–0442

NEW PALTZ

Jingle Bell Farm
1 Forest Glen Road
(845) 255–6588

NEWBURGH

Morgan House
12 Powelton Road
(845) 561–0326

WALDEN

Heritage Farm
163 Berea Road
(845) 778–3420

WALLKILL

Audrey's Farmhouse
2188 Brunswyck Road
(845) 895–3440

WINDHAM

Hotel Vienna
107 Route 296
(518) 734–5300

REGIONAL TOURIST INFORMATION– THE CATSKILLS

CATS,
P.O. Box 527,
Catskill 12414,
(518) 943–3223 or (800) NYS–CATS
www.catskillgetaways.com

Delaware County Chamber of Commerce,
114 East Main Street,
Delhi 13753,
(800) 642–4443
www.delawarecounty.org

Greene County Promotion Department,
Route 23B,
Catskill 12414,
(800) 355–2287
www.greene-ny.com

Sullivan County,
100 North Street,
City Government Center,
Monticello 12701,
(800) 882–2287
www.scva.net

Places to Eat in the Catskills

BEARSVILLE

The Bear Cafe
Route 212
(845) 679–5555

DELHI

Quarter Moon Cafe
53 Main Street
(607) 746–3112

HIGHLAND

The Would Restaurant
120 North Road
(845) 691–9883

KINGSTON

Le Canard Enchaine
278 Fair Street
(845) 339–2003

Armadillo Bar & Grill
97 Abeel Street
(845) 339–1550

SAUGERTIES

Cafe Tamayo
89 Partition Street
(845) 246–9371

WALTON

Miller's Barbecue and Apple Place
29735 State Highway 10
(607) 865–4721

WOODSTOCK

Mt. Gate Indian Restaurant
4 Deming Street
(845) 679–5100

New York City and Long Island

New York City needs no introduction—certainly not a cursory one of the length we're permitted here—except to note that this is where the most beaten of the state's paths converge. With one top-echelon attraction after another packed into the city, where do we find the lesser-known places of interest?

The answer is everywhere. One of the first things the traveler should realize about this city is that it is far more than a backdrop for the Statue of Liberty, the Metropolitan Museum of Art, Yankee Stadium, and their like. And natives often have to be reminded that New York isn't just a vast and cacophonous machine that reinvents itself daily. It is, in fact, a place with nearly 400 years of history, where Dutch farmers and quirky poets and future presidents have lived, and where people are concerned with Indian artifacts and Tibetan art and the minutiae of local history as well as with capital-C Culture.

As for Long Island, the main thing for people who don't live here to remember is that it's worth going to even if it isn't on the way to anything else. Starting near the city and heading east, we'll visit an assortment of historical sites and museums, along with places that remind us of the natural beauty and maritime flavor of Long Island before fast carpentry and fast food transformed so much of it into a vast suburb.

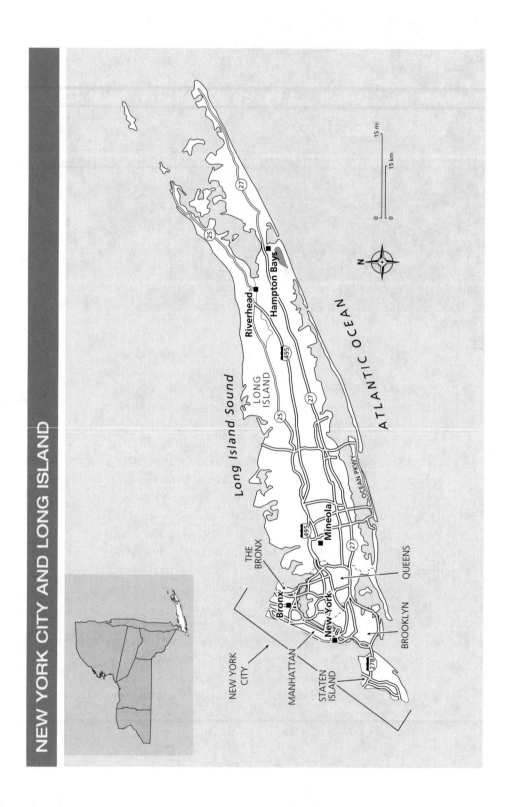

NEW YORK CITY AND LONG ISLAND

New York City

Looking for an offbeat tour of New York? Volunteers at **Big Apple Greeter** all have one thing in common: They know and love their city and want to share their knowledge—at no cost—with you. These volunteers are matched with visitors (individuals or groups of up to six) according to languages spoken and interests and will spend two to four hours showing you the neighborhoods throughout the five boroughs where New Yorkers live and work. They know where to find the best restaurants, flea markets, and lesser-known attractions.

Big Apple Greeter, 1 Centre Street, New York City, (212) 669–8159, www .bigapplegreeter.com, is a free public service. Be sure to contact them *at least* a month in advance of your arrival; appointments are strictly subject to the availability of volunteers. A visit request form is on the Greeter Web site.

Bruce Kayton specializes in tours of another sort—**Radical Walking Tours**. He focuses on the progressive alternative history of places such as Greenwich Village, City Hall, Harlem, and Wall Street, where people like Emma Goldman, Sacco & Vanzetti, the Black Panthers, and Abbie Hoffman made their mark on the New York legend. Mr. Kayton conducts Radical Walking Tours on Sunday from March through December. Tours last 2½ to 3½ hours; the fee is $10. Call him at (718) 492–0069 for information.

River to River Downtown Tours offers yet another option. Several years ago lifelong Manhattan resident Ruth Alscher-Green, a former teacher, "traded in her ruler for a pair of Reeboks" and now conducts two-hour walking tours of Lower Manhattan from the Hudson River to the East River, focusing on its art, architecture, and history. She's knowledgeable and enthusiastic—the aunt you always wish you had when you arrive in town. Ruth charges $35 per person, $50 for two, offers a special group rate, and will tailor her tour to your

AUTHORS' FAVORITES— NEW YORK CITY AND LONG ISLAND

Alice Austen House

Deep Hollow Ranch

Isamu Noguchi Garden Museum

Jacques Marchais Museum of Tibetan Art

Maxilla & Mandible, Ltd.

Pollock-Krasner House and Study Center

Riverhead Foundation for Marine Research and Preservation

Studio Museum in Harlem

An Unexpected Invitation

In the fall of 1985, my friend Chris Maynard and I paddled a canoe around Manhattan Island. As we were passing one of the big piers on the Hudson, Chris said to me, "That's where Malcolm Forbes keeps his yacht. There's one place we'll never be invited."

A year later, Mark Singer of the *New Yorker* did a "Talk of the Town" piece on our urban canoeing exploits, and Chris repeated his line. A few months after that, each of us received an engraved invitation in the mail. Malcolm Forbes had just launched his new yacht, Highlander V, and was planning a party and harbor cruise for the dedication. Notes accompanying the invitations, signed by the legendary publisher, explained that he wanted to rectify our notion that the Forbes flagship lay outside our realm of social acceptability.

It was a wonderful party and a wonderful cruise out past the newly refurbished Statue of Liberty. Chris was on a photography assignment in Europe, but the Schellers were there, heralded aboard with all the other celebrities by one of Malcolm Forbes's kilted bagpipers.

—Bill Scheller

interests. Contact her after 9:00 A.M. at Apt. 19U, 375 South End Avenue, New York City 10280, (212–321–2823).

Want to see what makes ***Times Square*** tick? A free ***walking tour*** leaves from the Times Square Visitors Center at 1560 Broadway (between 46th and 47th streets) every Friday at noon. For information of all sorts about Times Square, check out www.timesquare bid.org, (212) 768–1560.

getitatadiscount

Those people you see in line at TKTS (212–768–1818) in Times Square at Forty-seventh Street and Broadway are queuing up for half-price tickets to Broadway shows.

Of all the first-rank museums in the city of New York—institutions that can lay justified claim to being the most comprehensive of their kind—perhaps the least well known is the Smithsonian Institution's ***National Museum of the American Indian,*** George Gustav Heye Center. Nowhere else can we learn so much about the indigenous peoples who first called home the West Indies, and North, Central, and South America.

George Heye was an heir to an oil fortune who early in his life worked as a railroad construction engineer in the Southwest. In 1897 he bought the first of his Indian artifacts, a contemporary Navajo buckskin shirt, and from that point went on to develop a collecting mania that encompassed all things native from Alaska to Tierra del Fuego. He bought items that had just been made (including, it is said, the clothes off Indians' backs), and he bought archaeological finds dating from long before the European discovery of America. Heye founded his museum in 1916, and it opened to the public six years later. At that stage the collector owned some 400,000 objects; today the museum has more than a million individual items.

Exhibits at the museum are arranged geographically, according to the regions inhabited by the major indigenous peoples of North America, the West Indies, Central America, and South America. Also, there are numerous items associ-

Beaded Buckskin Dress,
National Museum of the
American Indian

ated with individuals—Sitting Bull's war club, Crazy Horse's feather headdress, Geronimo's cane, among others. Much of the collection must be kept in storage, but the astounding variety of material that is on display should surely convince visitors that this is *the* museum of the peoples of the New World.

Throughout the year Native musicians, dancers, artists, and elders present both formal and informal programs designed to help visitors better understand Indian cultures.

The National Museum of the American Indian, George Gustav Heye Center, Smithsonian Institution, Alexander Hamilton U.S. Custom House, One Bowling Green, New York City, (212) 668–6624, is open daily except Christmas from 10:00 A.M. to 5:00 P.M. and Thursday until 8:00 P.M. Admission is free.

More than 2,000 photographs, a large collection of artifacts, original documentary films, and individual narratives are utilized to create a picture of Jewish life and culture from the late 1880s to the present at the ***Museum of Jewish Heritage, A Living Memorial to the Holocaust*** in Battery Park City overlooking the Statue of Liberty and Ellis Island.

The museum focuses on three areas: the customs and traditions of Jewish life a century ago, the war against the Jews, and Jewish renewal in the postwar era. They combine to create a vivid image of the people of yesterday and today.

The Museum of Jewish Heritage, A Living Memorial to the Holocaust, 36 Battery Place, New York, (646) 437–4200, is open Sunday through Tuesday and

Among the Earliest Arrivals

The country's oldest Jewish congregation, Congregation Shearith Israel ("Remnant of Israel"), dates to September 12, 1654, when a group of newly arrived Jews from Spain and Portugal held a New Year service in New Amsterdam. The oldest gravestone in the congregation's first cemetery, at 55–57 St. James Place, bears the date 1683. The remains of many colonial-era Jews interred here had to be moved to newer cemeteries in Manhattan to make room for road construction.

Thursday 10:00 A.M. to 5:45 P.M.; Wednesday 10:00 A.M. to 8:00 P.M.; Friday and the eve of Jewish holidays 10:00 A.M. to 3:00 P.M. It is closed Saturday, Thanksgiving, and major Jewish holidays. Admission is $10.00 for adults and $5.00 for students and seniors. Admission is free on Wednesday from 4:00 to 8:00 P.M. For ticket information call (212) 945–0039.

In the mid-1800s Lucas Glockner, a German-born tailor, bought a lot at 97 Orchard Street on the Lower East Side that measured 25 by 100 feet. The lot was originally intended for single-family town houses, but Glockner erected a six-story tenement with apartments for twenty-two families as well as two storefronts in the basement. Each floor featured four three-room apartments with a total of 325 square feet each. Only one of the three rooms had windows.

Because it was the convention in the area for landlords to offer a free month's rent at the beginning of a year's lease, frequent moves were customary. Although 1,100 people have been documented as living at 97 Orchard Street between 1863 and 1935, a more realistic estimate is that 10,000 people from more than twenty-five nations lived there during its seventy-two-year residential service.

Ninety-seven Orchard Street is the first tenement to be preserved in America, and it is the site of the *Lower East Side Tenement Museum*, whose mission is to "promote tolerance through the presentation and interpretation of the variety of urban immigrant experiences on Manhattan's Lower East Side, a gateway to America." Visitors see apartments restored to interpret the lives of immigrant families who lived here over the years. The museum also hosts a series of weekend walks through the historic Orchard Street area. "The Streets Where We Lived" helps visitors learn how different immigrant groups shaped, and continue to shape, the Lower East Side.

All programs at the Lower East Side Tenement Museum, (212) 431–0233, begin at the Visitor Center, 90 Orchard Street, at the corner of Broome Street. The Visitor Center is open Monday through Friday 11:00 A.M. to 5:30 P.M.; Saturday and Sunday 10:45 A.M. to 5:30 P.M. Public tours are offered Tuesday through Sunday, September through June, and on Monday in July and August. Tickets are $10.00 for adults; $8.00 for students and seniors. Tickets can be purchased in advance on Ticketweb: www.ticketweb.com or by phone at (800) 965–4827. Same-day tickets may be available at the Visitors Center. Tours fill up, so be sure to reserve in advance. Free parking for the museum is available on Broome Street between Norfolk and Suffolk Streets. Have your parking stub validated at the box office.

The ***Lesbian, Gay, Bisexual and Transgender Community Center,*** located in Greenwich Village, is the largest of its kind on the East Coast, and second largest in the world. Among the services offered are a free welcome packet with maps and community information; an information and referral staff on duty throughout the center's open hours; and Internet access at the David Bohnett Cyber Center. The center also runs a Trans Coffeehouse for transgendered individuals and a popular ongoing movie night, Trans Cinema Arts. The National Museum of Lesbian, Gay, Bisexual and Transgender History and the National Archive of Lesbian, Gay, Bisexual and Transgender History, also located at the center, sponsor regular exhibits, publications, and scholarly research activities.

The Lesbian, Gay, Bisexual and Transgender Community Center, 208 West 13th Street, New York; (212)620–7310; www.gaycenter.org, is open daily from 9:00 A.M. to 11:00 P.M.

Back in Buffalo, a couple of chapters ago, we saw where the most momentous turn in ***Theodore Roosevelt's*** life took place—the house where he was inaugurated president of the United States. Here in the city you can see where his life began, at the ***Theodore Roosevelt Birthplace National Historic Site.*** The building that stands here today is a faithful reconstruction of the

Qui Plantavit Curabit
The Roosevelt Arms, Theodore Roosevelt Birthplace

ANNUAL EVENTS IN NEW YORK CITY

For a complete listing, check the Web site: iloveny.com.

JANUARY

Three Kings Day Parade in Spanish Harlem,
(212) 831–7272

FEBRUARY

New York Armory Antiques Show,
(212) 742–1180

Westminster Kennel Club Dog Show,
(212) 682–6852

MARCH

New York Flower Show,
(800) 553–2121

St. Patrick's Day Parade,
(212) 484–1222

APRIL

Easter Parade on Fifth Avenue,
(800) NYC–VISIT

New York International Auto Show,
(800) 282–3336

MAY

Bay Fest and Blessing of the Fleet,
(718) 646–9206

Bike New York,
(212) 932–BIKE

New York Open Judo Championship,
www.newyorkopenjudo.com

JUNE

Family Solstice Celebration,
(212) 267–9700

JVC Jazz Festival,
(212) 501–1390

JULY

Battery Fourth of July Celebration,
(212) 488–2163

AUGUST

Brighton Jubilee,
(718) 891–0800

brownstone row house in which TR was born on October 27, 1858. It was built following the ex-president's death in 1919, replacing a nondescript commercial building that had gone up only three years before, when the original Roosevelt home was torn down.

Open to the public since 1923, and a National Historic Site since 1963, the reconstructed Roosevelt home is furnished in the same style—and with many of the same articles—familiar to the sickly lad who lived here for the first fourteen years of his life. The president's widow and his two sisters supervised the reconstruction, recalling room layouts, furniture placement, and even interior color schemes. The result is a careful study not only of the environment that produced the scholar and improbable athlete who would become a rancher,

**Howl! Festival of East Village Arts
(including Charlie Parker Jazz
Festival),**
www.howlfestival.com

Harlem Week,
(212) 283–3315

U.S. Open Tennis Tournament,
(718) 760–6200 or (800) GO–TENNIS

SEPTEMBER

Columbus Day Parade,
(212) 249–9923

Feast of San Gennaro,
(212) 768–9320

New York Super Boat Grand Prix,
(305) 296–6166

Tugboat Festival,
(212) 245–0072

West Indian American Parade,
(718) 773–4052

OCTOBER

Blessing of the Animals,
(212) 316–7400

Greenwich Village Halloween Parade,
(800) NYC–VISIT

NOVEMBER

Macy's Thanksgiving Day Parade,
(212) 494–5432

New York City Marathon,
(212) 423–2249

DECEMBER

First Night,
(212) 484–1222

Radio City Christmas Spectacular,
(212) 307–7171

**Rockefeller Center Tree
Lighting Ceremony,**
(800) NYC–VISIT

police commissioner, Rough Rider, New York governor, and president but also
of the lifestyle of New York's more comfortable burghers in the middle of the
last century. Finally, the "new" Roosevelt house stands in stubborn contrast to
the modern buildings that surround it, reminding us of just how completely the
neighborhoods of New York have thrown off one persona after another.

The Theodore Roosevelt Birthplace National Historic Site, 28 East Twentieth Street, New York City, (212) 260–1616, is open Tuesday through Saturday
9:00 A.M. to 5:00 P.M. Guided tours are given on the hour; last tour at 4:00 P.M.
Closed on federal holidays. Admission is $3.00 for adults; children under 18 are
admitted free. There is no charge for educational groups, but reservations must
be made at least two weeks in advance.

Taxi Tips

Yellow medallion cabs are the only authorized taxis in New York City.

There are more than 12,000 yellow medallion cabs in the city.

Cabbies from 85 different nations drive the city's cabs.

If the cab's center roof light is not lit, it's not available.

One fare covers all passengers. The fare starts at $2.00 and jumps 30 cents for each additional ⅕ mile. The charge is 30 cents per 90 seconds in slow traffic or while stopped, and a 50-cent surcharge on rides between 8:00 P.M. and 6:00 A.M. Any bridge or tunnel tolls are paid by the passenger, who should be informed of this before the start of the trip. Cabs can issue printed receipts, helpful if you leave something behind.

There's a flat rate of $35 plus tolls and tip (generally 15 to 20 percent) to transport passengers from John F. Kennedy Airport to Manhattan. The fifteen-minute ride generally takes fifty to sixty minutes.

For more information call 212–NYC–TAXI.

You didn't expect to find this one in a little town up in the Mohawk Valley, did you? The ***Museum of Sex*** is a New York City institution dedicated to the "history, evolution, and cultural significance of human sexuality." Its holdings include the Ralph Whittington collection of erotica, a trove assembled by a distinguished former curator of a prestigious museum; and artifacts from the nearby Harmony Theater, formerly known as the Melody Burlesque. Recent special exhibitions have included offerings such as *Sex Among the Lotus: 2500 Years of Chinese Erotic Obsession.* Knowledgeable museum personnel lead walking tours through Manhattan's formerly raffish Tenderloin District, with former brothels and dance halls among the highlights.

The Museum of Sex, 233 Fifth Avenue (at 27th Street), New York; (212) 689–6337 (ticketing: 866–MOSEXTIX) is open Sunday to Friday, 11:00 A.M. to 6:30 P.M. (last ticket sold at 5:45 P.M.); Saturday 11:00 A.M. to 8:00 P.M. (last ticket sold at 7:15 P.M.); closed Thanksgiving and Christmas. Admission is $14.50; $13.50 for students and seniors. Walking tours cost $12.00; call for schedules.

There's no question that Americans are an industrious lot—New York City itself is a perfect example. But the fabulous collection of paintings, drawings, sculpture, textiles, furniture, functional and decorative arts, photographs, and contemporary environmental works on display at the ***American Folk Art Museum*** is testament to the fact that man cannot live by bread alone—the soul, too, needs nurturing.

The museum, founded by a group of collectors in 1961, is devoted to preserving the country's rich folk heritage. The collection, dating from the middle eighteenth century to the present, reflects the museum's increasingly broad definition of the field of folk art. The museum presents special exhibitions and events throughout the year and publishes *Folk Art* magazine, the only publication in the country covering the growing field of American folk art.

The American Folk Art Museum, Two Lincoln Square (Columbus Avenue between Sixty-fifth and Sixty-sixth Streets), New York City, (212) 977–7298, is open Tuesday through Sunday 11:30 A.M. to 7:30 P.M. and Friday until 8:00 P.M. Closed Monday, Christmas Day, New Year's Day, and Thanksgiving and closes early on July 4th. Admission is free. A second location at 45 West Fifty-third Street (212–265–1040) hosts an ongoing program of changing exhibits.

Is it possible to tour a building that no longer exists? The answer is yes, sort of, if the building is Pennsylvania Station—not the dreary modern terminal that crouches beneath Madison Square Garden, but the mighty neoclassical edifice that the Pennsylvania Railroad and McKim, Mead, and White built in 1910 to echo the Baths of Caracalla and stand, perhaps, for centuries. Demolished barely more than fifty years later in what the *New York Times* rightly called a "monumental act of vandalism," old Penn Station was nevertheless too deeply embedded in the sinews of Manhattan to have disappeared altogether. Like the Roman edifices that inspired it, its ghostly fragments lurk beneath its modern successor; indeed, they are part of what still makes today's Penn Station work.

Find out just what we're talking about when you take the 34th Street Partnership's **Penn Station Tour,** a ninety-minute walk through time that reveals the physical remains of what was once—along with still-glorious Grand Central

And You Thought Traffic Was Bad!

Here's how Josiah Quincy, president of Harvard University, described a stagecoach trip from Boston to New York via the Post Road in the eighteenth century:

"The carriages were old and shackling, and much of the harness of ropes. We reached our resting place for the night, if no accident intervened, at 10 o'clock, and after a frugal supper, went to bed with a notice that we should be called at three which generally proved to be half-past two, and then, whether it snowed or rained, the traveller must rise and make ready, by the help of a horn lantern and a farthing candle, and proceed on his way over bad roads, sometimes getting out to help the coachman lift the coach out of quagmire or rut, and arrive in New York after a week's hard travelling, wondering at the ease, as well as the expedition, with which our journey was effected."

Underground Info

Almost 6,000 cars—the world's largest subway fleet—operate over 714 miles of track in four of New York's five boroughs (Staten Island has no subways) and stop at 469 stations.

A subway token costs $1.50 and is good for a ride of any distance.

Cash is not accepted at turnstiles. Either buy a token at the booth or purchase a MetroCard, an electronic fare card. The MetroCard is also sold by vendors throughout the city that display a MetroCard sign. More than 200 of the city's busiest stations accept the card, which offers reduced rates on MTA subways and buses. See "Keep on Busin'" on page 204 for more information.

Up to three children under 44 inches tall can ride the subway free when accompanied by an adult.

The subway operates twenty-four hours a day, seven days a week.

For information call (718) 330–1234.

Station—one of the grand entrances to New York City. You'll see the pink granite and herringbone brickwork that once paved the station's carriage drive peeking through fake modern tile; discover the last of the iron-and-brass staircases that preceded escalators as a means of accessing the train platforms; stand opposite the only remaining original elevator cage; and look down at a patch of the original glass bricks that allowed sunlight to filter from the upper levels of the station to the tracks below. Along the way, architectural historian John Turkeli will tell the story of the rise and demise of the New York terminus of "The Standard Railroad of the World."

As of this writing, the Penn Station Tour is offered on the fourth Monday of each month (reservations required); participants gather at the 34th Street Partnership's Tourist Information Kiosk in the Penn Square Rotunda (there is no charge). To confirm schedules and reserve a space, contact the 34th Street Partnership, 500 Fifth Avenue, New York; (212) 719–3434; www.34thStreet.org. The Partnership also offers guided tours of 34th Street, and provides information for self-guided tours of Herald Square, Greeley Square, the gargantuan neoclassical central Post Office that stands on Eighth Avenue opposite the Penn Station/Madison Square Garden complex, and the Empire State Building Observatory.

Children of all ages as well as serious collectors will want to head down to Greenwich Village to *Classic Toys*, which houses an awesome collection of old and new toy and miniature figures (soldiers, animals, Wild West, railroad

Just a Short Sprint from One of the Outer Boroughs . . .

New York City's first automatic restrooms are located in Herald Square Park and Greeley Square Park, in Midtown's 34th Street District. Use of the modern facilities costs 50 cents.

station) and vehicles (cars, trucks, planes, racing, and construction). The inventory ranges from the newest in plastic cowboys and dinosaurs, to collector's items made more than one hundred years ago, to exquisite miniature knights in armor rendered by an English member of the Guild of Heralds.

Classic Toys, 218 Sullivan Street, New York City, (212) 674–4434, is open daily from noon to 6:00 P.M.

Looking for an unusual souvenir? Perhaps the horn of an impala (*Aepyceros melampus*), the skeleton of the Look Down fish (*Selene vomer*), or the skull of a Tokay Gecko (*Gecko gecko*) will do. **Maxilla & Mandible, Ltd.,** the world's only osteological store, is a natural-history and science emporium with 19,000 square feet of showroom, laboratory, workshop, and storage facilities. All of their specimens are unique, anatomically accurate, and obtained from legal and ethical sources. They're at 451–5 Columbus Avenue, New York City, (212) 724–6173, and are open Monday through Saturday 11:00 A.M. to 7:00 P.M. and Sunday 1:00 to 5:00 P.M. January through March the shop is closed Sunday and Monday; July through September, it's closed Sunday. Closed major holidays. Check out the Web site at www.maxillaandmandible.com—it's the *Felis catus*'s pajamas.

An Act of God

In 1870 the American actor Joseph Jefferson went to a church near the spot where the Empire State Building now stands to arrange for a friend's burial service. Upon learning that the deceased was an actor, the rector suggested Jefferson make arrangements at a church around the corner. Jefferson is said to have replied, "Thank God for the little church around the corner," and that's how the Church of the Transfiguration at 1 East Twenty-ninth Street got its nicknames, "Little Church Around the Corner" and the "Actors' Church." Over the years grateful thespians, including Sarah Bernhardt, have worshiped here, and there are memorial windows to actors such as John Drew, Edwin Booth, and Richard Mansfield.

El Museo del Barrio is dedicated to highlighting the art and culture of Puerto Rico and Latin America. Its collection includes more than 8,000 works of art from pre-Columbian vessels to contemporary pieces. Among the holdings are the second-largest collection of Taino objects in the country, secular and religious pieces, including the outstanding collection of 360 *santos de palo* (carved wooden saints used for household devotions) and a superb exhibit documenting the history of print- and poster-making in Puerto Rico from the 1940s to the present.

El Museo del Barrio, Heckscher Building, 1230 Fifth Avenue at 104th Street, New York City, (212) 831–7272, is open Wednesday through Sunday from 11:00 A.M. to 5:00 P.M. Suggested donation is $6.00 for adults and $4.00 for seniors and students. No donation asked for children under 12.

Harlem is a place—rich in history, tradition, food, music, and bad press— where the majority of people go about their daily lives in peace, but tourists are usually too apprehensive to visit. An enterprising company called *Harlem Spirituals* offers a variety of specialized tours of the city, including: "New York Visions," which visits the landmarks of Manhattan, the Bronx, and Brooklyn; a one-to-two-day "Heritage Tour" of the city's African-American heritage; and a "Harlem on Sunday Tour," which includes a church service and brunch at the famous Cotton Club. Reservations are required.

We Didn't Even Know They Had Teal Lights Up There

We've all seen the upper stories of the Empire State Building lit in red and green for the Christmas season; or red, white, and blue on the Fourth of July. But those are just two of many special color combinations. Here are some others, with the lights indicated in bottom-to-top order:

Red, white, and green: Columbus Day

Black, yellow, and red: German Reunification Day

Red, yellow, and green: Portugal Day

Purple and white: Alzheimer's Awareness

Pink and white: Breast Cancer Awareness

Lavender and white: Gay Pride

Purple, teal, and white: Osteoporosis Awareness

When no particular day, week, or event is being recognized, the building's tower is illuminated by plain white lights.

Harlem Spirituals, 1697 Broadway, #203, New York City, (800) 660–2166 or (212) 391–0900; www.harlemspirituals.com, offers tours in English, French, German, Italian, and Spanish, as well as other languages, based on availability.

The **Studio Museum in Harlem** was founded in 1967 as a working and exhibition space for African-American artists. Today, in a 60,000-square-foot building, the country's first accredited African-American fine arts museum houses an extensive collection of nineteenth- and twentieth-century African-American art, twentieth-century Caribbean and African art, and traditional African art and artifacts.

But this building is more than a museum. It's a center for interpreting its contents to both children and adults. In addition to an artists-in-residence program and an outreach program for Harlem's public schools, the museum hosts numerous workshops, art and humanities programs, and special exhibits throughout the year.

The Studio Museum in Harlem, 144 West 125th Street, New York City, (212) 864–4500, is open Wednesday to Friday noon to 6:00 P.M.; Saturday 10:00 A.M. to 6:00 P.M.; Sunday noon to 6:00 P.M. Suggested donation is $7.00 for adults; $5.00 for students and seniors; none for under 12.

> ## itwouldhave stretchedalmostto themoon
>
> On March 1, 1962, New York City held its largest ticker tape parade: 3,474 tons were dropped along a 7-mile route to honor astronaut John Glenn.

It's 3:00 A.M. and you've got the hungry horrors. A few places in the Big Apple that never close include **Around the Clock Cafe,** 8 Stuyvesant Street at Third Avenue, (212) 598–0402, for American/Continental cuisine; **Yaffa Cafe,** 97 St. Mark's Place, (212) 674–9302, for a semi-vegetarian menu, salads, omelets, and great desserts; **Empire Diner,** 210 Tenth Avenue at Twenty-second Street, (212) 243–2736, for American/ eclectic fare, a piano bar, and sidewalk dining; and **Original Ray's,** 835 Seventh Avenue at Fifty-third, (212) 974–9381, for fresh-baked pizza.

Manhattan's only lighthouse—nestled underneath the George Washington Bridge on Jeffrey's Hook—served as a beacon to ships for twenty-six years. Built in 1880 on Sandy Hook, New Jersey, the 40-foot-tall **Little Red Lighthouse** was dismantled in 1917 when it became obsolete. It was reconstructed on Jeffrey's Hook four years later in an effort to improve navigation on the Hudson River and did its job until the stronger lights from the bridge again rendered it obsolete. When the Coast Guard tried to remove the lighthouse in 1951, supporters rallied to save it.

Today the lighthouse, with its forty-eight brightly painted cast-iron plates, is a part of the Historic House Trust of New York City, and visitors can climb the spiral staircase to an observation deck that looks out across the river at the Palisades. Exhibition panels at the base provide information about the river.

The Little Red Lighthouse, in Fort Washington Park at 178th Street, is open for public tours organized by the Urban Park Rangers, established in 1979 as a uniformed force of environmental stewards dedicated to enhancing the public's appreciation and enjoyment of the city's parks. The lighthouse tour is a part of the exploration of Fort Washington Park. For information call (212) NEW YORK or, if you're in the city, just dial 311 for information on Parks Department programs.

And now, on to the U.S. mainland—to the only borough of the city of New York not located on an island. This is the **Bronx,** a place that ought to be recognized as more than the home of Yankee Stadium and the place you cross on Route 95 to get from New England to the George Washington Bridge. To get a handle on the story of this one-time suburban retreat that became one of New York's most densely populated residential districts, visit the **Museum of Bronx History.** The museum is housed in a building of a style and period not often encountered in a city that has torn down and rebuilt itself with as much abandon as has New York—a fieldstone house built in 1758, looking as if it would be more at home on a farm in Bucks County, Pennsylvania, than in the borough of endless row houses and apartment buildings.

The Museum of Bronx History, 3266 Bainbridge Avenue at 208th Street, Bronx, (718) 881–8900, is open Saturday from 10:00 A.M. to 4:00 P.M., Sunday from 1:00 to 5:00 P.M., and weekdays by appointment. Admission is $3.00. The Bronx County Historical Society, which administers the museum and the Poe Cottage, offers tours of the Bronx, as well as a lecture series. Call for a schedule or check its Web site: www.bronxhistoricalsociety.org.

One chapter in Bronx history is an important part of American literary history as well. In 1846 a thirty-seven-year-old poet, short-story writer, and critic named **Edgar Allan Poe** rented a small wooden cottage, now known as the **Poe Cottage,** in Poe Park, East Kingsbridge Road and the Grand Concourse, not far from the campus of Fordham University (in Poe's day it was known as St. John's College). Part of the reason for his move was the fragile health of his wife; Fordham, Poe thought, was a more salubrious environment than the couple's former home in New York City. But Virginia Clemm Poe—who was also the writer's cousin— died of tuberculosis at the Bronx cottage early in 1847, leaving Poe in the state of despondency that accounted for his poem *Annabel Lee* and other melancholic verse.

Within a Hairsbreadth of Ending on a Sour Note

On May 9, 1891, Russian composer Pyotr Ilich Tchaikovsky mounted the podium at the grand opening of Carnegie Hall, conducted the orchestra in a selection of his works, and pronounced the acoustics "magnificent." The world-renowned building, constructed with funds donated by Andrew Carnegie, was almost demolished in 1960 to make way for an office building. It was saved at the last minute by a group of musicians and music lovers led by violinist Isaac Stern.

Poe maintained his residence in the Bronx after his wife's death, drinking heavily and trying to keep up with his bills by delivering an occasional lecture. It was while returning from one of his lecture trips that he died in Baltimore in 1849.

Sometimes the world takes better care of dead poets' residences than it does the poets while they are alive, and such was the case with Edgar Allan Poe. The rapidly growing Bronx quickly enveloped the Poe Cottage during the latter half of the nineteenth century, but in 1902 the city dedicated a park in his honor across the street from the house. The house was moved to the park eleven years later and has been open as a museum since 1917.

The Edgar Allan Poe Cottage, Grand Concourse and East Kingsbridge Road, Bronx, (718) 881–8900, is open Saturday 10:00 A.M. to 4:00 P.M. and Sunday 1:00 to 5:00 P.M. throughout the year. Admission is $3.00 for adults and $1.00 for children under 12.

Not all of the Bronx was gobbled up by developers in the decades following Poe's brief stay. There are, of course, the green expanses of the New York Botanical and Zoological Gardens, Van Cortlandt Park, and Pelham Bay Park. But a visit to the borough should also include a stop at ***Wave Hill,*** a twenty-eight-acre preserve in the Riverdale neighborhood at the northwest corner of the Bronx. Wave Hill is not wilderness but a section of the borough that remained in its natural state until the middle of the last century, when it was first acquired as a country estate. Today it is the only one of the great Hudson River estates preserved for public use within the city limits.

In 1836 New York lawyer William Morris bought fifteen acres of riverbank real estate in the Wave Hill area and built Wave Hill House, one of the two mansions that today grace the property, as a summer retreat. Thirty years later the Morris tract was acquired by publisher William Appleton. Appleton remodeled the house and began developing the gardens and conservatories for which the property would become famous. The gardens were brought to their apogee, however, by financier George Perkins, who bought the estate in 1893 and increased its size to eighty acres, with a scattering of six fine houses, including not only Wave Hill but also *Glyndor,* which had been built by Oliver Harriman. (Burned in 1927, Glyndor was rebuilt by Perkins's widow. Glyndor II, as it is known, is still a part of the Wave Hill property.) Perkins's gardener was the talented Albert Millard. Under his direction plantings on the estate were expanded to include eight additional greenhouses and exotic Oriental trees.

The attractions of Wave Hill for today's visitor include art exhibits, concert series, outdoor dance performances, and special events. But the essential reason for a trip to the old estate remains its lovely grounds, some manicured and some an approximation of the wild state of this stretch of Bronx shoreline. There are 350 varieties of trees and shrubs, plus the wild and cultivated flowers planted in three greenhouses, in formal and informal gardens, and along the pathways of the estate. A ten-acre section of woods has been restored as a native Bronx forest environment, complete with elderberries, witch hazel, and native grasses.

Wave Hill, 249th Street and Independence Avenue, Bronx (mailing address: 675 West 252nd Street, Bronx 10471), (718) 549–3200, is open in spring and summer, Tuesday through Sunday 9:00 A.M. to 5:30 P.M., and Wednesday (June and July only) until 9:00 P.M. In fall and winter Wave Hill is open Tuesday through Sunday 9:00 A.M. to 4:30 P.M. The greenhouses are open from 10:00 A.M. to noon and 2:00 to 4:00 P.M. It is closed Christmas and New Year's Day. Admission is free all day Tuesday and until noon Saturday. Other days admission is $4.00 for adults, $2.00 for seniors and students, and free for children 6 and under. Tours are given each Sunday at 2:15 P.M. The cafe is open for lunch and snacks.

The kids have been great. They've listened to you quote stanzas from "The Raven" and heard about Teddy Roosevelt's charge up San Juan Hill. If they're between the ages of two and ten, head over to the *Brooklyn Children's Museum.* Founded in 1899, it was the first museum in the world designed expressly for youngsters. It will give you a chance to stop worrying about them touching everything—here the philosophy is "touch and learn."

The museum, with a collection of more than 27,000 artifacts and specimens in ten galleries, is housed in a unique 35,000-square-foot underground structure and features a turn-of-the-twentieth-century kiosk entrance and a "stream" running the length of the "people tube," a huge drainage pipe that connects four levels of exhibit space. According to the museum's brochure, "exhibits combine 'hands-on' components and objects to aid in the exploration of natural science, culture and history"—which translates to "learn and have fun at the same time."

Be sure to include a visit to the rooftop amphitheatre and a greenhouse, created jointly with the Brooklyn Botanic Garden. There is a trolley-to-shuttle service between the Children's Museum, Brooklyn Museum, and the Botanic Garden.

The Brooklyn Children's Museum, 145 Brooklyn Avenue, Brooklyn, (718–735–4400; for information and directions, 735–4402), is open during the school year Wednesday, Thursday, and Friday 1:00 to 6:00 P.M.; Saturday and Sunday 11:00 A.M. to 6:00 P.M. (Longer hours during school vacations.) The Rooftop Theater is open 6:30 to 8:00 P.M. Admission is $4.00 per visitor; children under age 1 are free. Families are admitted free before noon on Saturday and Sunday, and on the first Thursday of each month.

After a $3-million restoration, the country's first public Japanese garden is truly an exotic refuge in the middle of Brooklyn. Designed in 1915 by Takeo Shiota, The Japanese Hill-and-Pond Garden at the ***Brooklyn Botanic Garden,*** is an urban retreat like no other in the metropolitan area. Visitors enter through an orange-red Torii gate into a magical world of azaleas, pines, and weeping cherry trees, where dwarf bamboo and irises edge a pond inhabited by bronze cranes and waterfalls cascade gently from recessed grottoes.

The Brooklyn Botanic Garden, 900 Washington Avenue, Brooklyn, (718) 623–7200, is open in spring and summer, Tuesday through Friday 8:00 A.M. to 6:00 P.M.; weekends and holidays 10:00 A.M. to 6:00 P.M. Fall and winter, hours are Tuesday through Friday 8:00 A.M. to 4:30 P.M.; weekends and holidays 10:00 A.M. to 4:30 P.M. Closed Monday, except on holiday Mondays, and closed major holidays. Admission is $5.00 for adults, $3.00 for seniors and students, and free for children 16 and under. Admission is free all day on Tuesday and on Saturday from 10:00 A.M. to noon. Senior citizens are admitted free on Friday.

Melancholy Survivor

At the Brooklyn Museum (200 Eastern Parkway), there's an outdoor sculpture garden devoted to artwork and architectural details removed from vanished New York City buildings. Here you'll find Adolph Weinmann's Night, an allegorical female figure carved from pink granite. Along with a companion named Day, she once drowsed against a massive clock at one of the entrances to McKim, Mead, and White's magnificent Pennsylvania Station, built in 1910 and lost to developers in 1963.

The Ultimate in Recycling

The Brooklyn Botanic Garden was founded in 1910 on the site of an ash dump. It now encompasses 12,000 plant species from throughout the world.

The Grand Prospect Hall is a building with a history:

- When it was built in 1892, it was the tallest building in Brooklyn.
- Its French birdcage elevator was Brooklyn's first passenger elevator.
- William Jennings Bryan appeared on stage when he was stumping for the presidency.
- *The Cotton Club* and *Prizzi's Honor* were filmed here.
- Enrico Caruso, Mae West, Lena Horne, and Fred Astaire performed here.

The French Empire–style Victorian confection features a breathtaking lobby, marble grand staircase, rococo-style gold-leafed opera theater, a domed ceiling, and a grand ballroom that can accommodate up to 2,000 people.

Throughout the years the hall has served as a music hall, a German opera house, a vaudeville theater, a dance hall, a boxing arena, and a professional basketball court. Today it is used as a convention center.

The Grand Prospect Hall, 263 Prospect Avenue, Brooklyn, (718) 788–0777, is available for weddings, meetings, and bar mitzvahs. But management will be delighted to give you an informal tour at no charge; just call in advance to make sure someone will be there. The Web site is www.grandprospect.com.

The Wildlife Conservation Society's ***New York Aquarium,*** on Brooklyn's ***Coney Island,*** is the oldest continuously operating aquarium in the country. It houses more than 10,000 specimens, including the only California sea otters outside of California, and the only aquarium-born beluga whales to survive past their first birthday.

The aquarium's Sea Cliffs, a 300-foot-long re-creation of the rocky Pacific coast, is now home to walruses; harbor, grey, and fur seals; sea otters; and black-footed penguins. Exhibits in Conservation Hall focus on the society's efforts to protect marine species around the world, replicating habitats in areas such as the Belize Barrier Reef, the Amazon River, the Coral Reef, and Lake Victoria. The Aquatheater features a 200,000-gallon pool where marine mammal demonstrations are held throughout the day.

The New York Aquarium, Boardwalk at West Eighth Street and Surf Avenue, Coney Island, Brooklyn, (718) 265–FISH, is open daily 10:00 A.M. to 5:00 P.M. (last tickets sold at 4:45 P.M.); Saturday, Sunday, and holidays 10:00

A.M. to 5:30 P.M. (last tickets sold at 4:45 P.M.). Admission is $11.00 for adults and $7.00 for senior citizens and children ages 2 to 12. Parking is $7.00 per car.

The amusement park that made Coney Island famous in the 1920s is gone. The boardwalk and rides that remain are dim reminders of its glory days. And so, too, are the famous freakshows that used to titillate the throngs on a summer's night. But *Sideshows by the Seashore* makes a valiant effort to re-create the thrill of a traditional ten-in-one circus sideshow with ten live acts and attractions in every show. Actors and performance artists have replaced the two-headed man and bearded lady with wonders like Robbie the Indian Rubber Boy, a twenty-year-old contortionist from Calcutta; and Eak "the illustrated man," an escape artist, geek, and snake charmer.

Sideshows is in a historic 1917 building that, in the 1950s and 1960s, was home to Dave Rosen's Wonderland Circus Sideshow, where oddities including Sealo the Seal Boy once performed. The Freak Bar in the lobby serves beer and there's a gift shop.

Sideshows by the Seashore, West Twelfth Street (head east on the boardwalk), Coney Island, (718) 372–5159, is open from Easter through late May from 2:00 P.M. until sundown on Saturday and Sunday with a small-cast version of the show. From late May through early September the full cast performs Saturday and Sunday from 1:00 through 10:00 P.M. (and sometimes later) and on

Keep on Busin'

The MetroCard electronic fare card can be used on any of the city's 3,700 blue-and-white buses, which run through five boroughs along more than 220 routes.

A one-day MetroCard FunPass, which allows all-day transportation on MTA subways and buses, can be purchased for $7.00. A seven-day MetroCard, which gives the holder a week of unlimited rides, is available for $21.00. A thirty-day card can be purchased for $70.00.

People with physical disabilities can use a wheelchair lift located near the middle of the bus. The bus driver will give these people a postage-paid envelope in which to pay their fare.

Riders can transfer for free between buses with intersecting routes. Request a transfer ticket from the driver when boarding.

For route or schedule information: (718) 330–1234 between 6:00 A.M. and 9:00 P.M. Web site: www.nyc.ny.us. For general information call (212) METRO CARD; outside the city call (800) METRO CARD.

Wednesday, Thursday, and Friday from 2:00 to 8:00 P.M. Performance times are subject to change due to weather, so call that day for specific information. Admission is $5.00 for adults and $3.00 for children under 12. Tickets can be purchased at the door only on the day of performance.

Next door to Sideshows is the **Coney Island Museum,** "a small but fascinating museum of Coney Island memorabilia." It's a wonderful hodgepodge collection of antiques and old rides and offers a great view of landmark rides including the Wonder Wheel (which itself offers fabulous views of Manhattan) and the legendary Cyclone roller coaster. The museum is small and is itself a work in progress, but it gives visitors a glimpse into the Coney Island of long ago. Admission is just 99 cents, and the museum is open Saturday and Sunday from noon to sundown, weather permitting. For information call (718) 372–5159.

akindcut,indeed

The first tree to be designated an official landmark by the New York City Landmarks Preservation Commission was the weeping beech tree now in Weeping Beech Park, Thirty-seventh Avenue between Parson Boulevard and Bowne Street, in Flushing. It was grown from a cutting taken from a tree at an estate at Beersal, Belgium.

"It is said that stone is the affection of old men," said American-Japanese sculptor Isamu Noguchi, explaining his obsession with the medium. Caress the smooth, cold stone of his pieces, and perhaps you'll understand. They're displayed in the **Long Island City** neighborhood of the borough of **Queens** at the **Isamu Noguchi Garden Museum,** a brick factory building the artist converted for use as a warehouse in the 1970s. Prior to the museum's opening, he added a dramatic open-air addition and an outdoor sculpture garden. Today more than 250 of his works, including stone, bronze, and wood sculptures; models for public projects and gardens; elements of dance sets designed for choreographer Martha Graham; and his Akari lanterns are exhibited in twelve galleries in the building.

Noguchi's major granite and basalt sculptures are displayed in the garden, as is his tombstone, under which half of his ashes are interred. The other half is buried in his garden studio in Japan.

The Isamu Noguchi Garden Museum, 32-37 Vernon Boulevard, Long Island City (entrance around the corner at 9-01 33rd Road) is open Wednesday through Friday 11:00 A.M. to 5:00 P.M.; Saturday and Sunday 11:00 A.M. to 6:00 P.M. Admission is $5.00.

The Queens Artlink Shuttle, (714) 204–7088, a free shuttle, runs on weekends from 11:30 A.M. to 5:00 P.M. between The Museum of Modern Art (MoMA),

P.S. 1 Contemporary Art Center, the American Museum of the Moving Image, Socrates Sculpture Park, and the Isamu Noguchi Museum.

Some of the metropolitan area's most exciting international art exhibits are hosted at *P.S. 1 Contemporary Art Center* in Long Island City. During exhibition openings artists who are receiving free workspace in the buildings open their studios to the public.

P.S. 1 Contemporary Art Center, 22–25 Jackson Avenue at the intersection of Forty-sixth Avenue in Long Island City, (718) 784–2084, is open Thursday through Monday from noon to 6:00 P.M. A donation of $5.00 for adults and $2.00 for students and seniors is suggested.

The great Louis Armstrong seems to have been a man always in motion, a jazz genius who roared out of New Orleans and spent the rest of his days as a citizen of the world. "Satchmo" was all of those things and more, but for nearly thirty years he did have a quiet place where he rested, rehearsed, and spent time with friends and family between recording sessions, club gigs, and concert tours. The *Louis Armstrong House* in Corona, Queens, was the trumpeter's modest, two-story home. He and his wife Lucille bought the house in 1943, and he lived there until his death in 1971 (Lucille passed away in 1983).

Meet Me at the Unisphere

Whose future did you like better—Ford's or General Motors'?

To anyone of a certain age who once lived in the New York metropolitan area, that question could only refer to the carmakers' giant exhibits at the New York World's Fair of 1964–65 (OK, GM also dabbled in prognostication at the 1939 Fair, also held at Queens' Flushing Meadow). We went to the fair to appraise competing visions of tomorrow, which really weren't all that different after all—plenty of space travel, undersea habitations, immaculate cities navigated by expressways and moving sidewalks, and effortless push-button living. None of these windows on the future revealed any glimpse of the World's Fair in a box on everyone's desk, which in thirty years would take browsers from one corporate "pavilion" to another at the speed of . . . well, at almost the speed of light.

But we wouldn't have believed it anyway, and besides, we came to the fair for other reasons as well—because the Century Grill gave us our first taste of chutney (on a hamburger, of all things), because the Vatican had actually sent over Michelangelo's Pieta, and because you could watch the Dance of the Nuts and Bolts at Chrysler. And because one national pavilion offered an experience that summed up New York for us then, as it does today: You went to the Belgian Village to buy an Italian ice, and it was served by a Chinese guy.

Now completely restored and open to visitors, the 1910 house holds a collection of Armstrong memorabilia, including scrapbooks, photos, and gold-plated trumpets. The home's furnishings remain much as they were during Louis and Lucille's lifetimes. A gift shop on the premises sells Armstrong CDs, books, postcards, t-shirts, red beans and rice, and other items.

thebigapple

The city's nickname was first coined in the 1930s by jazz musicians who used the slang word "apple" for any town or city they were touring. New York City, a major gig, was the Big Apple.

The Louis Armstrong House, 34-56 107th Street, Corona, Queens; (718) 478–8274 is open Tuesday through Friday 10:00 A.M. to 5:00 P.M.; Saturday noon to 4:00 P.M. (last tour at 4:00 P.M. each day). Admission is $8.00 for adults, and $4.00 for students and seniors.

The borough of Queens is New York's most residential neighborhood—or rather, collection of neighborhoods, each retaining its own distinctive character. One such neighborhood is *Flushing,* best known to many nonnative New Yorkers as the site of the 1939 and 1964 World's Fairs. The history of this district goes back well over 300 years, as a visit to the *Bowne House* will demonstrate.

John Bowne built the house that today bears his name in 1661. To get some idea of what the future outlying boroughs of New York were like in those days, consider that two years after the Bowne House was built, the town meeting of nearby Jamaica offered a bounty of seven bushels of corn for every wolf shot or otherwise done away with. But wolves weren't the only threat John Bowne faced. A Quaker, he openly challenged Governor Peter Stuyvesant's edict banning that religion by holding meetings of the Society of Friends in his kitchen. He was arrested and sent back to Europe in 1662 but returned to New York two years later, after having been exonerated by the Dutch West India Company, managers of the New Amsterdam colony.

Now the oldest house in Queens, the Bowne House reflects not only the Dutch/English colonial style in which it was originally built but also all of the vernacular styles with which it was modified over the years.

The Bowne House displays styles of furnishing and portrait painting as they developed over the first two centuries of its existence. Everything here belonged to the Bownes, making this property a unique documentation of one family's experience in New York virtually from the time of its founding to the beginning of the modern era.

In 1694 the Friends of Flushing Village—now part of Queens—moved their meeting out of member John Bowne's house to a newly erected *Quaker*

Meeting House. By 1717 the membership had grown so large that the Quakers built an addition doubling the size of the original structure. Since then the house has remained virtually unchanged—a perfectly preserved early American structure still being used as its builders intended.

The Quaker Meeting House, 137–16 Northern Boulevard, Flushing 11357, (718) 358–9636, is open for worship every Sunday from 11:00 A.M. to noon. All are invited to attend. Tours are conducted by appointment.

Queens Historical Society has designed a self-guiding *Flushing Freedom Mile Historic Tour* encompassing nineteen historic sites, including the Bowne House and the Quaker Meeting House. For a copy write them at 143–35 Thirty-seventh Avenue, Flushing 11354 or call (718) 939–0647.

A seventeenth-century Quaker going to a clandestine meeting at the Bowne House might seem to have little in common with a twentieth-century Tibetan Buddhist, but the two share a bond of persecution. One of the uglier aspects of the Maoist period in China was the annexation of Tibet and the suppression of its ancient culture and religion. Despite some recent liberalization on the part of the Chinese occupiers of Tibet, it is still an extremely difficult place to visit; and ironically, those Westerners interested in Tibetan art and religious artifacts have learned to rely on foreign rather than native Tibetan collections. One such collection is the *Jacques Marchais Museum of Tibetan Art* on Staten Island. The museum houses more than a thousand examples of

Tibetan religious art—paintings, carved and cast statues, altars, ritual objects, and musical instruments—each of which was created to aid in the meditation that is such an important part of Buddhism, especially as practiced in Tibet.

And who was Jacques Marchais? "He" was a woman named Jacqueline Coblentz Klauber who operated a Manhattan art gallery under the masculine French pseudonym. Klauber/Marchais had a lifelong interest in things Tibetan that she said originated in her childhood, when she would play with Tibetan figures her great-

Crowned Buddha, Jacques Marchais
Museum of Tibetan Art

grandfather had brought back from the Orient. She never traveled to Tibet, but she carefully added to her collection until her death in 1947.

With its terraced gardens, lily pond, and air of detachment and serenity, the Marchais Museum is indeed an appropriate setting for the religious objects that make up the collection, representing centuries of Tibetan culture.

The Jacques Marchais Museum of Tibetan Art, 338 Lighthouse Avenue, Staten Island, (718) 987–3500, is open 1:00 to 5:00 P.M. Wednesday through Sunday. Admission is $5.00 for adults, $3.00 for senior citizens and students, and $2.00 for children under 12. Group tours are available by appointment. Check www.tibetanmuseum.com for current exhibits and programs, and information on holiday closings.

Within walking distance of the Marchais Museum is a collection of buildings representative of cultural continuity rather than upheaval and transplanting. **Historic Richmond Town** is a collection of twenty-seven buildings, fourteen of them restored and open to the public on a seasonal basis, that reminds us that Staten Island has a richer history than might be suggested by the tract houses and refineries that characterize the present-day borough.

cityfacts

Approximately 30.3 million visitors come to New York City each year.

There are about 230 hotels with 59,000 hotel rooms, and 17,000 restaurants.

Each year more than 5,000 annual street fairs and block parties are held on the city's streets.

The total weight of the Statue of Liberty is 450,000 pounds.

Thirty percent of lower Manhattan is built on acreage created by landfills.

Thirty-six million phone calls are made in the city during an average business day.

Richmond Town seems like a country village far from the bustle of Manhattan, and with good reason—that's what it was, in the seventeenth and eighteenth centuries when these houses and community buildings were built. Among them are the "Voorlezer's [Teacher's] House," a Dutch-era one-room school; an old county courthouse; a general store; and a farmhouse. Many of the buildings are staffed by craftspeople working with period equipment. White clapboard farmhouses dot the property's one hundred acres, and a central museum houses exhibits of Staten Island–made products that reveal the history and diversity of New York's least populous borough. There are special events through the year, and nineteenth-century dinners are served on seveeral dates during the summer. Advance reservations are necessary; the cost is $45.00 per person.

Historic Richmond Town, 441 Clark Avenue, Staten Island, (718) 351–1611, is open Wednesday through Sunday 1:00 to 5:00 P.M. from the day after Labor

Day to June 30, with guided tours given at 2:30 P.M. on weekdays and at 2:00 and 3:30 P.M. on weekends (visitors must be on tours to enter buildings). From July 1 through Labor Day, hours are Wednesday through Saturday 10:00 A.M. to 5:00 P.M.; Sunday 1:00 to 5:00 P.M. In summer, tours are self-guided, with costumed interpreters along the way. Closed major holidays. Admission is $5.00 for adults, $4.00 for seniors, and $3.50 for children ages 5 to 17.

An authentic Chinese Scholar's Garden is one of the highlights at the lovely eighty-acre **Staten Island Botanical Garden** on the grounds of Snug Harbor Cultural Center. It's an environment of wood, rocks, water, a variety of plants, and nineteenth-century furniture in the style of the Ming Period, all carefully composed to create an air of quiet meditation. Other displays include a Pond Garden; Heritage Rose, White, and Perennial Gardens; and a Sensory Garden designed to provide physically challenged persons with a garden experience. The garden, at 1000 Richmond Terrace, (718) 273–8200, is open at no charge from dawn to dusk. The Chinese Scholar's Garden is open Tuesday through Sunday, 10:00 A.M. to 5:00 P.M. with an admission fee of $5.00 for adults and $4.00 for seniors, students with I.D., and children under 12.

The 260-acre **Clay Pit Ponds State Park Preserve,** New York City's only State Park Preserve, allows visitors to step back in time to a Staten Island of 200 years ago. Preserved because of its unique geological, botanical, and historical significance, sands and clays were deposited here during the Cretaceous period nearly 70 million years ago. These, along with glacial deposits approximately 12,000 years old, provide a soil that supports a fascinating assemblage of plants such as black jack oaks, American chestnuts, and a variety of ferns in numerous

Remembering Emilio's

A lot of different people remember a lot of different things about New York in the 1960s—the World's Fair out in Flushing Meadow, be-ins in Central Park, Andy Warhol's "Factory," the last days of the Stork Club—but when I think back on summer nights in the city around 1968 or 1969, I think of Emilio's. Emilio's was a little Italian joint on Sixth Avenue in the Village, a long, narrow place with a bar in front, then a dining room or two, and then the kitchen, which you walked through to get to the patio out back. Emilio's patio was a little open square surrounded by ailanthus trees and brick walls, with three- and four-story buildings all around, and it was lit by Japanese lanterns. Many a night my friends and I sat there and ate lasagna or manicotti, drinking four-dollar bottles of Valpolicella, feeling like we were in the secret happy garden at the center of the most wonderful city in the world.

—Bill Scheller

habitats, including ponds, bogs, sandy barrens, freshwater wetlands, and fields as well as a large number of animals and birds including raccoons, screech owls, box turtles, and rufous-sided towhees.

During the 1800s a man named Abraham Ellis and his partner, Balthaser Kreischer, mined clay here: The men dug it out of a huge bare pit with shovels and pick axes, and donkeys hauled it on rails to the brickworks to the southwest. The clay was used to make such products as paints, dyes, and laundry bluing. When the mines closed, the pit filled with water and marsh plants thrived. Today, Ellis Swamp is home to vegetation, such as cattails and yellow pond lilies, and a mecca for wildlife, such as red-winged blackbirds, spring peepers, and, in early winter, mallard ducks.

dollarsandscents

Approximately 50,000 people shop at Bloomingdale's each day. Each day 500 ounces of fragrance are sprayed in the store.

The preserve has an excellent printed trail guide, which outlines several walks of varying duration of a half hour to an hour. They begin at the picnic area behind the Park Preserve Headquarters.

Clay Pit Ponds State Park Preserve, 83 Nielsen Avenue, Staten Island, (718) 967–1976, is open daily from dawn to dusk. Free seasonal environmental education programs are offered on Saturday. A working organic farm is open Monday through Saturday.

Fort Wadsworth, one of the country's oldest military installations, was first used during the American Revolution and was a key component of the New York Harbor defense system until the early 1970s. It became a National Park site and Lighthouse Center and Museum in 1995. Start your visit by viewing the introductory video at the visitor center before heading out on the 1½-mile trail around the site.

The Visitor Center at Fort Wadsworth, Bay Street, Staten Island, (718) 354–4500, is open Wednesday through Sunday, 10:00 A.M. to 5:00 P.M. Ranger-led tours are available Wednesday through Friday at 2:30 P.M.; Saturday and Sunday at 10:30 A.M. and 2:30 P.M.

In 1857, while Alexander Graham Bell was a ten-year-old boy living in Scotland, Antonio Meucci developed the first working telephone, transmitting a human voice over a copper wire charged with electricity. While he was busy inventing, he played host to his friend, the great Italian patriot Giuseppe Garibaldi. The globe-trotting Garibaldi, who not only campaigned to drive foreign powers from his beloved Italy but had also fought on behalf of Uruguay in its struggle for independence from Argentina, worked as a candlemaker on

Staten Island. He was yet to achieve his greatest victory, as the leader of the "red shirts" who liberated Sicily and southern Italy from Bourbon dynastic rule and set the stage for the ultimate defeat of the pope's temporal power and the incorporation of the Papal States into a secular Kingdom of Italy under the House of Savoy.

All this and more is explained at the ***Garibaldi-Meucci Museum,*** 420 Tompkins Avenue, Rosebank, Staten Island, (718) 442–1608. The museum, owned and operated by the Order of the Sons of Italy in America, the oldest organization of Italian-American men and women in the United States and Canada, is open year-round, Tuesday through Sunday 1:00 to 5:00 P.M. Admission is $3.00.

The oldest cultural institution on Staten Island is the ***Staten Island Institute of Arts and Sciences,*** founded in 1881 and headquartered in the small community of St. George just 2 blocks from the Staten Island Ferry Terminal. The institute's collection has been described as "eclectic"—and eclectic it is. Exhibits focus on the art, natural science, and cultural history of Staten Island and its people, drawing from the institute's collections of more than two million artifacts and specimens.

The art collection includes many fine works from ancient to contemporary periods, including works by Staten Island artists such as Jasper Cropsey, Guy Pene duBois, and Cecil Bell. Also included are pieces by internationally acclaimed talents such as Marc Chagall, Reginald Marsh, and Robert Henri, as well as decorative arts, furniture, clothing, and more. The natural history collections include 500,000 insects, 25,000 plant specimens, and geologic, shell, and archaeological specimens. The archives and library comprise the largest holdings of Staten Island history and science anywhere. Public programs for all ages include weekly "Lunch & Learn" buffets.

The Staten Island Institute of Arts and Sciences, 75 Stuyvesant Place, Staten Island, (718) 727–1135, is open Tuesday through Saturday 9:00 A.M. to 5:00 P.M.

The Kid Made Out Alright

In 1810 a sixteen-year-old Staten Island farm boy named Cornelius Vanderbilt borrowed $100 from his father to buy a small boat for ferrying passengers and freight across the Narrows to Manhattan. By the time of his death in 1877, "Commodore" Vanderbilt had parlayed that initial investment into a steam-ship and railroad fortune of $100 million—not bad, even by the standards of twentieth-century capitalism.

OTHER ATTRACTIONS WORTH SEEING IN NEW YORK CITY AND ON LONG ISLAND

NEW YORK CITY

American Museum of the Moving Image,
Thirty-fifth Avenue at Thirty-sixth Street,
Astoria, Queens,
(718) 784–4520

Bronx Zoo/Wildlife Conservation Park,
Bronx River Parkway–Fordham Road,
Bronx,
(718) 367–1010

Central Park Zoo,
Sixty-fourth Street and Fifth Avenue,
New York,
(212) 861–6030

Empire State Building,
Thirty-fourth Street and Fifth Avenue,
New York,
(212) 736–3100

Forbes Magazine Galleries,
62 Fifth Avenue,
New York,
(212) 206–5548

Museum of Modern Art,
11 West Fifty-third Street,
New York,
(212) 708–9400

Museum and School of Fine Arts,
1083 Fifth Avenue at Eighty-ninth Street,
New York,
(212) 369–4880

New York Botanical Garden,
200th Street and Southern Boulevard
(Kazimiroff Boulevard),
Bronx,
(718) 817–8700; for directions,
(718) 817–8779

New York Public Library,
Fifth Avenue and Forty-second Street,
New York,
(212) 869–8089

North Wind Undersea Institute,
610 City Island Avenue,
Bronx,
(718) 885–0701

St. Patrick's Cathedral,
Fifth Avenue at Fiftieth Street,
New York,
(212) 753–2261

and Sunday noon to 5:00 P.M. Suggested admission is $2.00 for adults and $1.00 for students and senior citizens. Children under 12 are free. Special tours and programs, including gallery tours, guided ferry rides, St. George walking tours, and formal classroom programs, are available to groups.

Clear Comfort, one of the picturesque suburban "cottages" that dotted the shoreline of nineteenth-century Staten Island, was the home of Alice Austen (1866–1952), one of the country's first female photographers. The house was extensively renovated by her father, John, over a period of twenty-five years. By the time he was finished, he had transformed the rundown eighteenth-century Dutch farmhouse into a magnificently landscaped Carpenter Gothic cottage.

LONG ISLAND

American Merchant Marine Museum,
Steamboat Road,
Kings Point,
(516) 773–5000

Belmont Park Race Track,
Hempstead Turnpike and Cross Island
Parkway,
Belmont,
(516) 488–6000

Hofstra University Museum,
Emily Lowe Gallery,
Hempstead Turnpike,
Hempstead,
(516) 463–5672

Long Island Children's Museum,
Garden City,
(516) 222–0207

Montauk Point Lighthouse,
Montauk Point State Park,
Montauk,
(631) 668–2544 or (888) MTK–POINT

Nassau County Museum of Art,
One Museum Drive,
Roslyn Harbor,
(516) 484–9338

Old Westbury Gardens,
Old Westbury,
(516) 333–0048

Sagamore Hill National Historic Site,
Cove Neck Road,
Oyster Bay,
(516) 922–4788

Splish Splash Water Park,
Riverhead,
(631) 727–3600

Vanderbilt Museum,
180 Little Neck Road,
Centerport, (631) 854–5555

Walt Whitman Birthplace
State Historic Site,
246 Old Walt Whitman Road,
Huntington Station,
(631) 427–5240

Alice lived in the house until illness and financial problems forced her to move in 1945. In the 1960s a group of citizens launched a successful effort to save Clear Comfort, and an exact restoration based on hundreds of Austen's photographs was completed in 1985. The home was designated a New York City Landmark in 1971 and a National Historic Landmark in 1993.

Today the gingerbread-gabled home overlooking the Narrows—the shipping channel for the Port of New York—serves as a gallery for her wonderful photographs documenting life in turn-of-the-twentieth-century America. Changing exhibitions exploring themes inspired by her work and times often use images from the Staten Island Historical Society's Alice Austen Collection of nearly 3,000 negatives. A video narrated by Helen Hayes tells the story of *Alice's World.*

The **Alice Austen House,** 2 Hylan Boulevard, Staten Island, (718) 816–4506, is open Thursday through Sunday from noon to 5:00 P.M. and closed major holidays and the months of January and February. There is a suggested donation of $3.00.

Long Island

East of New York City, beyond the borders of the boroughs of Brooklyn and Queens, Long Island stretches from the populous cities and towns of Nassau County to the beaches and New England–style villages of Suffolk County. Beginning in the Nassau County city of **Hempstead,** our first stop is the **African American Museum.**

Founded in 1970 under the auspices of the Nassau County Department of Recreation and Parks in response to growing awareness of the contributions of blacks on Long Island, the Black History Exhibit Center recently changed its name to the African American Museum and altered its emphasis to include interpretive exhibits of traditional and contemporary native African culture as well as local American black history and lore.

The black experience in New York State is by no means concentrated in New York City; nor is it a phenomenon largely associated with twentieth-century migrations from the South. A hundred years ago and more, blacks were farming, whaling, and working at crafts and small businesses on Long Island. Their ancestry, in many cases, dated back to the seventeenth- and eighteenth-century days when slavery—though not as widespread as it would become in the South—was still practiced in New York and the New England states.

The African American Museum tells the story of Long Island's blacks through displays of photographs and artifacts, lectures, workshops, and performing arts. Local artistic talent is especially promoted. African-oriented exhibits and special programs have included shows devoted to West African crafts, art from Sierra Leone, African toys, and black artistic expression in South Africa.

The African American Museum, 110 North Franklin Street, Hempstead, (516) 572–0730, is open Wednesday through Saturday 10:00 A.M. to 5:00 P.M.; Sunday 1:00 to 4:45 P.M.; Wednesday evening 6:00 to 9:00 P.M. Admission is free.

Another Hempstead attraction is not really in Hempstead but in the south-shore village of **Lawrence,** just across the New York City limits from Far Rockaway, Queens. This is **Rock Hall Museum,** a 1767 mansion built by Tory merchant Josiah Martin.

Rock Hall represents the high-water mark of late Georgian architecture in this part of the country, particularly in its interior detailing. The paneling and mantels, as well as much of the eighteenth- and early nineteenth-century furniture and the replica of a colonial kitchen (the original kitchen was in an outbuilding), came down virtually unchanged to our own time. Josiah Martin's family, having come through the revolution none the worse for being on the wrong side, lived here until 1823. The following year Thomas Hewlett bought Rock Hall; his family lived in the mansion for more than a century after his death in 1841. In 1948 the Hewletts gave the place to the town of Hempstead—presumably then a larger municipal entity—for use as a museum.

Rock Hall Museum, 199 Broadway, Lawrence, (516) 239–1157, is open year-round, Wednesday through Saturday 10:00 A.M. to 4:00 P.M. and Sunday noon to 4:00 P.M. Admission is free.

With 8½ miles of waterfront, *Freeport* calls itself "the Boating and Fishing Capital of the East." Woodcleft Avenue, informally known as *Nautical Mile,* is rumored to have once been a haven for bootleggers, pirates, and other scoundrels. Today it is a mecca for sightseers, browsers, and seafood lovers. Restaurants, pubs, fish markets, and gift shops line the avenue, and one of the Island's largest charter/sport fishing fleets sails out of the harbor daily in season.

If your idea of dolls begins and ends with Barbie and Ken, expand your horizons with a visit to *Dear Little Dollies.* More than 6,000 dolls fill every nook and cranny of the 5,000-square-foot store. Barbie is here—but so are one-of-a-kind dolls and limited editions by contemporary artists such as Yolanda Bello and Paul Crees; ethnic dolls; and midpriced dolls from makers including Seymour Mann, and Ashton-Drake Galleries. Prices range from $20 to $14,000. Dorothy and Louis Camilleri, owners of Dear Little Dollies, host numerous artist signings in the shop and special shows in the gallery. They also offer a mail-order service; call or check the Web at www.dldollies.com.

Dear Little Dollies, 418 Bedford Avenue, *Bellmore,* (516) 679–0164, is open Monday through Saturday 10:00 A.M. to 6:00 P.M., and Sunday from noon until 5:00 P.M.

On Long Island's south shore in *Seaford,* is a museum and preserve dedicated to life on the island as it was lived even before the era of farm and village life. The *Tackapausha Museum and Preserve* is an eighty-acre introduction to the ecology and natural history of the Northeast's coastal woodlands. Tackapausha is named after a sachem (chief) of Long Island's Massapequa Indians, a group that by and large managed to live on this land without greatly affecting its wildlife, its plant communities, or the balance of natural forces.

ANNUAL EVENTS ON LONG ISLAND

MARCH

Shakespeare Festival,
Hofstra University,
(516) 463–6644

MAY

Civil War Encampment,
Old Bethpage Village,
(516) 572–8400

JUNE

African American Street Fair,
Hempstead,
(516) 483–2000

Antique & Classic Boat & Car Show,
West Sayville,
(631) HIS–TORY

Harvest of the Bays,
Hampton Bays,
(631) 728–2211

Nassau County Fair,
(516) 794–9303

Strawberry Festival,
Mattituck,
(631) 298–2222

JULY

Annual Fireworks Extravaganza,
Shelter Island,
(631) 749–0399

Hamptons Greek Festival,
Southampton,
(631) 283–6169

Hamptons Shakespeare Festival,
Montauk and Southampton,
(631) 267–0105

Independence Day Celebration,
Old Bethpage Village,
(516) 572–8401

AUGUST

Hampton Classic Horse Show,
Bridgehampton,
(631) 537–3177

Railroad Festival,
Riverhead,
(631) 727–7920

Summer Fair,
Amagansett,
(631) 283–4600

SEPTEMBER

Hempstead Town's Festival by the Sea,
Hempstead,
(516) 483–2000

Historic Seaport Regatta,
Greenport to Sag Harbor,
(631) 477–1383

Shinnecock Pow-Wow,
Shinnecock Reservation,
(631) 283–6143

OCTOBER

Hamptons International Film Festival,
East Hampton,
(631) 324–4600

Haunted Lighthouse,
Montauk Point,
(631) 668–2544

DECEMBER

Big Duck Holiday Lighting Ceremony,
Flanders,
(631) 854–4970

Holiday Traditions and Candlelight Evenings,
Old Bethpage Village,
(516) 572–8400

The Tackapausha Museum is a small facility designed to serve as an introduction to the plants and animal life of the preserve itself. Exhibits explain the relationship between habitat groups, the differences between diurnal and nocturnal animals, and the changes in life patterns brought about by the different seasons. There is also a small collection of native animals, housed in as natural a setting as possible.

The preserve itself is a lovely piece of land, incorporating a variety of ecosystems. A self-guiding trail (pick up the interpretive map at the museum) takes visitors through the different environments.

The Tackapausha Museum and Preserve, Washington Avenue, Seaford 11783, (516) 571–7443, is open Tuesday through Saturday 10:00 A.M. to 4:00 P.M. and Sunday 1:00 to 4:00 P.M. Admission is $4.00 for adults; $1.00 for children; free for children under 4.

At our next stop we find plentiful evidence of the relentless trend toward suburbanization that has characterized this place during the past forty years. But we also find an institution that has set as its goal the preservation of as much as possible of the old, rural Long Island way of life. ***Old Bethpage Village Restoration*** is a re-creation of the world as it was long before there was a Levittown or Long Island Expressway. In fact—at least as far as its buildings are concerned—it is the architectural equivalent of a wildlife preserve. Starting in the middle 1960s, the curators of the village (it's managed by the Nassau County Department of Recreation and Parks) began moving threatened colonial and early nineteenth-century structures here, where they could be set up in a close approximation of a Long Island village of the Civil War era. There are now nearly fifty buildings on the site, all of them having been chosen to represent typical domestic, commercial, and agricultural structures of the era.

Quilting in the Noon Inn, Old Bethpage Village Restoration

All of those buildings without people and activity would make for a rather dry museum, so Old Bethpage Village has been staffed with historically attired guides and craftspeople. There's even an Old Bethpage Village militia, which will presumably come in handy if the place is ever attacked by a contingent from the Genesee Country Village or the Farmers' Museum at Cooperstown.

hailsuburbia

Levittown, the country's first instant suburb, was created in 1947 when 17,400 freestanding houses were erected.

Old Bethpage Village Restoration, Round Swamp Road, Old Bethpage, (516) 572–8400 (recorded message) or 572–8 401, is open Wednesday through Saturday 10:00 A.M. to 4:00 P.M. and Saturday and Sunday 10:00 A.M. to 5:00 P.M. Call for November and December hours. Closed January and February. Closed holidays except Memorial Day, July 4, Labor Day, and Columbus Day, when the restoration is closed the day after. Admission is $7.00 for adults and $5.00 for children and senior citizens (ticket sales end one hour before closing). Call for information on special presentations and events.

The **Gold Coast,** up on the north shore of Long Island, was created during the Roaring Twenties by families such as the Vanderbilts, the Chryslers, the Phippses, the Woolworths, and the Guggenheims, who built great mansions there. For information on which ones are open to the public for tours, call the Long Island Convention and Visitors Bureau, (800) 441–4601.

Sands Point Preserve overlooking Long Island Sound has something for both mansion and nature lovers. A large portion of the 216-acre property was owned by railroad heir Howard Gould at the turn of the century. He built the Tudor-inspired **Hempstead House** and **Castlegould,** the enormous turreted stable and carriage house that now serve as a visitors' center. In 1917 the Daniel Guggenheim family purchased the estate, and in 1923 Harry Guggenheim, Daniel's son, built the Norman mansion **Falaise** (the French word for cliff) on his share of the family property.

Today the property is owned by the Nassau County Department of Recreation and Parks, which preserves it not only as a focus of historical interest but also for the preservation and public enjoyment of its natural surroundings. Castlegould features large traveling natural history exhibits that change twice a year, plus interactive exhibits changing on a six-month basis. There are six marked nature trails; two of them are self-guiding, and one follows the shoreline. In addition to numerous geological phenomena, such as glacial erratics (large granite boulders dropped from the ice during the last continental glaciation about 20,000 years ago), there is a wide range of plant and bird life within the preserve. Kids will enjoy following the special Dinosaur Trail, with its replicas of real fossilized dinosaur tracks. Pick up trail maps at the visitors' center in Castlegould.

Sands Point Preserve, 95 Middleneck Road, Sands Point, (516) 571–7900 or (518) 571–7901, nature trails are open daily from 10:00 A.M. to 5:00 P.M. A gate fee of $1.00 is collected between Memorial Day and Labor Day. Falaise is open for tours from early May through late October, Wednesday through Sunday hourly between noon and 3:00 P.M., with an additional tour at 3:30 on weekends. Tours are limited to twenty people, and admission is on a first-come, first-served basis. Tickets are $6.00 for adults and $4.00 for seniors; children under 10 are not permitted. Hempstead House is open weekends from early May through late October, 12:30 to 4:00 P.M.; visitors should note that at press time, Hempstead House's famous collection of Wedgewood china is not on display. Special natural history exhibits in Castlegould are $4.00 for adults, $3.00 for children and seniors. Both Falaise and the Hempstead House are closed during the September Medieval Festival.

The *Holocaust Memorial & Educational Center of Nassau County,* on the 204-acre Welwyn Preserve, hopes to "foster a greater understanding of the causes and consequences of one of the darkest periods in world history." The center hosts ongoing exhibits and has a 1,850-volume library. It's at 100 Crescent Beach Road in *Glen Cove,* (516) 571–8040, and is open Monday through Friday 9:30 A.M. to 4:30 P.M. and Sunday 11:00 A.M. to 4:00 P.M. Admission is free.

Planting Fields Arboretum is the legacy of William Robertson Coe, a British-born insurance magnate who purchased this property in 1913. Coe immediately set about making his 409-acre estate into as complete a farm-garden-arboretum as possible. He began building greenhouses in 1914 (Coe Hall, the great house on the property, did not go up until 1919–21) and imported his camellia collection in 1917. The camellias couldn't make it through a Long Island winter, so a special greenhouse was built for them. Coe set up a working dairy and kept pigs and chickens as well. (Milk and produce from Planting Fields were donated to the needy during the Great Depression.)

islanditems

The largest island adjoining the continental United States, Long Island is approximately 118 miles long and 20 miles wide at its widest point.

Long Island has more than 150 beaches; the largest is 2,400-acre Jones Beach.

With almost 2.7 million people, if Long Island were a city, it would be the fourth largest in the nation.

King Kullen, the country's first supermarket, opened on Long Island in 1930.

They'll Never Win a Beauty Contest

The Eastern Hellbender, largest salamander in North America, is a denizen of only two river drainages in New York State—the Susquehanna and the Allegany. How large are we talking about? Hellbenders can grow to an astounding 29 inches, and their diet of worms, crayfish, and carrion can see them through a seventy-year lifespan. The short-legged, flat-bodied amphibians are nocturnal and fully aquatic, spending daytime under rocks or overhanging stream banks. They are entirely harmless.

But it was trees and shrubs that most commanded Coe's attention, and they were the subject of some of his greatest extravagances. The copper beech on the north lawn, for instance, was moved here from Massachusetts by barge and a team of seventy-two horses when it was already 60 feet high. Working with master landscape gardeners such as A. Robeson Sargent and James Dawson of Olmsted Brothers, Coe created grand allées of trees designed to frame the views from the house, and he established rambling azalea walks. As late as the 1950s, in the last years of his life, Coe planted the rhododendron park, which remains one of the outstanding features of Planting Fields.

From April through September (except on Labor Day and July 4) visitors can tour Coe Hall daily noon to 3:30 P.M. The fee is $5.00 for adults and children over 12, $3.50 for seniors, $1.00 for children ages 7 to 12, and free for those under 7. For tour information call (516) 922–8670.

Planting Fields Arboretum, 1039 van Buren Street, **Oyster Bay,** (516) 922–9200, is open daily 9:00 A.M. to 5:00 P.M. There is a $6.00 entry charge per car daily from May 1 through Labor Day and on weekends and holidays from Labor Day through the end of April. Closed Christmas.

> 'Tis advertised in Boston, New York and Buffalo,
> Five hundred brave Americans a-whaling for to go,
> Singing "Blow, ye winds in the morning,
> Blow ye winds heigh-o,
> Heave away, haul away, and blow, winds, blow."

So goes the old chantey.

But where would these brave whalers ship out from once they had answered the call? Most often they would go down to the sea at New Bedford or Nantucket; if they began their hard voyages on Long Island, most likely their home port would be Sag Harbor. But there were also smaller whaling ports on Long Island, such as **Cold Spring Harbor.** Here today the **Whaling Museum** celebrates the skills and adventures of the town's own whalers as well as those of other men who worked in this arduous industry from colonial times through the nineteenth century.

The Whaling Museum houses a large collection of the implements used in the whale "fishery," as it was known. Here are harpoons, lances, and the tools used in separating blubber from whale carcasses. A permanent exhibit, "Mark Well the Whale," details the history and impact of whaling on the locality. The museum features the state's only fully equipped nineteenth-century whaleboat with original gear; an extensive collection of the whaler's art of scrimshaw; and "The Wonder of Whales" conservation gallery for children.

awhaleofadeal

The first pastor of East Hampton's "Old Church," which was built in 1717, received for his salary "forty-five pounds annually, lands rate free, grain to be first ground at the mill every Monday and one-fourth of the whales stranded on the beach."

The Whaling Museum, Main Street, Route 25A, Cold Spring Harbor, (631) 367–3418, is open daily from Memorial Day through Labor Day; closed Monday during the rest of the year. Hours are 11:00 A.M. to 5:00 P.M. Admission is $4.00 for adults $3.00 for seniors and students 5 to 18; families (parents and children) $12.00. Free for military personnel and children 5 and under. On Sunday from 11:00 A.M. to 1:00 P.M., admission is by donation only.

The **DNA Learning Center,** the educational arm of Cold Spring Harbor Laboratory, is the world's first biotechnology museum. Two- and three-dimensional displays, computer multimedia, videos, and other elements are utilized to teach

Whaling Museum

visitors about genes in a presentation called "The Genes We Share," free Monday through Friday 10:00 A.M. to 4:00 P.M. and Saturday noon to 4:00 P.M.

DNA Learning Center, 334 Main Street, Cold Spring Harbor, (516) 367–5170, presents "Long Island Discovery," a twenty-eight-minute multimedia presentation exploring the history and heritage of Long Island. During the school year it is shown Monday through Saturday at 10:00 and 11:00 A.M. and 1:00 P.M. During the summer it is presented Monday through Friday at 10:00 and 11:00 A.M. and 1:00 P.M.; Saturday at 1:00 and 3:00 P.M. Call for exhibition hours. Admission is free.

The dog that helped Richard Nixon become president is interred under a small granite stone at the *Bide-a-Wee Pet Cemetery* in *Wantagh.* Checkers the cocker spaniel died in 1964, and we're not sure why the future president, who never lived on Long Island, chose to bury him here. But here he rests alongside about 50,000 other deceased pets. The cemetery is on Beltagh Avenue opposite Wantagh High School. Checkers is buried in plot #5.

Don't miss a visit to the National Landmark *St. James General Store*, 516 Moriches Road, St. James, (631) 862–8333. In business since 1857 it's the oldest continuously-operating general store in the country and looks just as it did in 1890. More than 4,000 items, many of which are nineteenth-century reproductions including handmade quilts, salt glaze pottery, hand-carved decoys, penny candy, exotic teas, and bonnets, fill the store's venerable shelves. The store is open daily except Monday from 10:00 A.M. to 5:00 P.M.; closed January and February.

hopaboard

Two year-round ferry lines cross Long Island Sound from Connecticut to Long Island: Cross Sound Ferry, Inc., (631) 323–2525 or (860) 443–5281, operates between New London and Orient Point; Bridgeport & Port Jefferson Ferry Co., (631) 473–0286, runs between Bridgeport and Port Jefferson. Both rides take approximately seventy- five minutes each way.

The village of *Stony Brook* on Long Island Sound has it all: a scenic location, a fascinating history, great food and lodgings, museums, and terrific shopping. And it owes its present-day success primarily to one man, Ward Melville, whose vision helped the rural village to successfully metamorphose into a suburban center while still retaining its historic integrity. His plan, unveiled to the community in 1939, called for relocating businesses and homes so as to open the view to the harbor. The shops were moved to a "shopping center" at the head of the village green, and today more than forty of the trendiest shops on Long Island are housed at the *Stony Brook Village Center.* Up the road the *Three Village Garden Club Exchange* features two floors of antiques and collectibles.

So Who's Buried There?

At 5,344 feet, Mt. Marcy is the highest point in New York State—and, of course, in Essex County. But which is the lowest "high point" in any of New York's sixty-two counties? That would be a spot in Greenwood Cemetery, in King's County, otherwise known as Brooklyn. Mt. Marcy looms over the big borough at a towering 220 feet.

Stony Brook's ***Three Village Inn***, built in 1751, was until 1867 the home of Captain Jonas Smith, Long Island's first millionaire sea captain. Today it's a charming inn and restaurant, a winner of the *Wine Spectator* Award of Excellence, featuring homemade breads and desserts and house specialties such as cold plum soup, pan-roasted chicken breast stuffed with ham and Monterey Jack cheese, baked lobster pie, and, every Sunday, a "Thanksgiving" turkey dinner with all the trimmings. The Inn is at 150 Main Street, Stony Brook; www.threevillageinn.com. To make a room or meal reservation (breakfast, lunch, dinner, and Sunday brunch), call (516) 751–0555.

Within walking distance of the inn, at 1200 Route 25A, is the ***Long Island Museum of American Art, History and Carriages,*** a museum complex housing the ***Margaret Melville Blackwell History Museum,*** featuring American decor in miniature in a gallery of fifteen period rooms and one of the country's finest collections of antique decoys, plus a new exhibition, every two or three months, on a historical theme; the ***Dorothy and Ward Melville Carriage House,*** with its world-renowned collection of more than ninety horse-drawn carriages; and the ***Art Museum,*** exhibiting American art from the eighteenth century to the present, as well as collected works of American genre painter William Sidney Mount (1807–68). There are also a 1794 barn, an 1867 carriage shed, an 1875 blacksmith shop, an 1877 one-room schoolhouse, and a colonial burying ground. The museums are open daily in July and August; the rest of the year they're open Wednesday through Saturday 10:00 A.M. to 5:00 P.M. and Sunday noon to 5:00 P.M. Closed Monday (except Monday holidays) and Tuesday. Also closed New Year's, Thanksgiving, Christmas Eve, and Christmas Day. Admission is $7.00 for adults, $6.00 for seniors, $3.00 ages 6 to 17, $3.00 for college students with ID; under 6 free. Admission covers everything on the nine-acre grounds. For information call (631) 751–0066.

A must-see before leaving town is the working ***Gristmill*** on Harbor Road, built circa 1751 and renovated through the efforts of Ward Melville in 1947. The mill is open in May and June and September through December on weekends noon to 4:30 P.M.; in July and August Friday, Saturday, and Sunday noon to 4:30

P.M. Admission is $2.00 for adults and $1.00 for children under 12. For information call (631) 751–2244. The Ward Melville Heritage Association, which operates the mill, also offers Discovery Wetlands Cruises; call (631) 751–2244 for infor,mation and ticket prices, or reserve online at www.wardmelvilleher itage.org.

Like Planting Fields in Oyster Bay, the south shore's **Bayard-Cutting Arboretum State Park** is another rich man's estate that has become a mecca for those who enjoy majestic trees and beautiful gardens. The arboretum, which is virtually adjacent to the state-managed **Connetquot River State Park Preserve,** was once the property of one of New York City's ablest financiers. William Bayard Cutting (1850–1912) was a lawyer, railroad director and president, banker, insurance executive, and philanthropist noted for having built the first block of Manhattan tenements to feature indoor plumbing.

In his leisure time (whenever that might have been), Cutting enjoyed himself by improving his Long Island retreat. He built the sixty-eight-room Tudor mansion that stands on the arboretum grounds in 1886, with a few decorative touches by his friend Louis Comfort Tiffany. (Visitors can enter the mansion, the former dining room of which houses a well-maintained collection of mounted birds.) When it came to landscaping, Cutting placed a good deal of trust in another friend, the great Harvard botanist and silviculturist Charles Sprague Sargent. Together with none other than Frederick Law Olmsted, Sargent was responsible for much of the appearance of the Cutting estate and, subsequently, the arboretum.

The Bayard-Cutting Arboretum State Park is an especially pleasant place for a quiet stroll, even for those not well versed in tree species. Azaleas and rhododendrons grow here in profusion. The streams and ponds, with their ducks and geese and graceful little footbridges, are reason enough to spend an afternoon at the Cutting.

The Bayard-Cutting Arboretum State Park, Route 27A, Great River, (631) 581–1002, is open Tuesday through Sunday 10:00 A.M. to sunset. Admission is $6.00 per car; free from November through March. Admission includes a tour of the first floor of the mansion; from September through May, tours of the newly restored second floor are given on Sunday at 2:00 P.M. for an additional $4.00 charge.

Within a few miles of the Bayard-Cutting Arboretum, on the Great South Bay that divides the barrier beach of Fire Island from the Long Island mainland, is the village of **West Sayville,** with its **Long Island Maritime Museum.** The whalers of Cold Spring Harbor were by no means the only brave Long Islanders to go down to the sea to pursue their quarry; here in West Sayville, men went out into dangerous waters to harvest the more prosaic but nonetheless important oyster. The maritime museum, in fact, includes a restored vintage 1907 oyster house and has among its holdings the largest collection of small craft on Long Island. There is also a restored boat-builder's shop, illustrative of the skill and care that went into the building of these essential commercial vessels. Other exhibits focus on the tools of oystermen over the years.

It isn't all oysters at the Long Island Maritime Museum. Displays of yachting and racing memorabilia, model boats, and artifacts related to the lifesaving service of the nineteenth century round out the museum's collection. Duck and other shorebird decoys, an integral part of American folk art in shoreline communities well into this century, are also on exhibit. The Bayman's Cottage depicts the style of living at the turn of the century.

onbeyondbabylon

In 1901 Guglielmo Marconi sent his first radio transmission from Fire Island Avenue in Babylon.

Long Island Maritime Museum, Route 27A, West Sayville, (631) HIS–TORY is open Monday through Saturday 10:00 A.M. to 3:00 P.M. and Sunday noon to 4:00 P.M. Admission is $4.00 for adults, $2.00 for seniors and children.

Fire Island National Seashore stretches for 32 miles from *Robert Moses State Park* on the west to *Smith Point Park* on the east. Both parks are accessible by car, but the seventeen communities sandwiched in between can be reached only by boat or on foot. Designated a "forever preserved wilderness area," the seashore is home to a variety of bird and animal life, including herons, wild geese, and deer (be alert for deer ticks, carriers of Lyme Disease, when you're in high grass). Among the must-see spots on the barrier island are *Sunken Forest* at Sailors Haven, *Watch Hill,* and *Smith Point.* For information contact the National Parks Service at (631) 289–4810. *Fire Island Lighthouse,* east of Robert Moses State Park (631–661–4876), which began guiding ships to New York Harbor in 1826, is open for tours daily from 9:30 A.M. to 5:00 P.M. in July and August. April through June, it's open weekends and holidays 9:30 A.M. to 5:00 P.M.

fireislandferry

No cars are allowed on Fire Island, home of Fire Island National Seashore, which stretches for 32 miles through 17 communities. The only way to get there is via ferry. For more information call Sunken Forest Ferry Service, (631) 589–0810, which operates from May to October.

September through mid-December, weekends 9:30 A.M. to 4:00 P.M. Reservations are recommended. The adjacent museum is open daily during months when the lighthouse is open; if no school groups are touring, it may be possible to tour the lighthouse. Admission to the museum is free. The cost to climb the tower is $5.00 for adults and $3.50 for children under 12, and $4.00 for seniors.

Elsie Collins's *1880 House* is a delightful, antique-filled bed-and-breakfast just a few blocks from *Westhampton Beach.* There are two large suites, each with its own adjoining sitting room and private bath in the farmhouse, and a third in an adjacent one-hundred-year-old barn. Guests can cool off in the swimming pool after a game of tennis or warm up by the fireplace after a brisk winter's walk on the beach. The B&B, at Two Seafield Lane, Westhampton Beach, (631) 288–1559 or (800) 346–3290, is open year-round. Rates, including breakfast, range from $125 to $150 in winter; $150 to $175 spring and fall; and $175 to $250 Memorial Day through Labor Day. A two-night minimum (three nights on holiday weekends) appllies in summer. Also four- and seven-day rates are available.

If your poodle has always wanted to sleep in the same bed as Jack Nicholson did, we've got a great place for you: the **Southampton Inn.** This hostelry goes beyond being pet (and family) friendly: Fifi can actually have breakfast with you in the library. But the place isn't going completely to the dogs: the ninety-room Tudor-style hotel offers elegant accommodations, fine dining, conference facilities, a heated swimming pool, all-weather tennis, a fitness room, a game room, and beach access. If you're not a pet person, ten Romance Rooms (off limit to pets, kids, and smoking) have been set aside in a separate building.

The Southampton Inn, 91 Hill Street, Southampton; (800) 832–6500; www.southamptoninn.com, is open year-round. Rates for a double range from $119 to $199 off-season; $149 to $459 from May to October.

In 1954 abstract expressionist painter Jackson Pollock moved with his bride, artist Lee Krasner, to a two-story 1879 shingled house overlooking Accabonac Creek. He lived here until his death in 1956, painting some of his most famous pieces in the studio he converted from a barn.

Today, at the *Pollock-Krasner House and Study Center*, visitors can tour the artists' studio, which contains a documentary photo-essay chronicling Pollock's evolution as an artist and detailing his working methods, and their house, including their furniture and personal library, as well as Pollock's extensive collection of jazz albums.

The Study Center, established to promote scholarship in twentieth-century American art, houses a growing art reference library built around the personal papers of those who witnessed the birth of abstract expressionism.

The Pollock-Krasner House and Study Center, 830 Springs Fireplace Road, *East Hampton,* (631) 324–4929, is open June, July, and August 1:00 to 5:00 P.M.; call for appointments the rest of the year. Tours are given every hour on the hour. Admission is $5.00 adults (guided tours $10.00), under 12 free. State and city university students, faculty, and staff are also admitted free.

Who you gonna call if you come across a stranded sea creature? ***Riverhead Foundation for Marine Research and Preservation,*** of course. The foundation is in charge of rescuing any whale, porpoise, dolphin, seal, or sea turtle stranded anywhere in New York. Established in 1980, the organization has handled more than 2,000 strandings, including the first and only successful rehabilitation and release of a baby sperm whale.

The Visitor Center briefs people on what to do if they find a stranded creature (don't attempt to push the animal back into the water or obstruct the blowhole; do notify the foundation and keep crowds away). It also has exhibits on sea turtles, harbor seals (when available), and other sea life.

Riverhead Foundation for Marine Research and Preservation's Visitor Center, 467 East Main Street, ***Riverhead,*** (631) 369–9840, is open from 10:00 A.M. to 5:00 P.M., daily July through Labor Day and weekends only the rest of the year. Admission is $4.00 for adults and $2.00 for children. The twenty-four-hour stranding hotline is (631) 369–9829. Visit its Web site at www.riverhead foundation.org. The foundation also operates seal-watching cruises from mid-January to mid-April; also seal walks (check Web site for details).

Why is there a giant duck on the side of the road just outside the town of ***Flanders?*** For the same reason there's a huge elephant on the Jersey shore: to attract tourists. The 30-foot-long, 20-foot-high white duck was built in 1931 by a local entrepreneur who was the proprietor of one of the area's numerous duck farms. Today the ***Big Duck*** houses a shop run by Friends for Long Island's Heritage and is a great place to stock up on duck collectibles and souvenirs. It's on Route 24, and open May 1 through Labor Day, daily (except Monday) from 10:00 A.M. to 5:00 P.M. Hours are subject to change. For information call (631) 852–8292.

At ***Slo Jack's Miniature Golf,*** Long Island's oldest, the windmill has been turning since 1960. It's the miniature course of our dreams, complete with a wishing well, paddle wheels, and a 1960s drive-in restaurant (car service no longer offered) that serves up hamburgers, hot dogs, soft-serve ice cream,

Give or Take a Few Decades . . .

Montauk Point Light was erected in 1796 on the recommendation of President George Washington, who calculated that it would stand for 200 years on its location some 300 feet from the sea's edge. Today, the 110 ½-foot tower—first in New York State and fourth-oldest in the United States—is only 100 feet from the water, which nibbles steadily at the tip of Long Island. Anti-erosion efforts have been implemented to protect the historic structure, which has already outlasted Washington's estimate of its lifespan.

Mexican food, and local seafood. Official season at Slo Jack's Miniature Golf, 212 West Montauk Highway, **Hampton Bays,** (631) 728–9601, is Memorial Day to Labor Day, but the restaurant is open March through Christmas, and unofficially the course is also open during that period. Both are open 10:00 A.M. to 11:00 P.M. There's also a surf shop on the premises.

America's oldest cattle ranch isn't out west—it's on the South Fork of Long Island. Established in 1658, **Deep Hollow Ranch** puts a different spin on Long Island beach life. Instead of lolling around on the beach at East Hampton, seeing and being seen, try one of Deep Hollow's ninety-minute guided trail rides, which will take you over hill and dale and along a lovely stretch of beach designated for horseback riding. Sprawling across 4,000 acres of land owned by Suffolk County, the ranch offers horses for all levels of riding skill along with English and western saddle lessons and pony rides for the kids, who will also enjoy the petting farm stocked with baby animals. In summer Deep Hollow offers nightly chuck wagon rides and barbecues and a dinner theater in July and August. When you hit the trail at Deep Hollow, you'll be following in history's hoofprints: Teddy Roosevelt camped here with his Rough Riders after the Spanish-American War. The ranch (P.O. Box 835) is in **Montauk** 11954, (631) 668–2744. Rides are offered year-round.

it'sexhausting

More than two million motor vehicles and 80,000 motor boats are registered in Nassau and Suffolk Counties.

Written up in major publications including *Gourmet* magazine and the *New York Times*, **The Lobster Roll Restaurant** (631–267–3740) is neither off the beaten path nor undiscovered. But the restaurant, an institution in these parts, gets consistently high marks for its fresh seafood, including salmon burgers and, of course, lobster rolls. It's right on Montauk Highway between **Amagansett** and Montauk: Look for the big sign that says LUNCH. (Actually, lunch and dinner are served daily in summer.)

If you're looking for peace and quiet, beautiful beaches, or simply a taste of island life, take a short ferry ride to **Shelter Island,** cradled between the North and South forks of Long Island. The car ferries leave from Greenport on the North Fork and North Haven on the South Shore. The Nature Conservancy owns nearly one-third of the 8,000-acre island, ensuring that this portion, at least, will remain unspoiled.

In 1871 a small group of Methodist clergy and laymen from Brooklyn purchased land on a bluff overlooking Shelter Island Sound. American landscape architect Robert Morris Copeland laid out plans for a camp meeting place, and four years later, the Union Church, intended by Copeland to be the camp's visual and social center, was built in the grove, a natural amphitheater that was also the site for an open-air preacher's stand and tents to accommodate the people who attended the early meetings.

Over the years 141 buildings in a variety of styles ranging from steep-gabled, delicately trimmed cottages to larger Stick, Queen Anne, and Colonial Revival homes were built here, and ***Shelter Island Heights Historic District*** "remains a unique embodiment of sensitive community development, based on respect for the natural landscape, a 19th century American ideal and practice."

There are four trails on the Nature Conservancy's ***Mashomack Preserve*** for nature study and bird-watching, varying in length from 1½ to 11 miles, and a barrier-free Braille trail for the visually impaired. In the village you can rent bicycles at ***Piccozzi's Bike Shop*** (631–749–0045), grab a bite at ***The Dory Restaurant*** (631–749–8871), have a lovely meal at the Victorian ***Chequit Inn*** (631–749–0018), or stop in at one of the other restaurants. By now you'll have fallen in love with the island and vowed never to leave. There are plenty of places that will put you up. The Chequit Inn also has guest rooms, as do a number of other places, including the ***Beech Tree House*** (631–749–4252), which has suites with full kitchens, and ***Shelter Island Resort*** (631–749–2001), overlooking Shelter Island Sound. For more information contact the Shelter Island Chamber of Commerce, Box 598, Shelter Island 11964, (631) 749–0399.

Long Island's North Fork is considered by many to be the "undiscovered" fork. Although it's far less crowded than the South Fork, it's quickly becoming a major tourist destination. But hop off the major highway (Route 25), and you'll discover some wonderful off-the-beaten-path surprises.

Cutchogue's Village Green on Route 25 is home to numerous historic buildings, including the beautifully preserved 1649 ***Old House,*** a National Historic

. . . And One Even Better

East Hampton's earliest white settlers were Puritans from Maidstone, Kent, who first landed in Salem, Massachusetts, and then continued on to found the Long Island town in 1649. In 1660 they acquired from the Montauk Indians "all the neck of land called Montauk, with all and every part and parcel thereof from sea to sea, from the utmost end of the land eastward to the sea-side, unto the other end of the said land westward, adjoining to the bounds of East Hampton . . . with meadow, wood, stone, creeks, ponds, and whatsover doth or may grow upon or issue from the same, with all the profits and commodities, by sea or land, unto the aforesaid inhabitants of East Hampton, their heirs and assigns, forever."

The price: £30 4s. 8d. sterling; in today's currency, approximately $1,000.

Landmark. Among the outstanding features of this English-style dwelling: the pilastered top chimney and the three-part casement window frames.

Take time to wander through the nearby **Old Burying Ground,** where many of the tombstones date back to the early 1700s and give a fascinating insight into the area's rich history. Among the stones:

> Rev. Thomas Payne
> B. 1723 / D. 10–15–1766

> Ah cruel death why didst thou strike so quick
> that guide the souls and healer of the sick
> them by to prize such useful death doth teach.

The Old House is owned and maintained by The Old House Society, Inc. and managed by the Cutchogue-New Suffolk Historical Council, P.O. Box 361, Cutchogue 11935, (631) 734–6977.

Today Cutchogue is rapidly becoming renowned for the numerous wineries that dot the road on both sides of town. Vintners have found the soil ideal for growing grapes, and the vines are thriving. The good news for tourists is that each vineyard has a tasting room and is delighted to have you stop by and sample its wares. You can meander from one to another on your own or retain the excellent services of Jo-Ann Perry, proprietor of **Vintage Tours,** who will tailor a tour to her customers' tastes or recommend one if they wish. She's a font of knowledge about both wine and local lore and combines a tour with a gourmet lunch on request. The basic tour begins at 11:30 A.M. (in her air-conditioned van). It costs $45 per person from November until Memorial Day and $55 per person from Memorial Day weekend until the first of December. Tours last from four to five hours. For information call her at (631) 765–4689.

Since 1976 folks have been stopping by the unprepossessing **Hellenic Snack Bar & Restaurant** (631–477–0138) on Route 25 in **East Marion** for some of the best Greek food on Long Island. Among the house specialties: *dolmades* (stuffed grape leaves), *spanakopita* (spinach pie), *moussaka,* and fried calamari. The desserts are all homemade, and fresh lamb, chicken, and pork are prepared on the outdoor rotisserie. The Hellenic is open for three meals daily.

Places to Stay in New York City and on Long Island

New York City (some booking services)

Bed and Breakfast Network of New York
(212) 645–8134 or
(800) 900–8134

Empire State B&B Association
www.esbba.com

Hotel Reservation Network Discount Rates
(800) 964–6835
www.hotels.com

Quikbook (hotels)
(800) 789–9887
www.quikbook.com

YMCAs,
(800) FIT–YMCA

AMAGANSETT

Mill-Garth Country Inn
23 Windmill Lane
(631) 267–3757

GARDEN CITY

Garden City International Hotel
45 Seventh Street
(516) 747–3000

LONG ISLAND

Dune Resorts, Montauk Amagansett, and East Hampton
(800) 684–DUNE

MONTAUK

Gurney's Inn Resort & Spa
290 Old Montauk Highway
(800) 8–GURNEYS or (631) 668–2345

Oceanside Beach Resort
626 Montauk Highway
(631) 668–9825

Shepherds Neck Inn
90 Second House Road
(631) 668–2105

PORT JEFFERSON

Holly Berry
415 West Broadway
(631) 331–3123

SHELTER ISLAND

Beach House B&B
P.O. Box 648
Shelter Island 11964
(631) 749–0264

Ram's Head Inn
108 Ram Island Drive
(631) 749–0811

Shelter Island Resort
Shore Road
Crescent Beach
(631) 749–4005

SOUTHAMPTON

Old Post House
136 Main Street
(631) 283–1717

WESTHAMPTON BEACH

Inn on Main
191 Main Street
(631) 288–8900

NEW YORK CITY AND LONG ISLAND

HANDY WEB SITES

General tourist information:
www.nycvisit.com

Virtual Tour of NYC:
www.nyctourist.com

New York City Parks:
www.nycgovparks.org

MTA (New York City subway):
www.mta.nyc.ny.us

Brooklyn Tourism Council:
www.brooklynx.org/tourism

Bronx Tourism Council:
www.ilovethebronx.com

Staten Island Tourism Council:
www.statenislandusa.com

Port Authority of New York and New Jersey:
www.panynj.gov

Places to Eat in New York City and on Long Island

NEW YORK CITY

BROOKLYN

Peter Luger Steakhouse
178 Broadway
(718) 387–7400

Junior's
386 Flatbush Avenue
(718) 852–5257
(Deli; cheesecake)

The River Cafe
1 Water Street
(718) 522–5200

Totonno Pizzeria Napolitano
1524 Neptune Avenue
(718) 372–8606

CITY ISLAND

Crab Shanty One
361 City Island Avenue
(718) 885–1810

MANHATTAN

Barney Greengrass
541 Amsterdam Avenue
(212) 724–4707

Calle Ocho
446 Columbus Avenue
(212) 873–5025
(Cuban cuisine)

Gotham Bar & Grill
12 East Twelfth Street
(212) 620–4020

Heidelberg
1648 Second Avenue
(212) 650–1385
(German cuisine)

NEW YORK INFORMATION

TRAVEL

New York State Division of Tourism
P.O. Box 2603
Albany 12220
(800) CALL–NYS
(outside U.S.: 518–474–4116)
www.state.ny.us
www.iloveny.com

New York State Department of Environmental Conservation
Room 679
50 Wolf Road
Albany 12233

General information:
(518) 457–3521

Campground information only:
(518) 457–2500

Camping reservations only:
(800) 456–CAMP
Call or write for free camping brochure.

New York Office of Parks, Recreation, and Historic Preservation
Empire State Plaza
Agency Building 1
Albany 12238
(518) 474–0456
Free guide to state parks and historic sites; brochures on biking, boating, snowmobiling.

(800) 456–CAMP
Camping and cabin reservations for state-operated sites.

New York State Hospitality and Tourism Association
(800) ENJOY–NY
Reservations at member hotels throughout the state.

Empire State Passport
Passport
State Parks
Albany 12238
One-time annual charge allows unlimited vehicle entrance to all state parks.

Il Mulino
86 West Third Street
(212) 673–3783
(Italian cuisine)

Nobu
105 Hudson Street
Tribeca
(212) 219–0500
(Japanese cuisine)

Patsy's
236 West 56th Street
(212) 247–3491
(Italian cuisine)

Shun Lee Palace East
155 East Fifty-fifth Street
(212) 371–8844
(Chinese cuisine)

Sylvia's
328 Lenox Avenue
Harlem
(212) 996–0660
(Soul food)

Terrace in the Sky
Butler Hall
400 West 119th Street
Harlem
(212) 666–9490
(French cuisine)

Union Square Cafe
21 East Sixteenth Street
(212) 243–4020

Vong
Lipstick Building
200 East Fifty-fourth Street
(212) 486–9592

LONG ISLAND

GARDEN CITY

Ruth's Chris Steak House
600 Old Country Road
(516) 222–0220

TRANSPORTATION

Major Airports
Albany International Airport (oldest municipal airport in the country)

Greater Buffalo International Airport

Greater Rochester International Airport

JFK (New York City)

La Guardia (New York City)

Newark (NJ) International

Syracuse-Hancock International Airport

Trains
AMTRAK, (800) USA–RAIL

Metro-North, (212) 532–4900; service between Grand Central Station, New Haven, Long Island, and the Hudson Valley

Bus
Adirondack Trailways, (800) 225–6815

Greyhound, (800) 528–0447

New York Trailways, (800) 295–5555

Ferries
New York Waterway-Ferry and Bus System, (800) 53–FERRY

Staten Island-Ferry, (718) 815–2628

Temperature Averages
Low 26° F, High 77° F

Major Newspapers
Buffalo News (Buffalo)

Daily News (New York City)

New York Post (New York City)

New York Times (New York City)

Plattsburgh Press Republican (Plattsburgh)

Rochester Democrat and Chronicle (Rochester)

Syracuse Post Standard (morning)/Herald Journal (evening) (Syracuse)

Times Union (Albany)

Population
19,300,000 (2004 est.)

GREENPORT

Greenporter Hotel & Spa
326 Front Street
(631) 477–0066

HOLBROOK

Mamma Lombardi's
400 Furrows Road
(631) 737–0774

MONTAUK

Gosman's Dock
500 West Lake Drive
(631) 668–3243

OYSTER BAY

Canterbury Ales
Oyster Bar & Grill
46 Audrey Avenue
(516) 922–3614

PORT JEFFERSON

Golden Pineapple
201 Liberty Avenue
(631) 331–0706

PORT WASHINGTON

Yamaguchi
63 Main Street
(516) 883–3500
(Japanese cuisine)

SHELTER ISLAND

Rams Head Inn
108 Ram Island Drive
(631) 749–0811

SOUTHOLD

Coeur des Vignes Hotel &
Restaurant Français
57225 Main Road
(631) 765–2656

REGIONAL INFORMATION— NEW YORK CITY AND LONG ISLAND

Official NYC Guide,
(800) 692–8474
(KIT: $9.95 first class for guidebook,
larger map, postcards, tips; $5.95 third
class)

**New York Convention
and Visitors Bureau,**
810 7th Avenue,
New York 10019,
(800) 692–8474 or (212) 484–1222

Publishes New York Tour Package
Directory free of charge.

Public transportation (subway and bus)
information is available at subway token
booths, or by calling (718) 330–1234.

The bureau operates information booths
during summer months at Forty-seventh
Street and Broadway, open daily from
11:30 A.M. to 7:00 P.M.; at Fifty-second
Street and Seventh Avenue, open daily
10:30 A.M. to 6:00 P.M.

**Long Island Convention
and Visitors Bureau,**
330 Motor Parkway,
Hauppauge 11788,
(877) FUN ON LI or (631) 951–3900,
www.funonli.com

**Shelter Island Chamber
of Commerce,**
P.O. Box 598,
Shelter Island 11964,
(631) 749–0399,
www.onisland.com

**East Hampton Chamber
of Commerce,**
79A Main Street,
East Hampton 11937,
(631) 324–0362,
www.easthamptonchamber.com

Indexes

Entries for Museums and Parks and Nature Preserves appear in special indexes on pages 250–53.

GENERAL INDEX

Ace of Diamonds Mine and Campground, 88
Adirondack Forest Preserve, 35
Adirondack Guideboats Woodward Boat Shop, 53
Adirondack Museum, 48
Adirondack State Park, 55
African American Museum, 220
Akwesasne Cultural Center, 58
Albany, 73
Albany Institute of History and Art, 73
Albergo Allegria, 183
Alexandria Bay, 60
Al Forno Room, 15
Alfred, 109
Alfred University, 109
Alice Austen House, 220
Alice T. Miner Museum, 57
Allegany State Park, 135, 153
Allentown (Buffalo), 140
Alling Coverlet Museum, 119
Amagansett, 234
Amenia, 19
American Bounty Restaurant, 15
American Folk Art Museum, 198
American Hotel, 83
American Maple Museum and Hall of Fame, 64
American Museum of Firefighting, 26
Amherst, Jeffrey, 47
Amish Country, 152
Amish Country Fair, 153
Amsterdam, 77
Anchor Bar and Restaurant, 146
Anderson's, 146
Antique Boat Museum, 61
Apple Pie Bakery Cafe, 16
Arbor Hill, 108
Arcade, 155

Arcade and Attica Railroad, 155
Arnold, John, 38
Around the Clock Cafe, 203
Art Museum (Stony Brook), 229
Artworks, The, 51
Asa Ransom House, 138
Ashford Hollow, 154
Atlantic Kayak Tours, 24
Auburn, 126
Audubon Society of New York State, 170
Auriesville, 78
Aurora, 128
Avoca, 107

Bald eagles, 170
Baldwinsville, 128
Balloons Over Letchworth, 110–11
Ballston Spa, 38
Barker, 139
Barn Museum, 176–77
Barnum, Phineas Taylor, 13
Barton Mines, 45
Basom, 138
Bayard-Cutting Arboretum State Park, 230
Beaver Lake Nature Center, 128
Bed & Breakfast Wellington, 95
Beech Tree House, 235
Beekman Arms, 22
Belhurst Castle, 122
Bellmore, 221
Belvedere Mansion, 18
Bemus Point–Stow Ferry, 150
Bennett's Riding Stable, 43
Bennington Battlefield State Historic Site, 30
Bide-a-wee Pet Cemetery, 228
Big Apple Greeter, 191

Big Duck, 233
Bird's Boat Livery, 50
Bloomfield, 116
Blue Mountain Lake, 48
Boiceville, 177
Boldt Castle, 59
Bolton Landing on Lake George, 43
Bonnie Castle Farm B & B, 120
Books of Marvel, 105
Bouckville, 92
Bowne House, 212
Bread Alone, 180
Breeze (Rochester-Toronto ferry), 115
Brewery Ommegang, 87
Brewster, 12
Brimstonia Cottage, 83
Bristol, 108
Bristol Springs, 109
Bronck Museum, 182
Bronx, 204–6
Brooklyn, 206–10
Brooklyn Botanic Garden, 207
Brooklyn Children's Museum, 206
Broome County (carousels), 130
Brotherhood (winery), 167
Brown, John, 53
Buffalo, 135, 137–47
Buffalo & Erie County Public
    Library, 146
Buffalo Museum of Science, 144
Burchfield-Penney Art Center, 145
Burroughs, John, 177, 184
Burroughs Memorial State Historic
    Site, 185

Caboose Motel, 107
Cambridge, 30
Camp Santanoni, 49
Camp Shanks WWII Museum, 163
Canajoharie, 80
Canajoharie Library and Art
    Gallery, 81
Canandaigua, 117
Cape Vincent, 63
Carmel, 12

Carney's Antiques, 158
Carousels, 130
Carriage House Inn, 120
Cascade Mountain Winery and
    Restaurant, 19
Case Research Lab Museum, 126
Castle at Tarrytown, 8
Castlegould, 224
Catamount Cafe, 179
Caterina de' Medici Dining Room, 15
Catskill Fly Fishing Center &
    Museum/Hall of Fame, 171
Catskill Mountain Railroad, 178
Catskill Rose, 180
Cayuga Museum, 125
Cazenovia Lake, 91
Champlain Canal, 76
Chappaqua, 9
Charlie the Butcher, 146
Chaumont, 63
Chaumont Barrens, 63
Chautauqua, 150
Chautauqua Belle, 151
Chautauqua Institution, 150
Chazy, 57
Cheese Barrel, The, 171–72
Chequit Inn, 235
Chestertown, 46
Children's Museum (Utica), 89
Chili Doll Hospital, 113
China Rose, 23
Chuang Yen Monastery, 12
Church, Frederic Edwin, 25
City Hall (Buffalo), 140
Clarence, 138
Classic Toys, 200
Clark's Ale House, 94
Clausen Farms, 84
Clay Pit Ponds State Park
    Preserve, 215
Clayton, 61
Clemens, Samuel Langhorne (Mark
    Twain), 101, 141
Clermont (Livingston home), 24
Clermont (town), 23

Cold Spring, 164
Cold Spring Harbor, 226
Colonie, 75
Conewango Valley, 153
Coney Island, 208–10
Coney Island Museum, 210
Connetquot River State Park
    Preserve, 230
Conrad N. Hilton Library, 16
Constable Hall, 66
Constableville, 66
Constitution Island, 163
Cooper, James Fenimore, 14, 71, 84
Cooperstown, 84
Corning, 103–5
Coxsackie, 182
Crabtree's Kittle House Restaurant
    and Country Inn, 9
Crailo State Historic Site, 28
Crandall Theater, 27
Croghan, 64
Cropsey, Jasper F., 5
Croton Point Park, 10
Crown Point, 47
Crown Point State Historic Site, 46
Crystal Spa, The, 39
Culinary Institute of America,
    The, 15
Curtiss, Glenn Hammond, 106
Cutchogue, 235

Dai Bosatsu Zendo, 171
Darwin D. Martin House, 142
Davis, Alexander Jackson, 6, 14
Davis Memorial Carillon, 109
Dear Little Dollies, 221
Deep Hollow Ranch, 234
Delamater Inn, 22
Delaware and Hudson Canal
    Museum, 175
Depuy Canal House, 175
Dette Trout Flies, 182
D.I.R.T. Motorsports Hall of Fame &
    Classic Car Museum, 127

DNA Learning Center, 227–28
Donald M. Kendall Sculpture
    Gardens, 6
Dorothy and Ward Melville Carriage
    House, 229
Dory Restaurant, The, 235
Dover Plains, 20
Dunkirk, 148
Dunkirk Historical Lighthouse, 148
Durham Center Museum, 182

Eagle Bridge, 30
East Aurora, 156
East Durham, 182
East Hampton, 232
East Hartford, 31
East Marion, 236
East Meredith, 185
Eastman, George, 112
Eccentricities, 158
Eden, 147
Edward Hopper House, 163
1880 House, 232
Elbert Hubbard–Roycroft
    Museum, 156
Eldred, 170
Eleanor Roosevelt National Historic
    Site, 17
Electronic Communication
    Museum, 116
Ellington, 152
Elmira, 101
El Museo del Barrio, 202
Emerson Inn and Spa, 179
Empire Diner, 203
Erie Canal, 71, 77, 91–93
Erie Canal Museum, 93
Erie Canal Village, 90
Escoffier Restaurant, 15
Essential Elements, 86
Essex, 47
Essex-Charlotte Ferry, 47
Essex Inn, 47
Everson Museum of Art, 93

Falaise, 224
Farmers' Museum, 85
Fenimore Art Museum, 84
Ferd's Bog, 51
Fillmore, Millard, 157
Finton's Landing B&B, 107
Fire Island Lighthouse, 231
Fire Island National Seashore, 231
Fishers, 116
Fisher's O.K. Rock Shop, 27
Fishkill, 13
Flanders, 233
Flushing, 212
Flushing Freedom Mile Historic
    Tour, 213
Fly Creek Cider Mill & Orchard, 85
Fonda, 79
Fonda National Shrine of Blessed
    Kateri Tekakwitha, 79
Forest Lawn, 145
Forestburgh, 170
Fort Constitution, 164
Fort Klock Historic Restoration, 81
Fort Niagara State Park, 139
Fort Ticonderoga, 44
Fort Wadsworth, 216
Fountain Elms, 89
Franklin Graphics, 153
Frank Lloyd Wright houses
    (Buffalo), 142
Frederic Remington Art
    Museum, 58
Fredonia, 148
Freeport, 221
Friends Lake Inn, 46
Fulton County Museum, 79
Fulton, Robert, 23

Ganondagan State Historic Site, 116
Gardener's Cottage, 143
Garibaldi-Meucci Museum, 217
Garnet Hill Lodge, 45
Garrison, 166
Gaslight Christmas Shoppe, 158
Gaslight Village Cafe and Pub, 158

Genesee Country Village
    & Museum, 112
Geneva, 121
Geneva On The Lake, 122
George Barton House, 143
Germantown, 24
Gilmor Glassworks, 23
Glass Menagerie, 103
Glen Cove, 225
Glen Iris Inn, 110
Glenn H. Curtiss Museum, 106
Glens Falls, 42
Gloversville, 79
Glyndor, 206
Gold Coast, 224
Golden Hill State Park, 139
Gomez Mill House, 173
Goose Pond Inn, 46
Goshen, 168
Goshen Historic Track, 168
Gould, Jay, 7
Grand Onion, The, 56–57
Grand Prospect Hall, The, 208
Granger Homestead and Carriage
    Museum, 117
Grant, Ulysses S., 42
Grant Cottage State Historic
    Site, 42
Great Camp Sagamore, 50
Greystone, 47
Griffis Sculpture Park, 154
Gristmill, 229

Hammondsport, 106
Hampton Bays, 234
Hanford Mills Museum, 185
Harlem, 202
Harlem Spirituals, 202
Harness Racing Museum & Hall of
    Fame, 167
Harralds, 13
Harriet Tubman Home, 126
Hart House Inn, 61
Hastings-on-Hudson, 5
Hattie's, 40

Hellenic Snack Bar and
Restaurant, 236
Hempstead, 220
Hempstead House, 224
Herschell Carrousel Factory
Museum, 140
High Falls, 175
Hill Top Inn, 102
Hillsdale, 26
Hillside Inn, 158
Historic Palmyra, 119
Historic Richmond Town, 214
Historic Throop Drugstore, 82
Hoffman Clock Museum, 121
Hogansburg, 58
Holocaust Memorial & Educational
Center of Nassau County, 225
Horne's Ferry, 63
Horseheads, 111
Horseheads Historical Society
Museum, 111
House of Guitars, 114
Howes Cave, 82
Hubbard, Elbert, 156
Hubbell House B & B, 124
Hudson, 26
Hudson Antique Dealers
Association, 26
Hudson River Museum, 3
Hudson Valley Raptor Center, 21
Huguenot Street, 174
Hyde Collection, 43
Hyde Hall, 86
Hyde Park, 17

Ilion, 88
Inn at Lake Joseph, 169
Innisfree Garden, 21
Iroquois Confederacy, 55
Iroquois Indian Museum, 82
Iroquois National Wildlife
Refuge, 137
Irving, Washington, 7
Isamu Noguchi Garden Museum, 210
Ithaca, 128

Jacques Marchais Museum of Tibetan
Art, 213
Jamestown, 152
Jasco Minerals, 45
Jay, John, 10
Jello-O Gallery, 158
John Brown, 52
John Brown Farm State Historic
Site, 52
John Burroughs Sanctuary, 176
John Jay Homestead, 10
Johnson, William, 38
Jones Bakery, 152
Junior Museum, The, 29

Kaaterskill Falls, 181
Kaatsbaan, 23
Kaleidoworld, 178–79
Katonah, 10
Kent-Delord House, 56

Lake Luzerne, 43
Lake Placid, 51
Landmark Inn, 87
L. & J.G. Stickley, Inc., 92
Lawrence, 220
Le Chateau, 11
Le Roy, 158
Lesbian, Gay, and Transgender
Community Center, 195
Letchworth Museum, 110
Letchworth State Park, 110
Lewis Country Farms, 14
Lindenwald Haus, 102
Little Red Lighthouse, 203
Liverpool, 95
Livingston Manor, 171
Livingston, Robert R., and Livingston
family, 23–24
Lobster Roll Restaurant, The, 234
Lock 6, 76
Locktender's Cottage, 175
Locust Grove, 14
Lodge at Emerson Place, 179
Log Village Grist Mill, 31

Long Island, 220–36
Long Island City, 210
Long Island Maritime Museum, 230
Long Island Museum of American
   Art, History and Carriages, 229
Lorenzo State Historic Site, 91
Louis Armstrong House, 211
Lower East Side Tenement
   Museum, 194
Lowville, 66
Lucy-Desi Museum, 152
Lyndhurst, 6

MacKenzie-Childs, Ltd., 128
Madison-Bouckville Outdoor
   Antiques Show, 92
Manitoga, 165
Manlius, 93
Marcella Sembrich Opera Museum, 43
Margaret Melville Blackwell History
   Museum, 229
Margaretville, 172
Mark Twain Study, 101
Marketplace at Catskill Corners, 178
Marlboro, 173
Mashomack Preserve, 235
Matt Brewing Company, 89
Maxilla & Mandible, Ltd., 201
Mayville, 149
McClurg Museum, 149
McKim, Mead, and White, 18
McKinley, William, 141
Memorial Day Museum, 124
Memories, 170
Mennonite Heritage Farm, 65
Mid-Lakes Navigation Co., Ltd., 95
Middleville, 88
Millard Fillmore House National
   Landmark, 157
Millbrook, 21
Millerton, 23
Mills Mansion State Historic Site, 17
Minnewaska State Park Preserve, 172
Mohonk Mountain House, 176
Montauk, 234

Montcalm, Marquis de, 44
Moose River Recreation Area, 50
Morgan Samuels Inn, 119
Morse, Samuel F.B., 14
Mountain Depot, The, 152
Mt. Defiance, 45
Mt. Independence, 45
Mt. Lebanon, 27
Mt. Marcy, 35
Mt. Morris Dam, 111
Mt. Nebo Gallery, 30
Mt. Pleasant, 178
Mt. Tremper, 179
Mueller's Valley View Cheese
   Factory, 153
Mumford, 112
Munson-Williams-Proctor Arts
   Institute, 88
Muscoot Farms, 11
Museum of Bronx History, 204
Museum of Jewish Heritage, 193
Museum of Sex, 198

Nannen Arboretum, 154
Naples, 108
National Baseball Hall of Fame
   Library, 84
National Bottle Museum, 38
National Museum of Racing and
   Thoroughbred Hall of Fame, 40
National Museum of the American
   Indian, 192
National Shrine of the North
   American Martyrs, 78
National Soaring Museum, 102
National Women's Hall of
   Fame, 123
Nautical Mile, 221
Newark, 121
Newcomb, 55
New Hope Farms Equestrian
   Park, 169
Newington Cropsey Foundation
   Gallery of Art, 5
New Paltz, 172–77

New Skete Communities, 30
New World Home Cooking
    Company, 180
New York City, 189–220
New York Aquarium, 208
North American Fiddler's Hall of
    Fame & Museum, 65
North Chili, 113
North Creek, 46
North Creek Railroad Station, 46
North Elba, 53
North River, 45
North Tarrytown, 8
North Tonawanda, 147
Nyack, 163

Oak Orchard Wildlife Management
    Area, 137
Ogdensburg, 59
Olana State Historic Site, 25
Old Bethpage, 224
Old Bethpage Village Restoration, 223
Old Burying Ground, 236
Old Chatham, 27
Old Drovers Inn, 20
Old Dutch Church of Sleepy
    Hollow, 8
Old Dutch Church of Sleepy Hollow
    Burying Ground, 9
Old Forge, 50
Old Forge Hardware, 51
Old Fort Niagara, 139
Old House, 235–36
Old Kinderhook, 27
Old Rhinebeck Aerodrome, 22
Olde Bryan Inn, The, 38
Olean, 155
Olmsted, Frederick Law, 25
Olympic Center Sports
    Complex, 51
Onchiota, 55
Onteora, The Mountain House, 177
Open Artist Studio Tours, 10
Opus 40 and Quarryman's
    Museum, 180–81

Original American Kazoo
    Company, 147
Original Ray's, 203
Ossining, 9
Ossining Heritage Area Park Visitors
    Center, 9
Oyster Bay, 226

Paleontological Research
    Institution, 128
Palmyra, 119
Palmyra Historical Museum, 120
Panama, 151
Panama Rocks Scenic Park, 151
Papa Joe's Restaurant, 120
Parksville, 171
Pat Mitchell's Homemade Ice
    Cream, 131
Paul Smiths, 55
Pedaling History Bicycle
    Museum, 146
Peebles Island State Park, 76
Peekskill, 10
Peekskill Farmer's Market, 10
Penn Station Tour, 199
Penn Yan, 107
Peru, 57
Petrified Creatures Museum of
    Natural History, 87
Petrified Sea Gardens, 41
Philipse family, 4
Philipse Manor Hall, 4
Phoenicia, 178
Piccozzi's Bike Shop, 235
Pine Island, 168
Pipe Creek Farm B & B, 155
Planting Fields Arboretum, 225
Plattsburgh, 56
Poe Cottage, 204
Poe, Edgar Allen, 204
Pollock-Krasner House and Study
    Center, 232
Port Jervis, 169
Poughkeepsie, 14
Pratt Rocks Park, 184

Prattsville, 183
Pratt, Zadock, 183
P.S. 1 Contemporary Art Center, 211
Pulaski, 67
Purchase, 6
Putnam, Israel, 14
Putnam Historical Society
    Museum, 165
Putnam's Canal Store, 77

Q-R-S Music Rolls, 143
Quaker Meeting House, 212-13
Quarryman's Museum, 181
Queens, 210–13
Quilt Room, 107

Radical Walking Tours, 191
Raquette Lake, 50
Reformed Dutch Church, 184
Remington Arms Museum, 87
Remington, Eliphalet, 87
Remington, Frederic, 58
Remsen, 68
Rensselaer, 28
Rhinebeck, 22
Richfield Springs, 87
River to River Downtown
    Tours, 191
Riverhead, 233
Riverhead Foundation for Marine
    Research and Preserve, 233
Robert Louis Stevenson Memorial
    Cottage, 54
Robert Moses State Park, 231
Rochester, 114
Rock City Park, 155
Rock Hall Museum, 220
Rockefeller family, 9
Rockwell Museum of Western
    Art, 105
Rodgers Book Barn, 26
Roger Tory Peterson Institute of
    Natural History, 151
Rome, 90
Romulus, 125

Roosevelt, Theodore, 195
Rosalie's Cucina, 127
Rose Hill Mansion, 121
Rose Inn, 129
Roxbury, 184
Roycroft Campus, 156
Roycroft Inn, The, 157

Sackets Harbor, 64
Sackets Harbor Battlefield State
    Historic Site, 64
Salamanca, 153
Salamanca Rail Museum, 153
Salt Museum, 94
Sampson WW-2 Navy Museum, 125
Sam's Point Dwarf Pine Ridge
    Preserve, 172
Sands Point Preserve, 224
Saranac Lake, 52
Saratoga National Historical Park, 38
Saratoga Springs, 38
Saratoga, Battle of, 37–38
Saugerties, 25, 181
Saugerties Lighthouse, 181
Schein-Joseph International Museum
    of Ceramic Art, 109
Schoharie Crossing State Historic
    Site, 77
Schuyler Mansion State Historic
    Site, 74
Schuyler, Philip, and Schuyler
    family, 74
Seaford, 221
Seaway Trail Discovery Center, 64
Selkirk Lighthouse, 66
Seneca Falls, 123
Seneca-Iroquois National
    Museum, 153
Seneca Lake Wine Trail, 130
Seneca Log House, 85
Shaker Heritage Society, 75
Shaker Museum and Library, 27
Shaker settlement, 75
Shakers, 74
Sharon Springs, 83

Shelter Island, 234
Shelter Island Heights Historic
    District, 235
Shelter Island Resort, 235
Siamese Ponds Wilderness
    Region, 49
Sideshows by the Seashore, 209
Silas Newell's Provisions, 158
Sing Sing Prison, 9
Six Nations Indian Museum, 55
Skaneateles, 95
Sky Top Tower, 176
Slabsides, 176
Sleepy Hollow, 8–9
Slo Jack's Miniature Golf, 233
Smith Point, 231
Smith Point Park, 231
Sodus Bay, 120
Sodus Bay Lighthouse Museum, 120
Sodus Point, 120
Sonnenberg Gardens, 117
South Salem, 11
Southeast Museum, 12
Southhampton Inn, 232
Springfield, 86
St. Andrew's Cafe, 15
St. James, 228
St. James General Store, 228
St. Johnsville, 81
Staatsburg, 18
State capital, Albany, 73
Staten Island, 213–20
Staten Island Botanical Garden, 215
Staten Island Institute of Arts and
    Sciences, 217
Steuben, Frederick von, 67
Steuben Memorial State Historic
    Site, 67
Stillwater, 37
Stillwater Reservoir, 51
Stockton, 149
Stockton Sales, 149
Stony Brook, 228
Stony Brook Village Center, 228
Stormville, 13

Strong Museum, 113
Studio Museum in Harlem, 203
Stull Observatory, 109
Sugar Loaf, 168
Sugar Loaf Arts and Craft
    Village, 168
Sunken Forest, 231
Sunnyside, 7
Syracuse, 93–95

Tackapausha Museum and
    Preserve, 221
"Tango at the Cat," 179
Tannersville, 181
Tarrytown, 7
Taylor Wine Museum, 107
Tekakwitha, Kateri, 79
Theodore Roosevelt Birthplace
    National Historic Site, 195–96
Theodore Roosevelt Inaugural
    National Historic Site, 141
Thirty Mile Point Lighthouse, 139
Thousand Islands Inn, 62
Three Village Garden Club
    Exchange, 228
Three Village Inn, 229
Ticonderoga, 44–45
Tiffany, Louis Comfort, 127
Tifft Nature Preserve, 145
Times Square walking tour, 192
Timespell, 130
Tonawanda Wildlife Management
    Area, 137
Totem Indian Trading Post, 177–78
Town Tinker, The, 178
Toy Town Museum, 157
Troutbeck, 19
Troy, 29
Tuthilltown Gristmill & Country
    Store, 173

Union Church of Pocantico Hills, 9
Upper Hudson River Railroad, 46
Utica, 88

Vagabond Inn, 108
Valentown Museum, 115
Van Wyck Homestead Museum, 13
Vaux, Calvert, 25
Verizon Sports Complex, 52
Veterans' Park Museum, 148
Victor, 116
Victorian Doll Museum, 113
Vintage Tours, 236
Visitor Interpretive Center, 55
Vitrix Hot Glass Studio, 103

Walloomsac, 30
Walter Davidson House, 143
Walter Elwood Museum, 77
Warner House, 164
Wantagh, 228
Washingtonville, 166
Watch Hill, 231
Waterford, 76
Waterford Flight, 76
Waterford Historical Museum and Cultural Center, 76
Waterloo, 124
Waterloo Terwilliger Historical Museum, 124
Watkins Glen, 130
Watkins Glen State Park, 130
Wave Hill, 205
Webb's Candy Factory, 149
Weedsport, 127
Wellesley Island, 60
West Chazy Pottery Studio, 58
West End Gallery, 105

West Falls, 155
West Park, 176
West Point, 164
West Point Foundry, 164–65
West Sayville, 230
Westfield, 149
Westhampton Beach, 232
Whaling Museum, 226
Whetstone Gulf State Park, 66
White Inn, 148
Willard Memorial Chapel, 126–27
William Heath House, 142
William Phelps General Store Museum, 119
Wilton, 42
Wing's Castle, 21
Wings of Eagles, 111
With Pipe and Book, 52
Wizard of Clay Pottery, The, 111
Wolcott, 120
Woodstock, 180
Woodstock Guild, 180
Wright, Frank Lloyd, 142
Wurtsboro, 170
Wurtsboro Airport, 170
Wyoming, 158

Yaffa Cafe, 203
Yarborough Square, 57
Ye Jolly Onion Inn, 169
Yonkers, 3
Youngstown, 139

Zadock Pratt Museum, 184

MUSEUMS

Adirondack Museum, 48
African American Museum, 220
Akwesasne Cultural Center, 58
Albany Institute of History and Art, 73
Alice T. Miner Museum, 57
Alling Coverlet Museum, 119
American Folk Art Museum, 198

American Maple Museum and Hall of Fame, 64
American Museum of Firefighting, 26
Antique Boat Museum, 61
Art Museum (Stony Brook), 229
Barn Museum, 176–77
Bronck Museum, 182
Brooklyn Children's Museum, 206

Buffalo Museum of Science, 144
Burchfield-Penney Art Center, 145
Burroughs Memorial State Historic
    Site, 185
Camp Shanks WWII Museum, 163
Canajoharie Library and Art
    Gallery, 81
Case Research Lab Museum, 126
Catskill Fly Fishing Center &
    Museum, 171
Cayuga Museum, 125
Children's Museum (Utica), 89
Coney Island Museum, 210
Crown Point State Historic Site, 46
Delaware and Hudson Canal
    Museum, 175
D.I.R.T. Motorsports Hall of Fame &
    Classic Car Museum, 127
DNA Learning Center, 227
Donald M. Kendall Sculpture
    Gardens, 6
Durham Center Museum, 182
El Museo del Barrio, 202
Elbert Hubbard–Roycroft
    Museum, 156
Electronic Communication
    Museum, 116
Erie Canal Museum, 93
Everson Museum of Art, 93
Farmers' Museum, 85
Fenimore Art Museum, 84
Fort Klock Historic Restoration, 81
Fountain Elms, 89
Frederic Remington Art
    Museum, 58
Fulton County Museum, 79
Ganondagan State Historic Site, 116
Garibaldi-Meucci Museum, 217
Genesee Country Village &
    Museum, 112
Glenn H. Curtiss Museum, 106
Granger Homestead and Carriage
    Museum, 117
Grant Cottage State Historic Site, 42
Hanford Mills Museum, 185

Harness Racing Museum and Hall of
    Fame, 167
Harriet Tubman Home, 126
Herschell Carrousel Factory
    Museum, 140
Hoffman Clock Museum, 121
Holocaust Memorial & Educational
    Center of Nassau County, 225
Horseheads Historical Society
    Museum, 111
Hudson River Museum, 3
Iroquois Indian Museum, 82
Isamu Noguchi Garden Museum, 210
Jacques Marchais Museum of Tibetan
    Art, 213
John Brown Farm State Historic
    Site, 53
John Jay Homestead, 10
Junior Museum, The, 29
Letchworth Museum, 110
Long Island Maritime Museum, 230
Long Island Museum of American
    Art, History and Carriages, 229
Lorenzo State Historic Site, 91
Louis Armstrong House, 211
Lower East Side Tenement
    Museum, 194
Lucy-Desi Museum, 152
Marcella Sembrich Opera Museum, 43
Margaret Melville Blackwell History
    Museum, 229
McClurg Museum, 149
Memorial Day Museum, 124
Millard Fillmore House National
    Landmark, 157
Munson-Williams-Proctor Arts
    Institute, 88
Museum of Bronx History, 204
Museum of Jewish Heritage, 193
Museum of Sex, 198
National Bottle Museum, 38
National Museum of Racing and
    Thoroughbred Hall of Fame, 40
National Museum of the American
    Indian, 192

National Soaring Museum, 102
National Women's Hall of Fame, 123
Newington Cropsey Foundation
   Gallery of Art, 5
North American Fiddler's Hall of
   Fame & Museum, 65
Opus 40 and Quarryman's
   Museum, 180–81
Original American Kazoo
   Company, 147
Paleontological Research
   Institution, 128
Palmyra Historical Museum, 120
Pedaling History Bicycle
   Museum, 146
Petrified Creatures Museum of
   Natural History, 87
Pollock-Krasner House and Study
   Center, 232
P.S. 1 Contemporary Art Center, 211
Putnam Historical Society
   Museum, 165
Remington Arms Museum, 87
Rock Hall Museum, 221
Rockwell Museum of Western
   Art, 105
Roger Tory Peterson Institute of
   Natural History, 151
Rose Hill Mansion, 121
Salamanca Rail Museum, 153
Salt Museum, 94
Sampson WW-2 Navy Museum, 125
Saratoga National Historical Park, 38
Saugerties Lighthouse, 181
Schein-Joseph International Museum
   of Ceramic Art, 109
Schoharie Crossing State Historic
   Site, 77

Schuyler Mansion State Historic
   Site, 74
Seaway Trail Discovery Center, 64
Seneca-Iroquois National
   Museum, 153
Shaker Museum and Library, 27
Six Nations Indian Museum, 54
Sodus Bay Lighthouse Museum, 120
Southeast Museum, 12
Staten Island Institute of Arts and
   Sciences, 215
Steuben Memorial State Historic
   Site, 67
Strong Museum, 113
Studio Museum in Harlem, 203
Tackapausha Museum and
   Preserve, 221
Taylor Wine Museum, 107
Theodore Roosevelt Birthplace
   National Historic Site, 196
Theodore Roosevelt Inaugural
   National Historic Site, 141
Toy Town Museum, 157
Valentown Museum, 115
Van Wyck Homestead Museum, 13
Veterans' Park Museum, 148
Victorian Doll Museum, 113
Walter Elwood Museum, 77
Waterford Historical Museum and
   Cultural Center, 76
Waterloo Terwilliger Historical
   Museum, 124
Whaling Museum, 226
William Phelps General Store
   Museum, 119
Wing's Castle, 20
Wings of Eagles, 111
Zadock Pratt Museum, 184

PARKS AND NATURE PRESERVES

Adirondack Forest Preserve, 35

Adirondack State Park, 55

Allegany State Park, 135, 153

Bayard-Cutting Arboretum State Park, 230

Beaver Lake Nature Center, 128

Connetquot River State Park Preserve, 230

Fort Niagara State Park, 139

Golden Hill State Park, 139

Griffis Sculpture Park, 154

Hudson Valley Raptor Center, 21

Innisfree Garden, 21

Iroquois National Wildlife Refuge, 137

John Burroughs Sanctuary, 176

Letchworth State Park, 110

Mashomack Preserve, 235

Minnewaska State Park Preserve, 172

Moose River Recreation Area, 51

Nannen Arboretum, 154

New York Aquarium, 208

Oak Orchard Wildlife Management Area, 137

Ossining Heritage Area Park Visitors Center, 9

Panama Rocks Scenic Park, 151

Peebles Island State Park, 76

Petrified Sea Gardens, 41

Planting Fields Arboretum, 225

Pratt Rocks Park, 184

Riverhead Foundation for Marine Research and Preserve, 228

Robert Moses State Park, 231

Sacandaga Park, 67

Sam's Point Dwarf Pine Ridge Preserve, 172

Sands Point Preserve, 224

Saratoga National Historical Park, 38

Siamese Ponds Wilderness Region, 49

Smith Point Park, 231

Sonnenberg Gardens, 117

Tackapausha Museum and Preserve, 221

Tifft Nature Preserve, 145

Tonawanda Wildlife Management Area, 137

Watkins Glen State Park, 130

West Park, 176

Whetstone Gulf State Park, 66

About the Authors

Bill and Kay Scheller are coauthors of *New Jersey Off the Beaten Path* and contributors to several National Geographic books. They have worked as correspondents for Fodor's and Insight guides, and for *Yankee* magazine's travel publications. They are the authors of *Best Vermont Drives* and *Best New Hampshire Drives*, published by their own Jasper Heights Press.